DISCARDED

African-Centered Schooling
in Theory and Practice

African-Centered Schooling in Theory and Practice

Edited by

DIANE S. POLLARD

CHERYL S. AJIROTUTU

Foreword by

EDGAR EPPS

BERGIN & GARVEY
Westport, Connecticut • London

Library of Congress Cataloging-in-Publication Data

African-centered schooling in theory and practice / edited by Diane S. Pollard and
Cheryl S. Ajirotutu ; foreword by Edgar Epps.
    p. cm.
  Includes bibliographical references and index.
  ISBN 0-89789-728-5 (alk. paper)
    1. African American Immersion Schools Evaluation Project.   2.
Afro-Americans—Education—Evaluation—Longitudinal studies.   3. Public
schools—Wisconsin—Milwaukee—Longitudinal studies.   4. Afrocentrism—United
States—Longitudinal studies.   I. Pollard, Diane.   II. Ajirotutu, Cheryl.
LC2731.A35   2000
371.829´96´073—dc21   99-055888

British Library Cataloguing in Publication Data is available.

Library of Congress Catalog Card Number: 99-055888
ISBN: 0-89789-728-5

First published in 2000

Bergin & Garvey, 88 Post Road West, Westport, CT 06881
An imprint of Greenwood Publishing Group, Inc.
www.greenwood.com

Printed in the United States of America

The paper used in this book complies with the
Permanent Paper Standard issued by the National
Information Standards Organization (Z39.48-1984).

10 9 8 7 6 5 4 3 2 1

Contents

Foreword

Edgar Epps

The education of black males has gained considerable attention in recent years (Hopkins, 1997; Kunjufu, 1990; Slaughter-Defoe & Richards, 1995). African American educators, community leaders, and researchers have been disappointed with the results of the major reform movements of the past two decades. Whether the focus is on higher standards, school-based management, restructuring schools, or a multicultural curriculum, the reform efforts have not had much impact on the educational achievement of black males. It has been observed in other research (e.g., Slaughter, & Epps, 1987) that for low-income urban African American children, the school experience is often discontinuous with early childhood development. Teacher expectations and the culture of the school often conflict with home experiences; competencies acquired in the home may not be valued in the typical classroom. The movement for African-centered education is based on the assumption that a school immersed in African traditions, rituals, values, and symbols will provide a learning environment that is more congruent with the lifestyles and values of African American families. A school based on African values, it is believed, would eliminate the patterns of rejection and alienation that engulf so many African American school children, especially males.

This book tells the stories of two African-centered schools, an elementary school and a middle school, in an urban public school system. The authors construe the events leading to the implementation of the African-centered schools as a continuation of the historical efforts of African Americans to obtain a viable education for their children. (Some of this history can be found in Anderson [1988]). It is informative that the major impetus for the schools came from African American educators and professionals in the black community. Because they are among the first models of African-centered public schools, these schools provide a valuable laboratory for assessing the viability of this form of education as an effective alternative to other reforms. It is indeed fortunate that the authors were able to study the implementation and development of the two schools and provide the basis for an understanding of the factors that enhance or impede the success of innovative reforms outside the educational mainstream. In reading the manuscript, I was impressed by the extend to which the factors affecting these schools mirror those that support or subvert other efforts to make schools more hospitable to African American children in general and males in particular.

The African-centered schools were originally conceived as "all male academies," but, as in other cities, legal and political obstacles resulted in a compromise: coeducational African-centered schools. The authors ask questions about factors that affect the implementation of African-centered education in each school. They look at the internal dynamics of the schools as well as the external factors that impact them. They ask questions about the perceptions of administrators and faculty, the role of teachers in implementing the model, and the role of bureaucratic policies and politics in determining the success or failure of the schools. The African-centered elementary school experienced relative success; the middle school encountered problems that undermined its success. What are the key differences in the implementation process that produced such disparate results?

The authors agree with other researchers (e.g., Edmonds, 1979) that a principal's leadership is the key to successful reform. The elementary school was fortunate to have stable committed leadership. The stability and longevity of the staff also helped to create the collaborative conditions conducive to successful implementation of the African-centered program. The principal envisioned a process in which the curriculum would be infused with African and African American history and culture. She also considered it important for the students to feel a sense of belonging to the school (a uniform policy was implemented). As with the effective schools movement, there was a strong emphasis on academic achievement. Teachers were encouraged to have high expectations for academic achievement among the students in their classes. I was delighted to read "Improving self-esteem is secondary to improving achievement." Many critics of African-centered schools and curricula dismiss these efforts as misguided attempts to boost self-esteem. The leadership of this school correctly placed the emphasis on academic achievement first; self-esteem and academic self-confidence will increase *after* children demonstrate competence in subject matter. It was noted that teachers' perceptions emphasized raising student self-esteem and building cultural pride. However, the academic emphasis was not subverted. Clarity of vision, stability of staff, and strong principal leadership appear to be the factors that contributed to the successful implementation of the African-centered model at the elementary school.

The middle school experience could be viewed as a textbook case study of all the things that can go wrong when attempting to introduce a new model of education and curriculum in a school building. The problems included lack of stability in leadership (no principal remained at the school for a sustained period of time) and faculty, the presence of a large number of long-term substitute teachers, tensions between staff and administrators, tensions among staff, union policies that restricted the number of African American teachers assigned to the school, and interference from the central administration and board of education. In addition, the staff had to overcome the negative image that was associated with the school before it became an African-centered school. The authors conclude that despite these setbacks, staff continued to be optimistic about the potential of the school. One reason for the optimism is the discontinuation of the union policy limiting the number of African American teachers. If a strong committed principal can assume the leadership of the school for several years and the staffing problems are overcome, it is possible that during the next five years, this school can develop the sense of community and mission needed for success.

I have not addressed the issue of the content of the African-centered curriculum. The specific content may vary from one setting to another. A common theme, however, is that the school should embrace the concepts of community and family. Essential to the ideas of African-centered education is the view that the child should feel at home in the school. The principal and teachers should be perceived as surrogate parents and mutual respect should govern the relationships of students to adult and adults to children. Parents and community members should feel welcome in the school. In short, this model is designed to counteract the traditional Eurocentric educational model that has resulted in the alienation of generations of African American children. The example of the elementary school in this book suggests that with committed and stable leadership and staff and minimal interference from the outside, the African-centered school can be a viable alternative to other types of educational reform. The strength of the model is that is goes beyond surface changes in curriculum and climate to implement a thoroughly grounded program that touches all aspects of the lives of children in schools. The example of the middle school serves as a reminder that any reform, no matter how soundly conceived, can be subverted by lack of leadership, poorly prepared teachers, and political and administrative interference. I hope that the experience of the elementary school will encourage others to implement reforms designed to make schools places that nurture African American children.

REFERENCES

Anderson, J. (1988). *The education of blacks in the South, 1860–1936.* Chapel Hill: University of North Carolina Press.

Edmonds, R. (1979). Effective schools for the urban poor. *Educational Leadership, 37,* 15–23.

Hopkins, R. (1997). *Educating black males: Critical lesson in school, community, and power.* Albany, NY: State University of New York Press.

Kunjufu, J. (October 10, 1991). The real issue about the black male academy. *Black Issues in Higher Education,* 63–64.

Slaughter, D. T., & Epps, E. G. (1987). The home environment and academic achievement of black American children and youth: An overview. *Journal of Negro Education, 56,* 3–20.

Slaughter-Defoe, & Richards, H. (1995). Literacy for empowerment: The case of black males. In V. L. Gadsden & D. A. Wagner (Eds.), *Literacy among African American Youth: Issues in learning, teaching, and schooling.* Cresskill, NJ: Hampton Press, Inc. 125–147.

Acknowledgments

The African American Immersion Schools Evaluation Project could not have been completed without the support and help of a number of people. We are pleased to take this opportunity to thank some of those who made it possible.

First, we extend our heartfelt thanks to the African American Immersion elementary school and the African American Immersion middle school. The administrators, teachers, and staff, as well as the students, always welcomed us, answered our questions patiently, and cooperated with our requests. In addition, we thank the parents of the students and the community members involved with the schools for their help in providing information to us.

We recognize that the immense task of documenting and evaluating these two schools during the five-year period of the study could not have been possible without extramural support. A grant from the Joyce Foundation of Chicago undergirded the project. A special thank you goes to Dr. Warren Chapman from the Program Office for his unwavering support of the project. In additon, we are grateful for funds from the Bader Foundation and the Milwaukee Education Trust for their support of specific project activities.

The University of Wisconsin–Milwaukee also contributed to our efforts. We appreciate the support from the School of Education and the College of Letters and Sciences, the Center for Teacher Education, Center for Urban Initiatives and Research, the UW System, the Institute for Race and Ethnicity, and the office of the Provost and Vice Chancellor. We are also grateful for the hard work of the clerical staff and students who worked with us on the project.

Finally, we thank our families.

Cheryl: To my grandmother, Mrs. Luvera Ridgeway, and the memory of my mother and father. Thank you for the guidance and support over the years. To my sisters and brothers, as a family we have always sustained each other through our joys and sorrows. Thank you for your unconditional love and support. And finally, to my daughter, Oluyinka, you made me smile and laugh over the course of this project.

Diane: To my parents, Elric and Clara Stewart for providing a strong and loving foundation for my life and work, and to my late uncle, James A. Bayton, who sparked my interest in research. My deepest gratitude is for my husband, Scott, whose unwavering support makes this and all projects possible and my children, Amina and Almasi, who make it all worthwhile.

Introduction

In 1990 when the Board of School Directors of Milwaukee made the decision to designate two of its schools as African American Immersion Schools, a national debate ensued. Educators, academicians, politicians, and other onlookers attempted to interpret the meaning and implications of this action at this juncture in the social history of American education. Both supporters and opponents of the establishment of the African American Immersion Schools were vociferous in making their positions heard in local and national media ("Milwaukee Creating 2 Schools for Black Boys," 1990; "Milwaukee School Plan Needs Support," 1990; "Motivate, Don't Isolate Black Students," 1990).

Despite the level of interest these schools engendered, what these responses most often missed was an understanding of the complex nature of urban education generally and the impact of African Americans' presence in those schools in particular. In addition, many of the respondents did not fully understand the specific factors in the city that led to the establishment of the African American Immersion Schools at this particular moment in history. This book describes and analyzes the establishment of two African American Immersion Schools and analyzes the first five years of their implementation. The purpose of the book is twofold: first, to position the schools within their specific context and, second, to link them to broader issues related to educating people of African descent effectively in urban schools. To accomplish these goals, the book combines an in-depth case study of the two African American Immersion Schools with commentary from leading educational researchers who have studied African-centered education and the education of African American children. We collected the data on which this book is based as part of a six-year, longitudinal, in-depth documentation and evaluation study of these two schools.

A BRIEF OVERVIEW OF THE CITY'S PUBLIC SCHOOLS

The history of the public schools in this city is embedded in the social and economic growth of Milwaukee. As early as the 1900s, the population of this midwestern city was overwhelmingly white, with only a small African American constituency. In 1910, African Americans comprised 0.2 percent of the city's population; this increased to 1.6 percent in 1945. By 1950, the African American population had almost doubled to 3.4 percent (Levin & Zipp, 1993). The migration of African Americans to this city, accompanied by an increasing flight of whites out of the city, continued, and by 1985, African Americans comprised 25.3 percent of the city population (Levin & Zipp, 1993). During this period, the public schools in this city experienced even more dramatic demographic changes. In 1970, the first year such figures were available, African Americans constituted 26 percent of the student population in the public schools, and whites made up 70.3 percent. By 1985, the white population had declined to 35.7 percent, whereas the African American population had grown to 52.6 percent (Levin & Zipp, 1993).

As in other large cities, schools in this urban community followed the tradition of creating attendance patterns based upon residential neighborhoods. The increase in the African American population in the city was accompanied by a concomitant increase in segregated neighborhoods and de facto segregation in the schools (Levin & Zipp, 1993; Trotter, 1985). According to Levin and Zipp, by 1975, 36 of the city's 155 public schools served predominantly African American student populations.

Efforts to desegregate Milwaukee's schools began in 1965. These efforts reached their peak in 1976 when the Federal District Court ruled in the case of *Amos v. Board of Education* that the schools were intentionally segregated and ordered the district to develop and implement a desegregation plan (Stolee, 1993). Although resistant, the district did develop a plan that relied on two general strategies within the city. One was to bus large numbers of African American students from overcrowded schools in predominantly black neighborhoods to schools in neighborhoods where, initially, most of the students were white. The second strategy was to create a number of "specialty schools," many located in predominantly black neighborhoods, to attract European American students. Despite these strategies, 20 elementary schools, 2 middle schools, and 1 high school, all located in poor, predominantly African American neighborhoods, were not desegregated. The court allowed these schools to operate with their predominantly African American student populations, although each of these schools was required to reserve spaces for white students, should they decide to attend them. Although the notion of desegregation continued into the 1980s and 1990s, the issue became less relevant as whites continued to flee the city's public schools and the population of African American and other students of color increased. By 1990, the year the Board of School Directors decided to establish the African American Immersion Schools, African Americans comprised over 60 percent of the public school population.

In addition to social changes, Milwaukee underwent significant economic changes during the 1980s and 1990s. These changes had important consequences for the schools. Prior to the 1980s, the city had enjoyed a strong economy, and African Americans as well as other groups relied heavily on industrial and manufacturing jobs. Beginning in the 1980s, however, this city began to experience deindustrialization on a large scale. Throughout that decade, factories closed and jobs were lost to other parts of the United States or to other countries where labor was cheaper; Milwaukee became one of the "rust belt" cities common to the midwestern and northeastern sections of the country. While this economic dislocation had widespread negative effects, its impact was felt most strongly in the African American community. African Americans had always had a tenuous position in the city economy (Levine & Zipp, 1993; Trotter, 1985), and deindustrialization led to economic devastation for this group. By 1986, Milwaukee ranked 46th of the 48 largest metropolitan areas in terms of the well-being of African Americans. Furthermore, it had the highest African American unemployment rate of any major metropolitan area in the United States (McNeely & Kinlow, 1987). This meant that the public schools experienced a significant increase in the numbers of very poor students, a trend that has continued to the present day.

THE ESTABLISHMENT OF THE AFRICAN AMERICAN IMMERSION SCHOOLS

In February 1989, the Milwaukee Board of School Directors established a Task Force to make recommendations regarding the educational and social crisis involving African American males in the schools and the community. The Task Force consisted of school personnel and students, representatives from higher education, community representatives, and parents. Between 1989 and 1990, the Task Force analyzed data from Milwaukee and a number of other urban school districts. As a result of their deliberations, the Task Force made a number of recommendations to the School Board. One was that two African American Male Immersion Schools, one elementary and one middle school, should be established to provide sites for the development of structural, curricular, and social initiatives aimed at meeting the needs and enhancing the achievements of African American students and African American males in particular (Milwaukee Public Schools, 1990).

These recommendations were accepted by the School Board in May 1990, and during the following year, June 1990 to August 1991, an Implementation Committee was established to develop plans to establish the African American Immersion Schools. Within the first two months after the Implementation Committee was established, an important change in the proposed schools was made. Following a challenge in the public arena to the legality of single-sex schools, along with some voiced concerns about the need to confront issues concerning African American girls, the decision was made to make these schools coeducational rather than solely for African American males. The African American Immersion elementary school was opened in September 1991, and the African American Immersion middle school opened in fall 1992.

THE AFRICAN AMERICAN IMMERSION SCHOOLS EVALUATION PROJECT

As the African American Immersion Schools were being planned, the public schools administration and the Implementation Committee noted that there was a need for a documentation and evaluation study of this experimental effort. We agreed to design and implement such a study, hereafter known as the African American Immersion Schools Evaluation Project. The African American Immersion Schools Evaluation Project is a six-year, longitudinal study of the first five years of implementation of the two African American Immersion Schools in this city. The African American Immersion Schools Evaluation Project is a distinguishing feature of this particular city's experiment with African-centered education. Although other similar efforts have been mounted in other cities, to our knowledge, no other has been accompanied by a long-term, in-depth evaluation study.

The African American Immersion Schools Evaluation Project had three overall aims: (1) to provide feedback to the school staffs and to local and national practitioners and researchers regarding the initial implementation and outcomes of these two schools, (2) to identify effective educational strategies that could be utilized in other educational settings, locally, nationally, and internationally, and (3) to contribute to knowledge about educating African American children effectively in public school settings.

The African American Immersion Schools Evaluation Project operated on the premise that an effective evaluation of the African American Immersion Schools needed to be holistic, participatory, and interdisciplinary. By *holistic*, we mean that the study should encompass all areas of school functioning and all participants. Thus we attempted to include information from all those involved in implementing these schools: administrators at both the school and district level, teachers, students, parents, and community representatives who volunteered to work with the schools.

Our study was participatory in that we worked collaboratively with school staff to shape the formative aspects of the evaluation. For example, we regularly participated in feedback sessions with school staff in which we reported our research activities and tentative findings and sought their suggestions. In addition, our early interviews with school staff regarding their perceptions of the directions for developing and implementing this particular African-centered educational model helped shape some of our subsequent data collection activities.

The interdisciplinary orientation of the African American Immersion Schools Evaluation Project derived from our backgrounds in educational psychology and anthropology. We integrated research traditions from both of our disciplines into the design of the study, utilizing a combination of qualitative and quantitative methods.

To organize the wealth of data that was collected in the African American Immersion Schools Evaluation Project, a schema consisting of five study areas was developed by the editors of this book. The articulation of this schema was guided by two factors. First, our experiences during the planning of the African American Immersion Schools indicated that these were important areas of interest. Second, our review of literature concerning educational reform as it related to African American children and African-centered education suggested that this schema provided meaningful categories for organizing data collection. The five study areas were

- *Administrative management strategies.* This component focused on identifying what school restructuring efforts and administrative activities were needed to support the development of an African-centered schooling experience in a public school setting.
- *Curriculum reform.* This component was concerned with the evolution of instructional practices as well as curriculum materials in the African American Immersion Schools. We asked what "best teaching practices" evolved as teachers infused the curriculum with African and African American history and culture.
- *Staff development.* In this component we were asked what kinds of staff development activities are needed to support teachers' development of an African-centered curriculum and accompanying pedagogical practices. In addition, we were interested in observing stability and change in school staffs' perceptions about this African-centered educational model and their roles in it.
- *Parent and community involvement.* The information gathered under this component was aimed at identifying how and in what ways parents and volunteers in the school from the community contributed to the development of the African American Immersion Schools.
- *Student growth and outcomes.* This component focused on assessments of the impact of this African-centered educational experience on the students. A variety of assessments were utilized including school records, instruments developed by the African American Immersion Schools Evaluation Project, and the voices of the students themselves as they discussed their experiences in these schools with us.

The African American Immersion Schools Evaluation Project collected data from the two African American Immersion Schools from September 1991 through May 1997. During this time, we visited the schools on a frequent and systematic basis not only during the regular school day but also during after-school extracurricular activities and programs. Our data collection measures included interviews, observations, surveys, archival information, and more formal assessment tools. Periodically, we met with district administrators to obtain their perceptions of the schools as well as to provide them with our preliminary impressions. Finally, we kept track of social and political activities within the community that had an impact on the schools.

This book reflects one of the thrusts of the African American Immersion Schools Evaluation Project: to link an in-depth analysis of the African American Immersion Schools in Milwaukee with broader issues related to implementing African-centered educational models in particular and culturally centered education in general. In keeping with this thrust, we believed it was important to develop opportunities in which other researchers and practitioners could reflect upon the work of the African American Immersion Schools in Milwaukee as well as our documentation and evaluation of them and provide us with feedback from a broader, national perspective. In some cases, these individuals visited the schools in Milwaukee individually. In others, they were part of an organized effort to provide us with feedback on the Evaluation Project.

In 1994, the African American Immersion Schools Evaluation Project hosted a working symposium entitled "Documenting the African American Immersion Schools: A Work in Progress." We invited a number of national experts who had conducted research on educating African American children and on African-centered education to meet with us and the school staffs to comment on the implementation of the schools and our documentation and evaluation of them to date. In addition to reviewing this specific project, this symposium helped us think through relationships between theory and practice in the development of African-centered education in public school settings. The panel members made several recommendations to us regarding refining our data collection procedures and offered both us and the school staffs perspectives representing broader conceptual frameworks for considering the implementation of African-centered schools in public settings.

The panelists at the working symposium later joined the editors of this volume in a presentation at the American Educational Research Association in 1995 in which the discussions at the symposium were further elaborated. In July 1996, the African American Immersion Schools Evaluation Project sponsored a national conference to which researchers, policy makers, and practitioners were invited to share information about African-centered education. Teachers at the elementary and middle African American Immersion Schools demonstrated some of their African-centered curriculum models. Several of the researchers returned to lead workshops at this conference.

We have invited several of these experts to contribute to this volume. Through this, we have attempted to link our in-depth analysis of the African American Immersion Schools in Milwaukee to broader issues concerning African American education in African-centered institutions as well as in other institutions in urban settings.

CONCEPTUAL FRAMEWORK FOR THE BOOK

This book provides the first comprehensive analysis and interpretation of the initial five years of implementation of two African-centered educational models in a public school setting. In this volume, we focus on the changes that occurred in the schools and their classrooms as staff attempted to infuse African and African American history and culture throughout these schools. We analyze the factors that affected the directions and degrees of change in each school, taking into account both the dynamics at work in the schools and external factors that impinged on them.

In this book, we focus on the perceptions of administrators and faculty as they were on the front lines of implementing this innovative reform effort. There are two important reasons for our focus on staff perceptions at these schools. The first has to do with the role of teachers in school reform initiatives. A criticism of many school reform initiatives was that they were often driven by top-down policies that stressed bureaucratic controls and accountability (Smylie, 1996). As such, these reform endeavors often did not include teachers in the process, did not have an effect on teachers' attitudes, beliefs, and practices, and ultimately, did not result in improved outcomes for students (Mirel, 1994; Taylor & Teddlie, 1992; Useem, Christman, Gold, & Simon, 1996). It has been argued that if reform and restructuring are to be effective, they must address a school's core cultural values and not just its organizational characteristics (Wehlage, Smith, & Lipman, 1992).

A second reason for this focus concerned the increasing cultural disparities between staff and students in schools serving poor African American children. Some researchers such as Irvine (1990) have described the issue of cultural mismatch between students and schools as a major factor underlying school failure among urban low-income African American students. In our study of the initial five years of operation of two African American Immersion schools, it quickly became apparent that the perceptions of teachers were a key factor in understanding their implementation. We analyzed how they both attempted to construct an African-centered educational model and responded to dynamics within the school and external forces impinging on them. Finally, because these schools are continuing to operate, we present the data described in this book as part of an ongoing, evolving process.

The African American Immersion Schools, as constituted in this particular city, represented a unique alternative for a public school setting. African-centered educational models had long existed in private schools (Ratteray, 1994). Furthermore, some attempts to implement African-centered models had been initiated prior to this experience. For example, in Baltimore, Maryland, selected first- and second-grade classes were designated for African American males and received African-centered instruction weekly (Narine, 1992). In Atlanta, Georgia, an attempt was made to institute African-centered education throughout the district (Irvine, this volume). Neither of these efforts approximated Milwaukee's effort, however. Here, the African-centered model was limited to two schools in the district. However, it encompassed the entire operation of these schools.

When the African American Immersion Schools were established, they had few theoretical or practical models to follow. Staff were required to conceptualize and develop the educational model to be utilized while implementing it. This had an impact on the design of the documentation and evaluation study of the schools. We could not begin our study by imposing any particular theoretical framework on our analysis of these schools. However, as we spent time in the schools, worked with our data, analyzed district activities, and read related literature, three major issues emerged that constitute the conceptual framework undergirding this volume.

First, the African American Immersion Schools in Milwaukee represent a contemporary example of a historical and ongoing effort by African Americans to realize their educational aspirations for their children. Anderson (1988) argued that African Americans have long viewed education as the major vehicle for freedom, independence, and individual and community improvement. Thus, they have exerted considerable effort to establish, control, or at least influence educational opportunities for their children. However, Anderson also documents that this has not always been a unified effort within the African American community. For example, he points out that in the 1800s there were debates among African Americans regarding the most effective ways to implement this vision. For example, Anderson (1988) describes the

Armstrong-Hampton idea of education, which focused on preparing blacks of the 1800s for manual and industrialized labor in the South. This idea was opposed by African American religious leaders of the time who established black colleges with traditional liberal arts curriculums to prepare blacks for leadership roles in the community. This debate foreshadowed the well-known Booker T. Washington–W.E.B. Du Bois debates of the late 1800s and early 1900s. In addition, African Americans were required to contend, and sometimes negotiate, with various white American factions who had their own ideas about the directions education for African Americans should take. Since whites often held the purse strings, their perspectives often could not be ignored, particularly in public sector schooling (Anderson, 1988).

Elements of these debates have continued within the African American community. African Americans have questioned whether the best education for their children should focus on "admission into white institutions versus the development of black institutions; integration versus pluralism, assimilation versus separatism, self determination versus external control" (Allen & Jewell, 1995: 79–80).

In this city, during the 1970s and the 1980s an increasing number of African Americans began to question existing school policies and call for alternatives to them. During this period, there was also an increase in the number of African Americans moving into positions of leadership in the public schools both as school principals and in the district administration. In addition, both educators and non-educators, aware of the high rates of school failure among African American students, began to advocate for institutional change. However, similar to earlier periods in history, the challenges to the status quo mounted by African Americans were not unified. The alternatives that were advocated included support for a voluntary inter-district city-suburban volunteer desegregation program, an attempt to create an autonomous predominantly African American district-within-a-district, and a burgeoning effort to institute a state-funded private school choice program aimed at central city students.

The African American Immersion Schools provided African Americans in this city with yet another alternative for the same aim: to educate African American children effectively. The notion of African-centered education had been evolving in the United States over a 200-year period (Adeleke, 1994; Ratteray, 1992). However, nationally, this paradigm was being reintroduced to conceptions of schooling for African American students (Asante, 1991; Eyo, 1991) around the time these African American Immersion Schools were being established. However, these schools were not viewed with uniform enthusiasm either within this community or nationally. As such, they had to compete with other educational interests both within local and national African American communities as well as with interests outside these communities.

The second major issue is that contemporary urban conditions are configured in a manner that often means that poor communities are not involved in the educational decision making that affects their children. Yet for a brief period in recent years, African American elite educators have had major influence in shaping the direction of educational reforms for poor urban communities. This paradoxical state of affairs was true in Milwaukee during the period 1987–1996, when the African American Immersion Schools came into being.

Wilson (1996) has argued that the disappearance of work in America's cities is associated with a number of other events that tend to leave the poorest parts of these cities isolated and powerless. He argues that as poverty becomes concentrated in particular areas of a city, citizens lose not only personal resources but also social resources such as access to information and the ability to monitor and control activities and events within their communities. Constrained by structural conditions that support widespread unemployment, residents of poor central city areas may begin to share perceptions of low self-efficacy with respect to their ability to have an impact on institutions in the community (Wilson, 1996). This analysis can be applied to the actions of poor community residents regarding public schools their children attend. In Milwaukee, the residents of the poorest communities had little voice in the decisions made about the schools that served their children.

While poor African Americans tended not to be involved in educational decision making having an impact on their children, in large cities around the United States, African American professionals were moving into leadership positions in public school hierarchies (Pollard, 1997). As these individuals moved into decision- and policy-making positions, they often began to address minority and African American education explicitly.

This was also the case in this city. In 1987, the deputy superintendent of the city's public schools was named acting superintendent, becoming the first African American to hold this post in the city. In 1988, this superintendent established a Minority Achievement Committee to make recommendations to the Board of School Directors for improving the achievement of minority students in the city's public schools. In its deliberations and recommendations, this committee noted the increase in the numbers of minority students as a continuing trend in the city's schools and called for interventions to take account of this increasing diversity.

In 1988, another individual was appointed superintendent of the public schools, becoming the second African American to hold this position. This individual made a number of sweeping organizational changes in the district that were, ostensibly, aimed at serving the increasingly culturally diverse and economically marginal student population. In addition, under this superintendent's tenure, the Task Force on African American Males was appointed, and the African American Immersion Schools were established. This expanded the efforts of the former acting superintendent to focus district priorities on the changed student population. The period of African American educational leadership in this city continued to 1995. Upon the resignation of this superintendent, another African American, a native of the city with a long history of activism, was appointed. However, this person only served for three years, and upon his resignation in 1995, the post of superintendent returned to European Americans.

During the initial five years the African American Immersion Schools were implemented, there were also marked changes in the School Board. In 1989 and 1990, when these schools were first proposed, some School Board members were strong advocates for them. However, over time, new School Board members were elected, and support for the concept of African-centered schooling eroded.

The changes in the superintendency and the School Board illustrate two points. First, the students served by the African American Immersion Schools—that is, poor African American children and their families—were not part of the decision making concerning these schools. Second, the schools were in a position to be strongly affected by the whims of external forces.

The third major issue is that the establishment of the African American Immersion Schools and other similar models in *public* school settings placed African-centered education as a viable and legitimate alternative to past and ongoing instructional practices that have failed to educate African American children effectively. As a result, although the African American Immersion Schools in this city were shaped by unique local conditions, they have relevant contributions to make to broader national and international efforts to understand and support the education of children of African descent.

A particularly critical aspect of any attempt to institutionalize African-centered educational models in urban public school systems concerns relationships between these particular models and large bureaucracies. African-centered educational models in the private sector had not had to cope with this issue; thus, once again, no models existed for either the African American Immersion Schools or the district in this city to follow. It is our contention that an analysis of the implementation of these schools will provide conceptually important information relevant to future efforts to establish African-centered educational efforts within bureaucratic school systems.

In summary, an in-depth analysis of the initial five years of implementation of the African American Immersion Schools in the public schools in this large urban midwestern city should inform researchers and practitioners interested in educating African American children more effectively. Our discussion of the documentation and evaluation of these schools in this book is aimed both at providing an in-depth analysis of these particular institutions and linking the processes observed in the African-centered efforts in Milwaukee to broader issues regarding meeting the educational needs of African American children generally and those in urban schools in particular. These dual aims are reflected in the schema for the remainder of this volume.

ORGANIZATION OF THE REMAINDER OF THE BOOK

This book is organized into two parts. In Part I, the case studies of the two African American Immersion Schools are presented. These case studies focus on the actions involved in implementing this unique public school experiment. The perceptions of school staff along with field notes from our observations of the schools, classrooms, and events at the district level are the primary sources of data. We describe the implementation process and analyze factors that affected it at the two schools.

Chapter 1 provides a more detailed discussion of the historical and social contexts that were precursors to the establishment of two African American Immersion

Schools in this school district. Chapters 2 and 3 provide detailed portraits of the African American Immersion elementary and middle schools, respectively. Chapters 4 and 5 offer analyses of the changes that occurred during the initial five years the schools were implemented. Chapter 4 focuses on school-level changes. Chapter 5 focuses on the classrooms and differentiates between surface and deep cultural change processes. Finally, in Chapter 6 we discuss the outcomes from the initial five-year implementation process at these schools. We conclude by identifying lessons learned from them and discussing the implications of these lessons for African-centered education in the public arena. The references for this Introduction and the first six chapters are located at the end of Part I.

Part II consists of chapters contributed by four researchers who have been involved with us during our study. They have visited the schools and/or participated in the symposium, the presentation at the American Educational Research Association, or the conference. A. Wade Boykin opens this part with a discussion of a theoretical context for African-centered education and the African American Immersion Schools in Chapter 7. In Chapter 8, Shirley Brice Heath takes up the issue of language in African-centered contexts. In Chapter 9, Gloria Ladson-Billings discusses pedagogical issues relevant to African-centered schooling. Finally, in Chapter 10, Jacqueline Jordan Irvine provides a critique of African-centered schooling efforts and raises a series of questions that need to be considered when implementing this cultural orientation in the public sector.

Our book concludes with an epilogue. We ended our data collection activities at the African American Immersion Schools in June 1997. However, since then, a number of events have occurred that have implications for the future of African-centered education in public schools both nationally and internationally. The epilogue discusses these events.

— PART I —

IMPLEMENTING
AFRICAN-CENTERED SCHOOLS
IN A PUBLIC CONTEXT

— 1 —

Historical, Social, and Cultural Contexts of the African American Immersion Schools

The African American Immersion Schools were established within an atmosphere of crisis. This crisis was based both on the general belief that education in the United States was in need of major reform and on the overwhelming evidence that existing school models and programs had failed miserably to educate African American children, particularly those in poor urban communities. The two African American Immersion Schools in Milwaukee, although viewed by some as controversial, were greeted by others with considerable hope and optimism. Educators, parents, and others who were supporters of these schools viewed them as educational innovations that might finally succeed where other school models had failed to educate African American children successfully.

The concept that the history and culture of African Americans could form the basis of an educational program is not new, particularly for African Americans in the United States. It is important, however, to understand the historical and contemporary contexts from which these schools emerged as well as the reasons underlying the establishment of the African-centered educational models in Milwaukee.

This chapter discusses the historical and contemporary contexts within which the African American Immersion Schools in Milwaukee were implemented. In this chapter, the following questions are addressed: (1) What were the precursors to Milwaukee's African American Immersion Schools? (2) What were the conditions in urban black America that led to or were associated with an increased interest in African-centered education on a national level? (3) What were the specific conditions or characteristics in Milwaukee that led this public school district to be one of the first to initiate an African-centered educational model? The answers to these questions will provide a perspective on the national and local contexts within which these schools emerged.

PRECURSORS TO MILWAUKEE'S AFRICAN AMERICAN IMMERSION SCHOOLS

The decision to implement African American Immersion Schools in the Milwaukee Public School District was not an obscure event nor an anomaly in the social history of education. Rather, it can be contextualized within a broader set of social, economic, and educational circumstances that have influenced urban centers like this one.

An important premise underlying public education, particularly in urban contexts, is that it can counter inequalities existing in the wider society (Bowles, 1977; Giroux & McLaren, 1989). However, educational researchers have pointed out that schools do not operate in a vacuum. Rather, they are important social institutions heavily influenced by prevailing political trends. It is argued that schools, along with other social institutions, serve as agencies whose function is to reproduce existing structural inequalities (Bourdieu, 1973; Levinson & Holland, 1996; Willis, 1981, 1983). More specifically, it is argued that there is a relationship between cultural reproduction and social reproduction. According to social reproduction theory, educational systems socialize clients to accept existing structures of power and symbolic relationships through the selective transmission of power and privileges. Hence, an educational system contributes to the reproduction of class structures and social relations.

This phenomenon is realized through the assumption of both overt and covert pedagogical practices (Bernstein, 1977; Levinson & Holland, 1996; Willis, 1981, 1983). Inherent in the social history of the United States as well as the city of Milwaukee is a persistent pattern that places African Americans in a separate and unequal social order. In many cases, these disparities are compounded by economic factors; however, the basic underpinning of this pattern is racially motivated.

Despite the persistence of this pattern, African Americans have a long history of attempting to use education as a means to gain access to resources necessary not only to survive but also to attempt to advance as a people in the United States. Faced with efforts by European American policy makers, first, to deny African Americans access to schooling and, second, to provide them with schools crippled by inadequate resources, African Americans fought back with persistent efforts to obtain access to educational resources that would serve their children effectively. This response has taken various philosophical perspectives. For instance, some have focused on access to the same educational institutions that European American children attended, whereas others called for black-controlled schools.

One major issue in the ongoing quest by African Americans for educational opportunity and access concerns the integration of their history and culture in the curriculum and in instructional processes and techniques. In most traditional schools, African American history and culture is ignored or exists at the margins of a Eurocentric curriculum. Attempts to remedy this situation have ranged from isolated add-ons of information regarding African Americans to curricula in which African American children are centered within their own cultural perspectives (Asante, 1991).

Interest in various aspects of African-centered schooling has existed for over 200 years (Ratteray, 1994). In the 1850s, African American activist Martin Delany presented views somewhat similar to those espoused by contemporary advocates of Afrocentrism in education (Adeleke, 1994). Originally, Delany, who lived from 1812 to 1885, argued that education should both liberate the mind and teach people the skills needed for economic survival. He also postulated that education could be used as a means of "moral suasion" to change the attitudes whites held toward African Americans. When he realized that this last postulation was not to be the case, Delany changed his views radically. He began to argue that blacks needed to control their children's education and that race and ethnicity should be the central constructs for the study of the African American experience in the United States. Similar to contemporary Afrocentrists, Delany argued that education should also be used to refute racist, colonialist perspectives (Adeleke, 1994). Other African American activists and theorists who demanded changes in education that would speak to the needs and interests of African American children included Carter G. Woodson, W.E.B. Du Bois, and George Padmore (Holmes, 1993). All of these philosopher–educators saw education as the primary source for political and social empowerment of African Americans and stressed the importance of African and African American history and culture in the schooling process (Holmes, 1993).

Another response to the denial of educational access experienced by African Americans was to develop independent schools as alternatives to the public schools. Some of these schools became another important precursor to contemporary African-centered educational models in public schools. Black independent schools existed as early as 1787 (Hoover, 1992). According to Ratteray (1992), independent schools were "created to protest social inequality, serve as examples of institution building and provide services to their communities" (139). African American independent schools varied widely with respect to their orientation and philosophy. While some developed an Afrocentric focus, others were virtually indistinguishable from the more traditional Eurocentric educational models (Ratteray, 1992). One example of an African-centered independent school was the Nairobi Day School, which existed from 1966 to 1984. This school, located in East Palo Alto, California, used African and African American history, culture, and language as the basis of its curriculum and made use of pedagogical techniques that responded to African American children's learning styles. The school demanded that teachers hold high expectations for its students, stressed skills-oriented instruction, and aimed to develop young people to be leaders committed to supporting the African American community (Hoover, 1992). When interest in African-centered schools in the public schools arose in the late 1980s and early 1990s, the only existing models were in independent schools.

Another precursor to the resurgence of interest in African-centered education in the 1990s came from both the civil rights advocates who fought for equal educational opportunities for black children and the Black Power, Black Nationalist, and Pan Africanist movements of the late 1960s and 1970s who framed their arguments in terms of black empowerment. The civil rights movement of the 1950s and 1960s focused on demands for African American access to resources and institutions, including schools from which blacks had been systematically excluded. A commonly held view is that a major goal of African Americans who fought for desegregated schools was assimilation into the dominant society with the implications that this involved adopting the dominant culture's norms and values. However, Dawkins and Braddock (1994) have suggested an alternative conceptualization. They argue that many African Americans have consistently sought "inclusion" in the political and economic arenas of society without ignoring or rejecting their culture.

The Black Power, Black Nationalist, and Pan Africanist movements evolved from the civil rights movements of the 1950s and 1960s. African Americans who held these perspectives rejected the assimilationist orientation attributed to some of the earlier civil rights activists and called for African American political and cultural control of their communities (Holmes, 1993). In addition, many of the cultural and political movements within the African American community during these years not only advocated community control of institutions but also questioned the validity of European American culture, particularly with respect to its meanings for African American students (Allen & Jewell, 1995). Allen and Jewell (1995) describe the conflicts between the largely African American community and the mostly European American teachers' union in the Ocean Hill–Brownsville School District in New York City in 1968 and 1969 as an example of the debate about who would set the agenda for African American education. Furthermore, these authors draw parallels between this conflict of the 1960s and similar conflicts between African American communities and white missionaries in the southern United States in the 1860s. Much of the impetus for African-centered education today focuses on the same issue: Whose agenda should schools for African American students follow?

Although the civil rights and Black Power movements held somewhat different perspectives with respect to the most effective means for black survival and empowerment in a racist, oppressive nation, there were interesting similarities in the educational outcomes of their activities. In many urban areas, one of the tactics of civil rights activitists who agitated for equal educational opportunity for African American children through school desegregation was the use of school boycotts and the establishment of alternative "freedom schools" for African American children. Often, these schools provided opportunities to teach children about African American history and culture. The authors of this volume participated in this freedom school movement in urban communities in the 1960s and 1970s.

Similarly, an offshoot of the Black Power, Black Nationalist, and Pan Africanist movements included the establishment of African-centered independent schools and other innovative educational programs such as the Black Panthers' free breakfast program, which often included the dissemination of educational information about African and African American history and culture. While most of these efforts were most often formalized in independent school settings, activists continued to argue forcefully that African and African American history and culture should be included in the curricula of public schools, particularly those that served African American student populations.

In summary, then, the African American Immersion Schools studied in this book were innovative but not new. An examination of the little-known history of African Americans reveals that views reflecting African-centered educational perspectives have existed for well over a century. Furthermore, efforts to provide educational programs in which African and African American history and culture are central have been implemented, often successfully, in the past. Most often, these efforts occurred in independent schools or in community-based organizations that operated programs that were tangential to the public schools. These African American Immersion Schools were unique, however, in that they represented one of the first attempts to formalize an African-centered perspective in the public school arena. At this point, we need to ask what the national and local conditions were in urban America that led to the establishment of these schools as alternatives for preparing African American children for the twenty-first century.

THE NATIONAL CONTEXT

In this section, we will describe the contexts surrounding the renewed interest in African-centered education nationally in the last decade of the twentieth century. Three major factors that are of key importance are: (1) the demographic changes in the country's landscape and concomitant political changes wrought by the federal government, (2) the emergence of the educational reform movement, and (3) renewed attention and scholarship by African American academicians concerning Afrocentrism and African-centered education. The interactions among these factors help us understand the reasons for the increase in the numbers of educators and parents who are advocating African-centered educational alternatives for African American children. While these factors have been observed throughout the United States, they are most evident in urban areas, which are the focus of this discussion.

Demographic, Social, and Educational Changes in the Landscape of the United States, 1950–1990

Despite assertions to the contrary, the United States has never been a culturally monolithic nation. Nevertheless, America's schools have presented a monolithic perspective. However, during the last half of the twentieth century, the pluralistic nature of this society has become increasingly evident. "In recent years, the United States has become less white, less 'European' and less bound by a single language" (Hacker, 1992, 167). In addition to the changes in the cultural characteristics of the population, there have been major economic dislocations during this period of time (McKenzie, 1991). These trends are especially evident in urban communities that have been characterized by a steady in-migration of African Americans and other people of color and out-migration of whites to suburban areas. At the same time, these in-migrants to cities have been faced with severe economic distress as industries have moved out of urban areas to suburbs, rural areas, or other countries (Rury, 1993). According to Wilson (1987), these major economic dislocations have resulted in critically high levels of unemployment, particularly concentrated in African American urban communities. This economic crisis has led to a variety of social problems that tend to accompany economic distress. This distress was compounded further by the actions of the Reagan and Bush administrations to limit the federal government's responsibility for implementing social and economic programs to help the poor (Jacob, 1991). Thus at the very time that many of these people were losing access to employment, job training, health, housing, and other social programs that might have helped them were being cut.

The impact of these demographic and economic changes on public schools has been profound. Narine (1992) noted that in 1954 only 10 percent of public school students represented people of color; however, by 1992, almost one-third of these students were people of color. Currently, in many large cities, such as Chicago, Illinois, Washington, D.C., Baltimore, Maryland, Philadelphia, Pennsylvania, and Milwaukee, Wisconsin, a majority of the public school students are African American. Indeed, it has been projected that by the year 2000 African American and other students of color will comprise majorities in more than 50 major cities in the United States (Frierson, 1990).

In addition, because of the economic dislocations in urban communities, large numbers of these children have grown up in conditions of poverty. The extreme nature of this poverty, combined with continuing discrimination and institutionalized racism, meant that many of these children lived under great stress (McKenzie, 1991). As Wilson (1987) noted, the role of schooling takes on quite different meanings when increasing numbers of students come from families that have experienced high levels of joblessness, economic stress, and accompanying social isolation. Unfortunately, however, schools have tended to ignore these children's situations, preferring instead to continue to apply pedagogical techniques that do not address their needs. Unable or unwilling to accommodate the needs of poor African American children, teachers often give up, and achievement declines.

Despite their increase in numbers, African Americans have had to struggle continuously to obtain an adequate education for their children. For almost 40 years, a major aspect of this struggle concerned the desegregation of public schools, first in the South and then in the urban North. Initially, many African Americans supported school desegregation efforts, viewing these possible avenues for improved educational opportunities. However, they may have underestimated the strength and intractability of European American resistance to sharing educational resources with African Americans as well as their determination to maintain their positions of privilege in this society (Allen & Jewell, 1995).

White resistance to desegregation took many forms. One was to remove white children from public schools. In many southern states, this was accomplished through the establishment of private schools for white students. In urban areas, European Americans fled to suburbs, thus recreating segregated schooling environments with relatively affluent schools in predominantly white suburbs and poorly financed and resourced schools serving African American and Latino/Latina children in central cities. Another type of resistance involved tracking in desegregated schools in which white students were placed in "higher" tracks and provided with more resources, whereas African Americans were relegated to stigmatized "lower" tracks or levels (Narine, 1992). Resistance to desegregation was also evident in school staffing and curricular policies. In many school districts, desegregation meant that African American teachers and administrators lost jobs to whites who maintained control over the curriculum available to students. Finally, because of segregated housing patterns and a lack of commitment by public officials to educational parity for African Americans, desegregation simply did not occur in many urban communities (Narine, 1992).

Observing the unanticipated consequences of the movement toward school desegregation, many African Americans began to question the wisdom of pursuing this direction as the primary possible solution to their continuing struggle for educational parity. Studies conducted in the late 1980s and early 1990s of school attendance patterns, particularly in urban areas, suggested that desegregation would not lead to viable educational opportunities for large numbers of African American children, particularly those concentrated in central cities. Citing a study by Orfield, Narine (1992) noted that, nationally, 63 percent of African American students attended schools in which people of color predominated. In the Northeast, one-third of African American students were in schools that were more than 99 percent black. In cases where desegregation did occur, such as Milwaukee, the burden of desegregating schools fell disproportionately on African American students who were bussed long distances, often to hostile school environments. Furthermore, as the school populations of cities have become dominated by African Americans and other people of color, the issue of desegregation including whites has become increasingly irrelevant. The demise of school desegregation as an issue was exacerbated with the Supreme Court decisions of *Board of Education of Oklahoma City v. Dowell* (1991) and *Freeman v. Pitt* (1992), which terminated federally mandated desegregation decrees in Tulsa and Oklahoma City, Oklahoma (Brown, 1993). These decisions will allow many communities to abandon all pretenses at desegregation. Understanding these trends, many African Americans began to look to other alternatives to help their children gain educational access and parity.

Despite the failure of school desegregation, it must be noted that much of the earlier interest of African Americans in this process derived from their knowledge that the segregated public schools their children had to attend frequently lacked the resources to provide adequate, effective educational experiences. This situation remained for the racially isolated schools the majority of African American children in urban areas attended in the 1990s. It has been argued that schools that serve predominantly African American communities have tended to be chronically underfunded (Narine, 1992). As a result, these schools often do not have the funds to hire personnel to serve the needs of the students or even to provide adequate educational materials and technology for their students.

In addition to a lack of resources, the schools serving predominantly or totally African American student populations are increasingly staffed by white teachers, many of whom do not understand and empathize with these students. This problem has been exacerbated during the past 30 to 40 years by a decline in the numbers of

African American teachers. During the period from 1970 to 1990, the percentage of African Americans in teaching declined from 12 percent to 8 percent. Furthermore, if these trends continue, it is projected that by the year 2000 African Americans will comprise less than 5 percent of elementary and secondary school teachers (King, 1993). This trend is counterbalanced by the steady increase in the numbers of African American and other students of color noted earlier in this chapter.

The lack of available African American teachers in schools in general, and particularly in schools in which African American students predominate, is important in at least two ways. First, African American teachers have often served as role models and parent surrogates for African American students. Second, they often bring to their classrooms beliefs in the efficacy of African American children, an ability to communicate with them, and the use of culturally relevant pedagogical strategies (King, 1993). On the other hand, white teachers, who do not share the culture of African American students, may not understand their behavior or appreciate the talents they bring to the school setting, especially if they have not had the opportunity to learn about African and African American history and culture.

In addition to these demographic characteristics, teachers of African American students, both black and white, may suffer from their own miseducation with respect to work with this population. Too often, in teacher preparation programs, the history and culture of African Americans as well as other people of color are ignored, and African American children are discussed only from a deficit perspective. As a result, many teachers enter these schools believing these students are incapacitated in some manner. They may abdicate their responsibility to teach these students altogether (Delpit, 1995), or they may set such low standards for achievement that their students find it difficult to compete in later schooling and in life (Narine, 1992). These beliefs are often exacerbated when the children are also poor.

In summary, then, the past 40 years have been characterized by major demographic changes particularly in urban communities. A most important aspect of this has involved an unprecedented increase in the African American presence in the nation's largest cities. The largest impact of these population shifts has been in urban public schools. In these cities, African Americans have continued their struggle to have their children educated effectively. During the 1960s and 1970s, much of this struggle revolved around school desegregation. In more recent years, it has become apparent that desegregation has failed to improve African American children's educational opportunities. At the same time, however, racially isolated schools continue to fail to educate African American children effectively. As the twentieth century began to draw to a close, it was becoming clear that traditional schools were not working for this population.

The Role of Educational Reform

Another force was at work, however. America's schools not only were failing African American children, other children of color, and poor children. There was an increasing perception that they were failing European American and middle-class children as well. The concerns about the education available to these latter groups were first presented in *A Nation at Risk* (National Commission on Excellence in Education, 1983), a report that indicted America's schools and became the impetus for an educational reform movement that continues to exist today. *A Nation at Risk* was followed by a spate of other reports that detailed the crises apparent in America's schools, identified the culprits believed to have caused these crises, and made recommendations for reforming and restructuring the nation's schools. Although most of these reports initially did not concern themselves with African American or other children of color, throughout the country, and particularly in urban communities, school reform became the watchword of the day. Districts began to experiment with new organizational structures and programs.

Despite this flurry of activity, African American children continued to suffer unacceptable levels of school failure nationally. Educational reform seemed to have little or no impact on their schooling experiences. Several writers have suggested reasons for the failures of educational reform for both African American and other children. Mirel (1994) argued that educational reformers had not considered the political issues inherent in significant educational change. Specifically, Mirel noted that reform necessarily challenges deeply held ideas about education and often engenders resistance. In a similar vein, Wehlage, Smith, and Lipman (1992) studied educational reform in four cities and found little change in fundamental core values in the schools. Rather, they found supplemental tinkering with activities that left the schools' traditional policies and values intact. In a major critique of the current educational reform movement, Berliner and Biddle (1995) argue not only that contemporary educational reform is based on misguided and suspect assumptions and assertions but also that most suggestions for reform fail to address the real issues facing today's schools. Indeed, a perusal of the educational reform literature indicates that much of it ignores the cultural and social changes that have occurred in today's student populations. As a result, many of these reforms fail to address the cultural bases of schooling as well as the current economic conditions, focusing instead on relatively narrowly defined aspects of teacher and student performance in traditional European-centered settings. Given this orientation in the educational reform movement, it is not surprising to find that African American children have not benefited from it.

In summary, the last decades of the twentieth century provided continuing evidence of the validity of reproduction theories of education for African Americans. In urban communities particularly, schools repeatedly failed to educate poor African American children so that they could participate in the social and economic systems of society. Further, neither the desegregation movement of the 1950–1970 period nor the reform efforts of the 1980s addressed these students' needs effectively.

However, an alternative perspective was being reinvigorated. African-centered perspectives were being reintroduced to conceptions of schooling for African American students. The philosophical and educational tenets of Afrocentrism and African-centered education had been discussed for several years (Asante, 1991, 1991–1992, 1992, 1993; Eyo, 1991; Harris, 1992; Holmes, 1993; Murrell, 1996; O'Daniel,

1994). Asante (1991) defined *Afrocentrism* as a paradigm in which the peoples of Africa and the African Diaspora and their worldviews were central to the schooling process. An Afrocentric perspective also attempts to present accurate portrayals of both the African past and the ongoing struggles of African peoples throughout the world (Akoto, 1994). African-centered education is defined as

> the codification or systematic expression of Afrikan [sic] people's will to recover, recreate, and perpetuate our cultural heritage. . . . [It] enriches our culture as it attempts to illuminate it and it enculturates the people whose collective and historical experiences shape and are shaped by it. (Akoto, 1994, 321)

An African-centered education, therefore, is derived from an Afrocentric worldview, that revisits and focuses on the ways in which African culture and people of African ancestry have contributed to the world (Eyo, 1991).

Asante (1992) argued that if African Americans were taught within the context of their own history and culture, they would find it easier to relate to the knowledge that was presented to them and would be more likely to see themselves as actual participants in the learning process rather than as observers of someone else's history and culture. He asserted that when students are able to use cultural and social referents from their own historical backgrounds, they will become empowered in their classrooms, will feel more confident about their schooling experiences, and will be more highly motivated to engage in the educational process (Asante, 1991–1992). Noting that Afrocentrism is one of a number of centered approaches, proponents of African-centered education argue that this approach represents a viable path toward the recognition of the pluralistic nature of society in the contemporary United States as well as the world. Through grounding in an African-centered perspective, with its teachings of recognition of and respect for diverse cultural perspectives, African American children are more likely to embrace what Asante (1991) calls a "nonhierarchical" multiculturalism in which they have a clear sense of their own place in history and thus are better able to understand their relations with other people of the world (172).

The writings of Afrocentric scholars and the increasingly evident pluralism in the United States, along with the mounting documentation of the failure of traditional American schools to educate African American students effectively, formed a backdrop for interest in African-centered educational programs as potentially viable alternatives. This was particularly true in urban areas where evidence of both cultural diversity among students and inadequate schooling was acutely visible. However, according to Wieder (1992), three events provided a strong impetus to this movement. These were (1) a conference that focused on the inclusion of African and African American content in the high school curriculum, held in Atlanta, Georgia, in 1989 and repeated in 1990, (2) the publication of the *Baseline Essays* by the Portland, Oregon, school system in 1989, and (3) the publication of a report by the New York State Minority Task Force entitled *A Curriculum of Infusion* in 1989. Interestingly, all three of these events led to consideration of the inclusion of an

African-centered perspective in public school settings. In addition, in some public schools, experiments in African-centered education were being implemented on a limited basis. One of the best known of these attempts was a program in the Baltimore Public Schools in which African American male elementary students were provided with experiences from an Afrocentric perspective for several hours a week (Narine, 1992). However, in 1991, many of the African-centered educational experiments were limited to pullout programs during the school day or after-school programs. In the private sector, however, African-centered schools were proliferating. Indeed, by the beginning of the 1990s it was estimated that over 350 African-centered private schools served over 50,000 African American students in the United States (Jackson, 1994). Clearly, however, the impetus was present for the implementation of African-centered educational models on a wider scale in public school settings. In the next section, we turn our attention to Milwaukee, which was one of the first public school districts in the nation to establish school-wide African-centered educational programs.

THE LOCAL CONTEXT

In many ways, Milwaukee mirrored the patterns found in other major urban areas in the twentieth century. During the first half of the twentieth century, Milwaukee, like many other cities, was characterized by a period of major economic expansion because of increasing industrialization (Levine & Zipp, 1993). Unlike other northern cities, however, during this period the African American population was quite small. Although African Americans migrated to Milwaukee in a steady stream between 1900 and 1950, this did not take place at a rate similar to that in such cities as Chicago, Philadelphia, and Detroit (Trotter, 1985). In 1920, African Americans comprised 0.5 percent of the city's population. By 1950, African Americans still made up only 3.4 percent of Milwaukee's population (Levine & Zipp, 1993). Milwaukee had one of the smallest African American communities among northern cities at that time (Trotter, 1985).

African Americans who migrated to Milwaukee during the first half of the twentieth century were greeted with an interesting situation. The city had attracted large numbers of ethnic white workers to its factories and plants and developed a strong labor movement. African Americans migrating to Milwaukee faced strong hostility from white workers and white capitalists. As a result, they were relegated to the lowest level of labor, domestic service and personal service jobs (Trotter, 1985). Furthermore, when times of economic distress fell upon the city, African Americans were hardest hit. For example, Trotter (1985) noted that during the depression years the unemployment rate for African Americans in Milwaukee was four times higher than that of whites. Furthermore, he noted, the unemployment rate for African Americans in Milwaukee was higher than that for African Americans in New York, Chicago, Detroit, and Cleveland. Thus, despite the fact that African Americans who migrated to Milwaukee were economically better off than if they had remained in the South, their position was always precarious.

In the 1920s, Milwaukee was a forerunner in national policy by being the first city in the nation to offer low-income housing projects. However, blacks were not allowed to participate in this innovation. By the mid-1920s, the Milwaukee Real Estate Association had organized to establish a "black belt" to contain its growing African American population to two wards in the city. Furthermore, these wards were commercially zoned, and no less than 15 junkyards coexisted within the neighborhoods with African Americans. These environmental factors, coupled with a deplorable lack of available decent housing, led to increased health risks (Dalke, 1990).

It should be noted that African Americans in Milwaukee did not passively accept the position to which they had been relegated. Passed over by most public policy reforms, blacks found that they had to organize and agitate independently for better conditions by the late 1920s. At that time, opinions as to the best strategies to improve the conditions of African Americans were as diverse as they are today. The Urban League focused on the task of improving housing and acquiring recreational facilities for black Milwaukeeans. Other groups included the National Association for the Advancement of Colored People (NAACP) and the Labor Council, later renamed the Progressive Labor League, which had strong socialist and communist ties. There was also a strong presence of the Universal Negro Improvement Association, an organization founded by Marcus Garvey. A final group, called the Republican Milwaukee Men's Organization, was aligned with the National Republican Party (Milwaukee Urban League, 1919-1979; National Association for the Advancement of Colored People, 1917-1970). This diversity of civic activist groups foreshadowed the current presence of differing alliances and perspectives among blacks in Milwaukee. More important, it informs our understanding of the dynamics that shaped the social milieu of this city.

The situation of African Americans in Milwaukee changed dramatically during the last half of the twentieth century owing to several factors. First, because of increased migration of African Americans to the city, combined with a new and rapidly increasing flight of whites to suburbs, the proportion of the African American population increased substantially. Second, as the numbers of African Americans in Milwaukee increased, there was a concomitant increase in segregation. European Americans were moving to suburban areas; however, African Americans were generally excluded from these areas because of discriminatory housing policies. These trends and policies led Milwaukee to the dubious distinction of being ranked first in the United States in the number of African Americans living in the central city and first among metropolitan areas in the United States in racial segregation in 1980 (McNeely & Kinlow, 1987).

Finally, deindustrialization combined with policies established by the Reagan and Bush administrations on the federal level in the 1980s and 1990s led to a marked increase in poverty among this city's African American population. This trend was exacerbated during the 1990s with the rise of state-regulated programs aimed at reducing governmental assistance to poor families. As indicated in the Introduction, these demographic and economic changes were reflected in the shifting racial composition of the city's schools. Specifically, the student population in these schools changed from predominantly European American in the 1950s to predominantly African American in 1990. Furthermore, by 1990, in many schools, the majority of these students were poor.

As the number of African American students increased, so did segregation in the schools. Milwaukee Public Schools maintained a neighborhood schools policy that, combined with the housing segregation policies in effect, resulted in racially isolated schools. Black teachers who were recruited to Milwaukee from other parts of the country in increasing numbers in the 1960s and 1970s were placed primarily in schools where African American students predominated. Furthermore, these schools received fewer resources than other schools. Finally, evidence of a racial gap in the performance of African American and European American students began to appear (Academy for Educational Development, 1967; McNeely & Kinlow, 1987).

While these changes were dramatic, they were not altogether unforeseen. Indeed, Cibulka and Olson (1993) argued that racial changes in the Milwaukee Public Schools population were noticeable in the 1940s, and there was a steady increase in the African American population in these schools through the 1950s and 1960s. The early reactions of the Milwaukee Public Schools Board and administration was to ignore these changes and to avoid confronting issues related to race. This "head in the sand" approach is most evident in a historical overview of the Milwaukee Public Schools entitled *Our Roots Grow Deep. 1836-1967* (Lamers, 1974). Throughout this description of the evolution of the public schools, there is not one mention of African Americans specifically. There is, however, a relatively extensive discussion of increased troubles in the schools during the 1960-1967 period. These increased troubles are attributed to an increase in the numbers of "newcomers and underprivileged" in the schools.

There is other evidence of the school system's apparent inability or unwillingness to deal with the changes that were occurring in its student population during this period. For example, according to Cibulka and Olson (1993), the school district conducted a study in 1961 and found major differences in the "learning conditions between inner city schools and other schools within the . . . system" (90). However, these authors noted that the district officials avoided any mention of race when discussing these findings; instead, the focus was on poverty of the children. Furthermore, the only attempt to remedy the inequities found between the two groups of schools was the establishment of compensatory education programs. Again in 1967, the school district and a citizens committee contracted with the Academy for Educational Development in New York for a study of conditions in the Milwaukee Public Schools. In its report, the Academy for Educational Development (1967) noted a number of problems and presented recommendations to alleviate them. Many of the problems noted stemmed from the district's failure to manage the increasing diversity of the student population. The report made note of the differences in educational achievement in schools that were populated predominantly by African American and other students of color versus those populated primarily by European American students. These differences in achievement were attributed to the school district's failure to meet African American and other students of color's educational needs. The school system was further criticized for having a system of neighborhood schools that did not meet the needs of the neighborhoods they served and for ignoring the cultural diversity of its clients. Some of the recommendations contained in this report were (1) to develop "Special Education Centers which would make effective use of the rich diversity of ethnic, cultural, and socioeconomic heritages within the Milwaukee community for the special study of music, art, science and mathematics" (1967, 43); (2) to decentralize curriculum, organization, and assessment to better meet the needs and interests of different neighborhoods; (3) to provide teachers with more training in the social sciences to increase their understanding of different students' cultural backgrounds; and (4) to increase the numbers of African American teachers and administrators in the schools (Academy for Educational Development, 1967). Although this report called for a major reduction in the racial isolation African American and other students of color experienced, many of the recommendations from the Academy for Educational Development's study foreshadowed the concerns underlying the establishment of the African American Immersion Schools almost three decades later.

Unfortunately, however, most of the recommendations made by this group were ignored by the school district. The Milwaukee Public Schools administration argued that its policy was "color-blind" even as racial isolation and accompanying inequities in schooling for students of color increased. Furthermore, it stood by its neighborhood schools policy with one curious exception: When predominantly black schools became overcrowded, Milwaukee instituted an "intact busing" policy in which African American students and their teachers were bused to less-crowded, predominantly European American schools but were kept completely separated from the children in these schools. Under intact busing, the African American children had separate classes, lunch, and recess periods from the European American children. This policy in which race was so paramount seemed most incongruous with the district's assertion that it maintained color-blind policies. Intact busing was introduced in the late 1950s (Stolee, 1993).

While educational conditions in predominantly African American schools deteriorated steadily even after the Academy's report in 1967, African American citizens did not sit by and accept these conditions. Rather, there was increased agitation for change. African Americans' efforts to gain improved educational experiences for their children were evidenced by several major directions between the 1960s and the 1990s. These directions were related and evolved from African Americans' frustrations with the educational system and included (1) protests, (2) desegregation efforts in both the city and metropolitan area, and (3) attempts to establish schools controlled by, or more responsive to, African Americans.

Protests

During the period from 1960 to 1965, African Americans in Milwaukee began to express their distress about the overcrowded and underresourced schools their children were consigned to in the central city. The failure of the School Board and the larger white community to recognize the inequities in schooling formally, along with their refusal to admit to the race-based policies that maintained these unequal educational opportunities, sparked a series of demonstrations and other activities of protest. Most of these protests were directed against the segregated status of Milwaukee's public schools. They took the form of school boycotts, the establishment of alternative freedom schools, and the formation of the Milwaukee United School Integration Committee (MUSIC), an organization that coordinated efforts to fight segregation (Stolee, 1993). These protest efforts, while resisted by educational, business, and political leaders as well as by many white citizens, did bring issues of African American education to the forefront in Milwaukee and led to efforts within the African American community for actual remedies to the unequal educational situations their children faced.

Desegregation Efforts

In 1965, attorney Lloyd Barbee, a leader in MUSIC and other protest efforts, filed suit in federal court alleging that the Milwaukee Public Schools intentionally maintained a segregated system (Stolee, 1993). This led to a protracted court battle during which the school district attempted to justify its status quo policies. Over a decade later, in 1976, federal courts found that the Milwaukee Public Schools were intentionally segregated and ordered that plans be developed to remedy this situation. Although the school district resisted, plans were developed to desegregate both student and teacher populations in the Milwaukee Public Schools (Stolee, 1993).

After the desegregation suit was settled and as implementation plans were developed and implemented, European American parents in Milwaukee, like their counterparts elsewhere, reacted by removing their children from the Milwaukee Public Schools in increasing numbers. While some of this movement was into parochial independent schools, much occurred as whites moved to the suburbs. As a result, resegregation began to occur steadily within the city. Proponents of desegregation, recognizing this, supported legislative efforts to establish interdistrict transfers of students at the state level. This led to the establishment of the Chapter 220 program, a voluntary program in which children of color in a city with a minority population of 30 percent or more could transfer to suburban districts with minority populations of 30 percent or less and white students from the suburbs could attend city schools (Stolee, 1993). The 220 program was initiated in metropolitan Milwaukee in 1976 with a small number of participating students. The program was initially resisted by many suburban residents and was kept quite small. However, a lawsuit was filed in 1984 by the Milwaukee Public Schools and the local NAACP arguing that the suburbs were resisting these desegregation efforts. This case was settled by consent decree in 1987 and led to a major increase in the numbers of students participating in this effort. By 1990, the Chapter 220 program included 23 suburban districts and Milwaukee. Over 8,000 students of color from Milwaukee were attending suburban schools, whereas approximately 1,000 white students from the suburbs attended school in Milwaukee (Compact for Educational Opportunity, 1993).

Local Efforts to Establish Black Schools

One of the early attempts to establish a culturally based schooling experience for African American students in Milwaukee occurred in the late 1960s and early 1970s. An African American principal at a predominantly black middle school gathered together a group of African American teachers. They developed a curriculum in which black history and culture were infused into social studies and language arts classes. Unfortunately, this effort was relatively short-lived. After protests from the teachers' union and some district administrators, the staff was dispersed to other schools, ending this brief experiment. However, the notion of specific educational experiences for African American students persisted.

The idea of culturally based schooling also began to take root in some independent schools in Milwaukee. Specifically, during the 1970s and 1980s the Roman Catholic Archdiocese announced that it would disband some central city Catholic schools that had become populated predominantly by African American children. After protests from the African American community, an agreement was reached with two of the elementary schools faced with this situation. They would become independent schools. Although the Archdiocese would continue to provide limited support, they would look to the community for the bulk of their funding. As these two schools became independent, they also took on certain characteristics of African and African American culture, reflecting the backgrounds of their student bodies. In these schools, the level and degree of infusion were quite limited, often to the names of buildings, celebrations of historical events, and some infusion of African American history into areas of the curriculum. However, they did offer an alternative for those African American parents who could afford them.

By the late 1980s, it had become apparent that desegregation within the city of Milwaukee would be quite limited. At about the same time, some African Americans were expressing dissatisfaction with Milwaukee Public Schools' desegregation policies, especially with the distances to which African American children were being bused. In addition, certain politicians at the state level were expressing dissatisfaction with the Milwaukee Public Schools in general. There were some suggestions put forth for breaking up the state's largest school district into smaller units.

One group took advantage of these trends and proposed the establishment of a district composed of the central city schools populated predominantly by African Americans. Although this would essentially have been a "black" school district, there was little or no discussion of instituting an African-centered educational focus to these schools. This proposition was greeted with considerable controversy from many quarters. Although the proposal was not implemented, it did highlight the existence of this fairly large group of predominantly African American schools, and it suggested an alternative to the desegregation model that had been dominant heretofore.

By 1989, the educational situation in Milwaukee was in a state of crisis. Desegregation was becoming increasingly meaningless as the number of students of color in the city increased. Yet large numbers of students were still being bused around the city. Achievement levels were falling precipitously for African Americans and other students of color. Increases in disruptive behavior in the schools were reported, and the Milwaukee Public Schools were beginning to be portrayed as dangerous sites of frustration and failure. The predominantly white teaching staff appeared unable to teach the increasingly culturally diverse student population. In addition, the district continued to implement a standard Eurocentric curriculum. Clearly, an alternative solution was needed.

SUMMARY AND CONCLUSIONS

The establishment of the African American Immersion Schools in Milwaukee reflected the failure of traditional school models, both locally and nationally, to educate African American students effectively. They represented an alternative model aimed at providing African American students educational experiences within the framework of their own history and culture. These schools had historical precedents with respect to both African Americans' continuing struggle to obtain educational parity, in general, and the existence of African-centered conceptions of schooling, in particular. A number of contemporary national and local factors converged, leading to the view that African American Immersion Schools could be considered as a viable alternative to the failures of the existing system. One of these factors was the changing demographic composition of urban public school student populations.

A second factor involved the increasing frustration of African Americans and others with the educational models that existed in the 1970s, 1980s, and early 1990s. It has been argued that the academic and applied interest in Afrocentricity was particularly propitious in the late 1980s and early 1990s because cultural politics had become an important battleground in which African Americans as well as other people of color were in a position to both question traditionally Eurocentric conceptions of the world and offer viable alternatives (Merelman, 1994).

In addition to reflecting these national trends, some factors unique to Milwaukee may have encouraged the establishment of the African American Immersion Schools. One factor was that Milwaukee had a history of cultural infusion, although this history ignored African Americans. Beginning in 1867, Milwaukee established bilingual German schools throughout the district. In 1912, bilingual schools featuring the Polish and Italian languages were established. All of these programs were terminated when the United States entered World War II (Lamers, 1974). However, the idea of culturally infused schooling made its reappearance in 1982 when German and French Immersion Schools were established as specialty schools under the Milwaukee desegregation plan. Later, a Spanish Immersion School was added. These events established a historical precedent for the introduction of African American Immersion Schools.

A second factor concerned the prior establishment of schools oriented toward African American students as one of the responses to the failure of desegregation in Milwaukee. It must be noted that these attempts did not truly reflect African-centered educational models. In the public middle school and the two independent elementary schools, African and African American cultural infusion was very limited. The attempt to form a black school district focused primarily on administrative changes and paid little attention to cultural infusion. When attempted in the public sector, these efforts were thwarted. In the private sector, however, these efforts have been quite successful. These efforts provide yet another precedent for the consideration of African American Immersion Schools in Milwaukee.

The events leading to and including the establishment of the African American Immersion Schools can be summarized in terms of the three major issues identified in the Introduction. First, they represented both the continuation of African Americans' historical efforts to obtain a viable education for their children. However, the controversy surrounding their establishment, even within the African American community, illustrated that this was not a unified movement. Second, the major impetus for the African American Immersion Schools came from African American educators and professionals in the black community. Yet they were targeted to poor African Americans who had little input into the decision to establish them. Third, the African American Immersion Schools, as among the first models in the public setting, raised the level of discussion of African-centered education as a potentially viable alternative. However, as part of a large school district, bureaucratic policies and politics had an important impact on them.

By 1990, the Milwaukee Public Schools recognized that they were in a state of crisis. The tried and true educational models of the past were not working, particularly for African American students. The idea of the African American Immersion Schools, while controversial, seemed a worthwhile experiment. As such, they offered promissory notes of hope for students for whom all else had failed as well as for those who theorized about the goals and benefits of Afrocentric schooling for African American children. Our documentation of the first five years of implementation of these schools not only describes the initial return on these promissory notes but also analyzes the reasons these initial outcomes were attained.

— 2 —

A Portrait of the African American Immersion Elementary School

When the bell rings, children begin to form single files as they wait patiently on the playground for their teachers to appear. As each teacher leads his or her class into the building, an observer cannot help but be impressed by the orderly manner in which they file into the school in their uniforms. As one enters the main door, a bright yellow wall with a colorful rainbow to the immediate right welcomes you to the school. As one walks through the hallways, the students' work decorates the walls. Throughout the school, one cannot help but notice the African-centered focus of the students' work ranging from Anansi artwork by first graders to biographies of famous African Americans written by third and fourth graders. Soon after the children have gone to their classrooms, a child's voice can be heard on the intercom throughout the school, announcing the following:

> Good morning, my name is___, and I will be your reader this week. Today is Tuesday, November 4. . . . On this day in 1979, Richard Arrington was elected the first African American mayor of Birmingham, Alabama. Our positive affirmation for the week is "Self-help is the best help." I repeat, "self-help is the best help." We will now have our pledges.

This announcement is followed by a chorus of students from an entire class who recite two pledges over the loudspeaker. In each classroom in the school, the rest of the students join in. First, facing a red, black, and green flag, the students recite the following African American Pledge of Allegiance:

> I pledge allegiance to the flag of African American people. Under God, I will protect freedom, generate unity, seek peace, honor our ancestors, and encourage and support the development and prosperity of people of African descent.

This is followed by the Pledge of Allegiance to the American flag. The lead student reader then says, "Thank you. [The principal] will announce today's birthdays, and remember, 'self-help is the best help.'" The names of students with birthdays are announced, and the children then turn their attention to classroom activities.

This ritual begins each school day at the African American Immersion elementary school, one of the first public schools in the nation where an African-centered focus was institutionalized as part of an effort to raise the academic achievement of African American children. This ritual is one of many examples of a school-wide activity that infuses African and African American history and culture into the ongoing daily life of the school.

THE SCHOOL SETTING

The African American Immersion elementary school was built in the early part of the nineteenth century. The large, three-story, brightly colored stucco building stands alone on a city block, surrounded by a paved-over playground and staff parking lot. The back of the building faces a busy thoroughfare, whereas the streets at the side and front of the school are primarily residential. Inside the school, the walls are painted in bright colors contrasting with highly polished wooden floors. Although the building is old, it is well kept. Each of the high-ceilinged classrooms on the first through third floors is large and bright with one wall of windows overlooking the playground.

Although large, the building uses every bit of its space to accommodate students in classes ranging from Head Start to the fifth grade. During the initial five years of the implementation of the African American Immersion model, when we documented and evaluated the school, student enrollment averaged 552. The classrooms are grouped by grade, with first graders taking up most of the third floor. Most of the second- through fourth-grade classes are located on the second floor, and the kindergarten students share the first floor with administrative offices. In one wing at the northern end of the building the two fifth-grade classrooms are located on either side of a large room that serves as a combination cafeteria, auditorium, and indoor gym. The basement of the building houses another kindergarten class, exceptional education classes, the science classroom, and a room shared by the art and music teachers. In one corner of the basement is the staff lounge, where teachers gather periodically throughout the day to meet, eat, and seek brief moments of respite from their hectic schedules.

The African American Immersion elementary school is located in one of the oldest African American communities in the city. Situated just north of the city's downtown area and what was formerly one of the country's largest breweries, this community was once a thriving center of housing and commerce for the African American settlers in this city (Trotter, 1985). By 1990, however, this community had become characterized by urban blight, decimated by the loss of jobs as large industries left the city and by neglect as the city withdrew services and resources. The main thoroughfare through this neighborhood, which passes the school, once had been the site of many small businesses; however, by 1991 it was characterized by large numbers of boarded-up and abandoned buildings.

This community had also experienced changes in the characteristics of its African American population. Many longtime residents were struggling to cope with economic losses and the concomitant downward mobility engendered by these. In addition, newer African American migrants to the city, who were often attempting to escape even more desperate conditions elsewhere, were moving into the community. As a result, the neighborhood was characterized by increasing transiency and poverty. This community was not unlike those found in almost all large cities in the United States.

In many ways, the African American Immersion elementary school reflected the community it served. As a neighborhood school, over 99 percent of the students were African American. Furthermore, many of the students came from poor families. In 1991–1992, the first year the African American Immersion School model was implemented, 89 percent of the students were eligible for free or reduced lunch. During the period of our study, this number rose steadily, and by 1995–1996, the number of students eligible for free or reduced lunch had grown to 98 percent (Milwaukee Public Schools, 1991–1992, 1995–1996). In addition, at the time this school was designated an African American Immersion School, it already was receiving supplemental funding available to schools with high numbers of poor students under the federal Chapter 1 and State P-5 programs. Each of these programs provided funds to schools with high proportions of students from poor families.

Finally, when this school was designated to implement an African-centered educational focus, indicators of student achievement were low. For example, in 1990–1991, the year before this particular experiment began, results from the Iowa Tests of Basic Skills showed that only 15 percent of fifth graders scored at or above the national average in reading, and only 28 percent achieved similar results in math. Only slightly more than half of the school's third graders, 57 percent, achieved a passing score on the state-administered reading test. In summary, then, at the time that an African-centered focus was initiated at this elementary school, a number of indicators suggested that it was typical of urban elementary schools serving poor African American children. The successful implementation of an African-centered focus depends on the efforts of the administrators and staff of a school. This was particularly important in the public school arena where there were few guidelines available to help administrators and teachers when this school was designated an African American Immersion School. As a result, the staff, who were required to develop and implement an African-centered educational focus simultaneously, were key to the outcomes of this particular experiment. Therefore, we will turn our attention to the characteristics of the staff at the African American Immersion elementary school. At this particular school, the principal and staff provided an anchor of stability for its transient student population and neighborhood.

CHARACTERISTICS OF THE SCHOOL PRINCIPAL

Clearly, a key component in any educational reform involves the roles taken by the chief school administrator. An assessment of six nationally based school improvement programs identified characteristics of effective administrators (Clark & Clark,

1996). Among these characteristics were the following: one who has a strong sense of the educational vision and purpose of the school, who communicates that vision to school staff and the community served by the school, and who supports and encourages personal and professional growth and empowerment among the staff. Studies of schools that were effective in educating African American students found principals with similar characteristics (Jones-Wilson, 1991; Moody & Moody, 1989).

An important aspect of our documentation and evaluation of the African American Immersion Schools involved annual interviews with the school principal. The annual interviews allowed us to gain insights into ways in which the principal perceived the school and shaped its direction. In this section, we will discuss data from the interviews with the elementary school principal in the first, third, and fifth years of our study.

The principal at this elementary school had held her position at the school for three years before it was designated an African American Immersion School. She applied to serve at the school when it was designated to implement an African-centered focus and was selected by the district administration for the job in April 1991. During the spring and summer of 1991, the principal worked with the Implementation Committee to help plan for the Immersion Schools. During the three years before this elementary school was an African American Immersion School, this principal had already begun some programs that were carried over as the school's focus changed. One of these was a career day when African American adults who worked in a wide range of jobs came to the school and visited classrooms. Another was a merit program. In each marking period, students were given 50 points to protect. Points were lost for poor behavior and work, whereas other points could be earned for positive academic and social performance. At the end of the marking period, students were rewarded for maintaining or protecting points. Both of these activities were maintained when the school's focus changed. The merit program's name was changed to *Zawadi*, a Swahili word meaning "reward."

During the initial five years that this elementary school operated as an African American Immersion School, the principal exhibited several consistent themes in her perceptions and leadership style. These included (1) a clear vision of what this particular African-centered educational model should be and an agenda for implementing that vision, (2) an active and flexible hands-on management style, (3) positive and empowering relationships with staff, (4) high expectations for academic achievement among the students, and (5) a perception of what constitutes school change.

Vision

This principal had some very clear ideas about how to operationalize the African American Immersion idea in this elementary school. One such idea involved the transformation of the school's curriculum. At an in-service for faculty and staff the week before the opening of the school, she announced to the staff: "Our process will be one of infusion. We will infuse our curriculum with African and African

American history and culture, and we will start with social studies and language arts this year and then move on." By defining the process of creating an African-centered focus as one of infusion, the principal provided the staff with a well-defined mechanism for transforming the curriculum. This process became the primary agenda for moving this school from a Eurocentric to an Afrocentric orientation.

A second important aspect of the principal's vision for this school concerned her perspective of the students. Her perspective was grounded in centering the child in the schooling process. Early in the first year of the implementation of the immersion concept, she articulated her goals for this new public school educational model:

> I am hoping that I am going to be able to have a group of young people who really have a real strong sense of who they are and, more importantly, what they want to become. Because I want them to be able to see themselves as growing and changing and learning, I want to expose them to different activities in school and out of school that are going to help them become the best woman or man they can possibly become.

In this principal's view, the school's transformation into an African American Immersion School was meaningless if the students did not see the value of this shift in their lives. Thus, it was important to her that new school policies made a difference to the students. This was evident in the following excerpt:

> [B]asically speaking, the whole atmosphere of the school is different. Staff and students, I think we all have set very high expectations for ourselves. By and large, we are all living up to those high expectations. . . . But the thing is, the children, by and large, seem to start their day off on a very positive note. They interact with each other more positively. The young men are really exerting themselves in terms of their leadership roles. It is really nice to see the cadets. They seem to have taken on a different maturity level, if that is at all possible. . . . They . . . used to play all the time. Everything was a joke. Now they seem to be taking school more seriously. . . . Their knowledge of different people and their past is growing. In terms of learning poetry, like "Hey Black Child" and the positive pledge and things like this, they have just sucked that up like sponges.

From this principal's perspective, it was very important that the students felt a sense of belonging to the school.

One of the ways this was accomplished was through the institutionalization of a school uniform policy. This policy was advocated by parents as well as the principal and staff and was implemented when the school became an African American Immersion School. The principal felt this policy had positive outcomes for the students.

> Uniforms have made a lot of difference in the basic decorum of the students. . . . They just feel proud because they know that they look good. Everywhere they go. . . . I took eight kids to the Hyatt for lunch for the Martin Luther King kickoff luncheon, and they got to stand up and show off their uniforms. They lit up the room, just with the way they felt about themselves.

The principal went on to say that the students "are really buying into this whole process. . . . They, in fact, are part of the process."

Management Style

This principal implemented her vision for the African American Immersion elementary school through a management style that involved active monitoring of school activities. She was a visible presence throughout the school: "If you are not willing to come out of this office and get to know your teachers, get to know your kids, the needs of your community, and build your school based on that, then you can't do the job." The principal frequently observed in teachers' classrooms and sometimes even took on the role of classroom instructor. She often used her observations to clarify for teachers the overall vision of this particular African-centered educational model.

> I only had a few instances of when I went in to observe teachers that I had to tell them, "No this wasn't what we were talking about. This is an add-on, or this is a worksheet." . . . In those instances, teachers and I have to sit down and discuss it. And there have been changes. In some instances, slow, but there have been changes.

Although this principal had definite ideas about the direction that the school should take, she was also flexible and willing to compromise policies and procedures in order to maintain harmony while pursuing the larger goal of developing an African-centered orientation. One example of this flexibility involved her reaction to some students' resistance to the school uniforms.

> The older kids resisted somewhat wearing uniforms every day. So that was one of the reasons we went to free dress day. Once a month, usually a Friday, they got to wear whatever they wanted to wear, and so did the staff. Everybody was excited about free dress day. And you would see when people wouldn't be dressed, "professional" people would say to them, "It is not free dress day." The expectation of dress has improved, risen, and we don't expect them to have on tennis shoes and jeans. So whenever they would see them, "Is today a free dress day?"

Similar flexibility was shown by the principal when teachers voiced concerns about a school organization policy that was instituted when the African American Immersion process began. The school was reorganized into families, small groups of teachers and their students. The school day was reorganized so that the teachers in each family would have joint planning times. In addition, there was an expectation that each family would implement joint activities for their students periodically. While the teachers supported the general idea of the family structure, they were not pleased with the way it was organized initially. The principal responded accordingly.

> I like the family structure. I think it is nice. It's been changed. . . . The first way I did it was I had cross grade groupings. . . . I had kindergarten and first [grades], and then I

had second and third and fourth and fifth, and it just didn't work. So I'm flexible. I said, "Let's go back to the drawing board." So we went to [same] grade levels the last two years, and it's been better.

Relationships with Staff

This principal recognized the centrality of the school staff to the success of this school experiment. She maintained high expectations for the staff and emphasized a collaborative model of interaction. For example, as the implementation of the immersion model got under way, she described the staff in the following manner:

> When I look at the overall structure of the school, I have to marvel at how well the people can work together when given the opportunity. The first-grade team always worked well together, but now with the family structure and the team time, we focus in on long-range planning, which is something we lost sight of with not having any planning time. Now they plan months in advance and share in the expertise that they bring to the profession.

When describing the high points of the first year of implementation, the principal noted a sense of cohesiveness among the staff: "I think . . . the feeling of family . . . has been created in the school. . . . It may be my perception, but [there is] the kind of feeling that we are in this together, that we can do it. We have everything that we need to do it."

This principal sought to empower the school staff by encouraging them to take initiative and work independently. As the following excerpt demonstrates, this required her to modify some of the ways she interacted with teachers.

> In January, we were focusing on Dr. Martin Luther King, and the kids wrote stories; they are doing a play. That was their work together. That took a lot off of me too because, at one time, I always thought I had to keep my staff on track, so I'd put things in the bulletin that we need to do this and that, but now they work as a team and I get notes on what they are doing. I knew they had it in them, and I sort of pushed them out of the nest, and they are doing nicely all alone. When we first started with the family structure, I did an outline to focus on the topic. I attended meetings about the first month, and I haven't been to one since. They give me their notes. . . . When you have the freedom, you have to have a lot of faith and believe in them and what they are doing. You keep a watchful eye from a careful distance. You don't want to smother them so they don't rely on you to make decisions.

Expectations for Student Achievement

In addition to stressing positive relationships with staff, this principal also had a keen understanding of the students she served, and she shaped her goals accordingly. It should be noted that although she recognized her students' backgrounds, she maintained high expectations for them.

It is very important that we teach our young people to be survivors . . . how to assess their situation and how to change those circumstances so that they become more favorable, so that they are not swallowed up in hopelessness. Critical thinking skills, problem-solving skills, are going to be very critical because they are going to have to make some choices. [We are] doing a lot of things around careers . . . what opportunities are out there for a poor black girl and poor black boy. [We are] teaching them that if they will engage in this educational process, give it their best shot, that these things that other people have realized can also become realities for them.

This goal of nurturing student achievement was consistently stated by the principal in our annual interviews with her throughout the initial five years of the program. For her, this was the highest priority: "When we talk about improved self-esteem, I think that will probably be a secondary goal almost as important as improved student achievement." The emphasis on student achievement, along with high expectations, began to have a payoff by the third year this school operated as an African American Immersion School:

But now, I feel we have tasted success. We had experience with the third-grade reading test, and we gained 57 points from the year previously. Even though it is a different set of children, it proves that learning is happening in our school, that children are making progress in our school, and that we do have some high-functioning people.

It should be noted, however, that this principal's definition of achievement focused on the development of higher-order thinking skills rather than simply the acquisition of basic skills:

Having them [the students] have a belief in themselves, believing that they can do and be anything if they put their minds to it and work hard at it. I really think that's what school is all about; more than having students that have A's and B's, having real high Iowa scores . . . is really having a well-rounded child who can think and analyze.

Perceptions of Change

In addition to her emphasis on the growth of her students, this principal expressed high expectations for the African American Immersion experiment from its beginning. Her expectations were accompanied by a strong sense that the development of an African-centered educational model involved a process of ongoing change. For example, in the middle of the first year when asked to describe the highlight of the first few months, she described the program as emerging successfully:

[I was able] to see ideas put into workable form in terms of curriculum, knowing the staff, working with the parents, kind of putting the pieces together. . . . That was the accomplishment of 1991 that I was most proud of. . . . It is everything I dreamed a school could be.

According to this principal, the staff's efforts to deal with change continued to have positive results as the school completed its third year of providing an African-centered education. In her description of that year, she stated, "The staff is really jelling. They are really becoming a cohesive team. They are working better together. They are sharing more information and setting very high expectations for themselves." The principal went on to discuss how she actively monitored change as she attempted to shape the direction of the school.

> I am adding and subtracting staff because of the fact that they have not found a niche within this organization, so I'm still having a little higher turnover than I would like. But I think once those people who really can't keep up with the pace have found someplace else that they want to go and we have replaced them with people who really are motivated and committed to this project, we can't help but keep getting better and better.

In the fifth year that this elementary school operated as an African American Immersion School, the principal spoke of the multifaceted nature of the changes that she perceived had occurred.

> Well, I think that as we look at where the school was eight or ten years ago . . . you 'd be able to come up with some things that happened. Even if you didn't know the history of what's behind the school . . . you'd be able to see a change. You have to know that the right people came together at the right place and the right time. Probably with the right attitude, right mind and some very significant strategies to make some very strong impacts. The significant thing for me is that we believed and we worked hard enough to make the kids believe and they worked hard enough to make some changes.

Finally, as the principal worked with this process during the initial five-year period the school operated as an African American Immersion School, she broadened her perspective on change beyond this particular school site.

> I think there is so much to be learned from this project that we could probably spend the next 25 years actually coming up with why it worked, but I know we don't have that kind of time. What we need to be about now is solidifying that it did work and finding out what we can share with others so they can start moving in that direction.

In summary, the principal at the African American Immersion elementary school was a force for stability and constancy during the initial five years that this school implemented an African-centered educational model. Because she had been at the school for three years prior to its designation as an African American Immersion School, she brought a sense of continuity to the process. Indeed, some activities she had already initiated were easily modified to take on an African-centered focus. This principal had a definite vision for the African-centered orientation of the school, and this was freely shared with staff. At the center of this vision were the students, who were viewed from a strengths rather than a deficits perspective. This principal's management style combined an active involvement with nurturing support of both staff and students. Finally, she saw the development and implementation of this African-centered model as an active and ongoing process of change. Each accomplishment was seen as simply opening the door to further modification and improvement of the school.

CHARACTERISTICS OF THE SCHOOL STAFF

As part of the planning for the elementary African American Immersion School, the Implementation Committee and the principal made several recommendations regarding staffing. These recommendations were based on the idea that the new African American Immersion School should attempt to meet the needs of the whole child. Thus, the school should respond not only to the academic but also to the psychological and social needs the child might have. As a result, it was recommended that the staff should include a full-time guidance counselor and a full-time social worker. In addition, the school was assigned a full-time implementor and librarian. The implementor position was being included in most elementary and middle schools in the district around this time. The staff was also augmented with full-time specialists in art, music, science, and physical education. In many elementary schools in this district, these staff positions are part-time, and counselors, social workers, and specialists often are assigned to two or, in some cases, three schools. The school used a onetime increase in funding to support these additional staff.

In addition to the provision of curricular support, the full-time specialists allowed for an aspect of school restructuring deemed to be of major importance to the success of the school: the institutionalization of staff planning time as part of the school day. The Implementation Committee as well as the principal recognized that the staff would have to develop an African-centered curriculum and pedagogy simultaneously with delivering it. This could not be accomplished without the provision of some time when faculty could plan together during the school day.

In addition to time for planning, the Implementation Committee had recommended that the faculty be required to visit the homes of their students. This would also have to be carried out during regular school hours. It was anticipated that these visits could be done while the students were in classes with the specialists.

These additional staff members provided important support to the implementation of the African-centered educational model at the African American Immersion elementary school. In addition to counseling activities, the guidance counselor took responsibility for organizing a number of school-wide activities, particularly ones that involved the broader community. The social worker assisted teachers with home visits during the first year of the program. The implementor was available to help teachers develop curriculum and also helped coordinate school-wide activities. The specialists provided important breadth and depth to the curriculum.

The implementation of an African-centered educational paradigm requires that teachers have knowledge of African and African American history and culture. Most teachers are not exposed to this knowledge as part of their preservice education. In recognition of this, teachers at both of the African American Immersion schools were required to complete a minimum of eighteen credits in African and African American history and culture within the first three years of their placement at these schools.

Like all schools in this district, the teaching staff at the African American Immersion elementary school was predominantly white. Prior to the time the African American Immersion Schools were conceived and implemented, the teachers' union had been successful in requiring the district to limit the number of African American teachers who could be placed at a single school to a number close to the percentage of African American teachers in the district as a whole. In 1991–1992, the numbers of African American teachers at any school could be between 18 percent and 23 percent of the entire faculty. This had been some cause for concern among the planners for this city's African-centered educational experiment because they wanted students to have more African American teachers, arguing that students needed to see more models from their own cultural background. Through negotiations with the teachers' union, during the initial five years the immersion schools were implemented, this cap was gradually raised and finally eliminated, but only for the two African American Immersion Schools. However, the racial composition at the African American Immersion elementary school did not change appreciably during this time.

To provide a greater African American adult presence at the elementary school, a large number of African American paraprofessionals were hired. In particular, in the first years, a number of these educational assistants were African American males.

A majority of the teachers who had been at the school in 1990–1991 chose to remain at the school when it was designated an African American Immersion School. Indeed, many of these teachers expressed considerable support for and excitement about this experiment. In addition, the faculty expressed strong support for the principal; several indicated that their decision to remain at the school was related to her selection to administer the African-centered program. In fact, during the first year the immersion model was implemented, of the 21 teachers who were interviewed, 14, or two-thirds, of them had worked at the school before. Some of the staff had served at this school for 15 or more years when it became an African American Immersion School. This meant that this school began as an immersion school with a relatively stable staff.

Our observations indicate that the stability and longevity of the staff of this school created the conditions for the sustained collaboration necessary to build an African-centered program. Because so many of these staff members knew each other and had worked together, they were able to move quickly into cooperative activities. A high level of cohesiveness already existed within the school. Furthermore, because relatively few new staff members came into the school as it began implementing the African-centered model, they could become assimilated to the school norms relatively easily.

Table 1 shows the percentage of staff who remained at this elementary school during the first three and first five years this school operated as an African American Immersion School. Three-fourths of the staff remained at the school during the crucial initial three years it was implemented as an African American Immersion School, and with the exception of administrators, over half stayed at the school during its first five years as an African-centered elementary school. This gave the school stability and allowed the staff to develop consensus and maintain consistency in defining and implementing their view of African-centered education. This level of stability was also supportive for the students at this school. The view of the entire school as a "family" was strengthened as students knew almost all of the teachers and were able to anticipate who they would interact with from year to year.

Despite the staff stability at the African American Immersion elementary school, there was a net decline in staff positions during the initial five years it operated as an African American Immersion School. Specifically, the number of administrators was reduced by one as the implementor left and was not replaced during the third year of the African American Immersion School experiment. This left the principal and assistant principal as the only administrators. The number of support staff, consisting of the counselor, psychologist, social worker, and speech pathologist remained the same over the five-year period. Interestingly, while the counselor, social worker, and speech pathologist, all remained at the school for the five years of the study period, a different school psychologist served the school in each of those years. During the first five years this school implemented an African-centered educational model, the teaching staff was reduced from 35 to 31, and the number of educational assistants declined from 23 in the first year to 17 in the fifth year.

These declines were caused by a steady decrease in funding that plagued the school after its first year of operation as an African American Immersion School. Initially, this school received $305,000 beyond its regular budget of approximately $342,000. However, these were one-time only funds, and no additional monies were provided after that first year. As a result, the principal and the Site-Based Management Team that determined school policy had to cut staff positions. With respect to staff losses, in some cases such as the library, they were replaced by educational assistants. The

Table 1
Staff Stability at the African American Immersion Elementary School (in percent)

	Stability for First Three Years	Stability for First Five Years
Administrators	75	25
Support staff	75	75
Teachers	78.8	54.8
Educational assistants	88.2	58.8

largest area of loss, the reduction in the number of educational assistants, had two negative effects. First, the classroom teachers lost valuable help. In addition, however, since most of the educational assistants were African American and many were African American males, students lost a number of potential role models. Regardless of these losses, however, overall the staff at the African American Immersion elementary school was generally stable, cooperative, and committed to the idea of building an African-centered instructional model.

TEACHER VOICES

During each year of the Evaluation Project, teachers at the African American Immersion elementary school were interviewed about their perceptions of the school, its clients, and their own pedagogical work. During the first year the school operated as an African American Immersion School two sets of teacher interviews were conducted—one toward the beginning of the year and the other at the end of the year. In the remaining four years of the documentation and evaluation study, teacher interviews were conducted only at the end of the year. Those interviewed included not only teachers but also support staff.

In keeping with the participatory and holistic nature of the Evaluation Project, we believed that it was important to understand how teachers defined the African American Immersion School concept and how they viewed this school experiment in broader contexts. To that end, we included several questions in the beginning of the year interviews held during the first year of our study. Following are the questions and the teachers' responses to them. It must be kept in mind that the responses reported here are from a representative sample of the teachers present during that first year.

In the beginning of the first year, we were interested in understanding how the teachers viewed the establishment of this African-centered educational model, which was at that time unique to public schools, in a broader context. We asked the teachers, "Why are African American Immersion Schools occurring now in history?"

The teachers' responses to this question revolved around three general themes. One theme was that the school was a response to societal problems. The second theme was that it was a response to the failure of public educational institutions to educate African American children effectively. A third theme revealed the teachers' commitment to the concept of an African-centered model.

With respect to the first theme, several faculty members felt this type of school was a response to a range of problems that existed in contemporary American society and that were seen as having a major negative impact on the African American community. One teacher spoke to the societal issues in the following response:

> I think it is because of the whole society as it is right now. My goodness, something's got to be done. We've got to turn this around. We are looking at crime statistics. We are looking at dropouts. We are looking at children being murdered on a daily basis. It's frightening. The status quo didn't work. So we've got to try something else.

Another staff member focused more directly on issues confronting poor urban African American youngsters in her explanation for the emergence of an African-centered focus in this public school at this time with the following response:

> Because black youngsters are in trouble—economics, homocide, pregnancy, maladjustment to school—[there is a] need for more alternative types of schools. Why have children changed so much? Because they haven't been given the culture through family institutions and churches.

A third teacher, who had worked at the school for more than a decade, echoed the previous two respondents but cautioned that the impact of this school model would not be seen immediately. She stated that African American Immersion Schools were occurring in the last decade of the twentieth century "because of increases in crime, drugs, dropouts, lack of preparation for jobs in kids. People want a quick fix. There won't be one."

The second theme argued by several teachers was that the school was a response to the failure of existing schools to educate African American children effectively. For example, one of the support staff members stated:

> It's kind of a political question. . . . I think the African American community, for one thing, has seen that the educational system hasn't been working for a great majority of the kids. And people want to have the kids educated, and this is another way of reaching them.

Another teacher saw the interest in the African American Immersion model as a continuation of struggles by blacks for equity in the city. This teacher responded to the question by stating, "I'm wondering if it's just the natural progression of things. See, when I was going to school, well, when I was in high school, for example, Groppi [a local activist during the Civil Rights era] was marching." Finally, one teacher located the establishment of the African American Immersion Schools at this point in time in terms of attitudes within the European American rather than the African American community.

> If you want a really honest response, I think what's happening right now is the white community has given up and they are just saying, "Go ahead and do whatever you want. We are not going to fight you to this extent because we have just sort of given up on what you are doing and do it your own way." It's back to the separatist, equal kind of concept of many, many years ago.

Although this teacher's reference to a return to separatism echoed the sentiments of some detractors of this African-centered model, his perspective was that this was not a negative thing. He said, "In some ways that makes it easier for us to operate because we are going to be left alone." Furthermore, this teacher's argument was rooted in a rejection of the "melting pot" philosophy, that was often advanced in more traditional schools, noting, "I think that time of everybody trying to live together and melt together and all that sort of stuff is pretty much over, at least for this particular cycle."

Finally, a number of teachers discussed their commitment to the concept of an African American Immersion School as they responded to this question. For example, one of the teachers who cited societal problems as a reason for the establishment of the school also added, "I think this is an excellent program. I hope it will be tremendously successful." Another applauded "the focus of the program on early intervention, not remediation" and stated that "this was a great opportunity to do this now. I'm excited about being here." Another teacher noted, "There are different schools for different people. We honor a multicultural society, although there isn't the bend toward the African American."

These responses just described were typical examples from the sample of teachers for whom we had interview data. It appears evident that they viewed the establishment of the African American Immersion School as an important moment in history. In addition, many of them perceived that larger societal forces, not just educational failure, contributed to the momentum to establish the school.

Another question that was asked only at the beginning of the first year of the African American Immersion School experiments was: "What special qualities does it take to be an African American Immersion School?" Almost all of the respondents to this question felt that specific characteristics of the staff were key ingredients necessary to establish an African-centered school experience. Three major characteristics of teachers were identified. One was that staff should be nurturing and caring toward the students. As one African American teacher stated, "First . . . it takes concern and care. You have to love them, you have to be persistent, stay on the case."

A second characteristic mentioned by a number of the teachers was knowledge about African and African American history and culture. A number of the teachers were very aware that their professional training had not prepared them for this kind of orientation. For example, one stated:

> You should be able to get the facts straight, not give the children false information and things like that. I'm doing a lot of studying myself. I told the children that I'm learning a lot along with you because I didn't have this privilege when I was growing up. I didn't get black history. I had one course in high school and one in college.

The third characteristic mentioned by respondents at this school was that staff had to be committed to the idea of implementing an African-centered emphasis. One teacher indicated an important quality was "a well-trained staff that wants to be here, that believes in the program." This teacher went on to indicate this was the case at the African American Immersion elementary school. She said, "We are enthusiastic. We believe that we will make a difference. We are charting new waters."

Some teachers stated that an important special quality of an African American Immersion School involved the role of parents. For example, one primary teacher who had been at the school for over 20 years stated the following: "I think probably the . . . biggest thing is a lot of contact with parents and a lot of getting parents into work with them."

A number of teachers combined several of these themes in their descriptions of the special qualities necessary for an African American Immersion School. The following examples are illustrative.

> I think, first, we need to start with having teachers have a background, a strong background. I think we also have to be very dedicated to this and know this is going to take a lot of work to start it out and to learn it and expect to do; you'd have to give more than 100 percent this year. We have to have resources, so I bought my own books about the [material] that I teach the kids. Of course, the kids and the parents have to be willing to be a part of this, or it isn't going to work either.

The teacher who gave this response was a relative newcomer to the school. The following response by a teacher who had taught at the school for over ten years echoed these sentiments.

> The first thing I would say they would have to have is a staff committed to the concept of immersing African culture into the curriculum. Also educated in African history and courses that deal with that. Also, you must have parent involvement. You must get the parents in and get them involved and get them excited about the curriculum.

To ascertain how the teachers and support staff understood the nature of this new school experiment, we asked, "What is an African American Immersion School?" In their responses, teachers discussed their vision for the school. Two themes emerged in their responses. One focused on describing how the school was expected to have an impact on students. The other concerned anticipated changes in school curriculum and climate.

In general, there was strong consensus that this was a school that developed and implemented a curriculum that incorporated African and African American history and culture. The reasons for doing this, in the teachers' views, were to increase students' self-esteem and help them develop pride in their culture. For example, a teacher characterized this endeavor as "a school where children are taught self-esteem. They learn about their past . . . their present . . . and what they can do in the future." In many cases, respondents felt this school should compensate for the Eurocentric focus of other educational models. For example, a teacher responded in the following manner: "I think it is trying to get the children to be proud of their heritage and letting them know that we are important and we have made so many important contributions, and we want them to know about this as well as the good along with the bad."

The other theme that became evident from teachers' responses to this question focused on their expectations with respect to changes in the school's curriculum and climate. The idea of infusing cultural information across academic subjects as well as an emphasis on cultural strengths rather than deficits was also evident. One of the specialists incorporated these perspectives:

> In my opinion, an African American Immersion School is a school where the culture, the beginning of the African American culture in all aspects, the art, music, the read-

ing, exploring the different sections of the African culture . . . should be incorporated into the curriculum. I also think that it deals with the positive aspects of the African Americans because a lot of times we hear just about slavery. And we only . . . get one month, in February, and after that, the kids don't hear or see anything of Black history.

One teacher noted the school's mandate to retain the district-wide curriculum while attempting to infuse an African-centered emphasis. "I see it as immersing the children's culture into the curriculum. We must teach the basic curriculum, but we must bring the African culture into it at any point we can. You know, tie it in through all subject areas." This same teacher was reinforced by the students' reaction to the new emphasis.

The exciting part to me is that the children are very excited. I did not know what their reaction would be because sometimes [when] you approach a child . . . many of them do not know that much about Africa. If they see a film where someone is dressed a little different, they react laughing and that type of reaction. They are very excited. When we do African folktales, they like to read it again. So I am finding that they are excited about this, and it just makes it exciting to teach.

One of the teachers emphasized the need for a change in school climate as well as curriculum with the following statement:

I kind of know what it isn't probably better than what it is exactly. What it isn't is a lot of curriculum changes. That is not the important thing I think has to happen here. The thing that has to happen, that is going to make this succeed or fail . . . is not exactly what we do with curriculum, although that is an important part of it. But it is more of the attitudes that we, as a staff, get for ourselves and how well we can incorporate parents into buying into what we are doing and what the children are doing. . . . If we can't get parents really buying into this whole program, then I think that we are doomed to failure. So it's an attitudinal change. It's a nurturing kind of change that needs to take place. It's away from the tests, more to what children are about and that kind of thing.

The teachers and support staff who were interviewed at the beginning of the first year that this elementary school operated as an African American Immersion School appeared to agree that this was a unique educational experiment. They focused on curriculum change as the major underpinning of an African American Immersion School but also perceived that their own dedication and commitment to the concept as well as to the children served were crucial elements to developing this model. They perceived that they were participating in an important historical moment; however, they were also aware that they did not have full public support for their endeavors.

We now turn to two questions that were asked of the teachers annually during each of the five years of the implementation of the Evaluation Project. The teachers' responses to these questions provide more information about the overall orientation of this school as an African-centered educational experiment. Here, we report teachers' responses to these questions at three points during our five-year documentation and evaluation study of these schools. The years for which data are reported include the first, third, and fifth years of our investigation. The first year's data provide a baseline and represent teachers' perspectives at the beginning of the process of implementing the African American Immersion model. By the third year at the African American Immersion elementary school, the staff had essentially established a modus operandi. In addition, in this year, the school had its first taste of success as an African American Immersion School. The students showed a marked improvement in performance on the statewide reading test given to third graders. Data from the fifth year provide a picture of the school at the end point of the Evaluation Project. It should be noted that in each of the three years discussed here the interviews were conducted with a representative sample of teachers and support staff at the school in that particular year. Because the sample of teachers interviewed varied slightly over the years, these data cannot be considered to be longitudinal.

The first of these questions is, "In your opinion, what are the goals of an African American Immersion School?" The teachers' responses to this question demonstrated a high level of consensus about what the goals of such a school should be. Furthermore, teachers tended to report very similar goals for the school in each of the three years we discuss. Two closely related themes emerged from our analysis of the teachers' responses to these questions.

The first theme was that a major goal of the African American Immersion School was to raise students' self-esteem and build cultural pride in them. This theme implicitly seemed to assume that these children had low self-esteem at the outset. For example, a European American teacher stated, "I think the main thing that we are trying to get at is student self-esteem. We have a long way to go." A number of the teachers argued that providing students with knowledge about their culture and history would enhance their self-esteem and other aspects of behavior. For example, an upper-level teacher stated, "The goals are to immerse the children in their own culture where [through] the school process, they can relate and see themselves right in the curriculum, promote positive self-esteem, good citizenship, and respect for others." Another teacher made a more direct link between cultural knowledge and self-esteem, with the following response to the question: "Well, one of our main goals is to raise the students' self-esteem through learning about their ancestral heritage."

The second theme also took enhancing self-esteem and cultural pride as central to the goals of the school but saw these efforts as tools to increase the students' academic achievement. Teachers believed that enhanced self-esteem was a cornerstone for academic achievement. One teacher described the benefits of improved self-esteem in the following manner:

> So if we can get students to feel good about themselves, that's . . . a two-pronged thing. Some of it is the hugging and kissing and the "I Am Somebody" kind of thing. But the other part of it is making them academically successful, so you've got to have your teach-

ing techniques in tune two ways. It's got to be the nurturing kind of thing and the other a solid academic program.

This theme was reported by some teachers in the first year and by an increasing number in subsequent years. One example came from a support staff person in the first year: "Well . . . we have been defining them [the goals] through staff meetings and things like that. But basically, as I see it, simply put, is to raise students' achievement via greater self-esteem through the African American ideal of [the] curriculum that they are trying to implement." This teacher noted that the definition of the goals was an ongoing group process among this school's staff, at least during the first year it operated as an African American Immersion School.

These two themes remained salient in subsequent years. By the third year, the goal of enhancing self-esteem and cultural pride had become codified in the school's mission statement. In addition, some teachers were describing how they operationalized this goal. The following examples illustrate this.

> Well, according to our mission statement, to promote self-esteem in our students and to give them a sense of pride in their heritage and in their culture and that's done by helping the students to realize that we were not just slaves, that we have made great contributions to society and to the world as a matter of fact, and I think that is real important. I think that is our main goal.

The previous response was given by a teacher who had been at the school since its inception as an African American Immersion School. The next response came from a teacher who was new to the school in its third year. This teacher described the goals in the following manner: "Well, I agree with the statement that is written on our newsletter every week that we are raising self-esteem through the African American heritage, and that means incorporating all aspects into all my subjects which I'm learning how to do."

Over time, an increasing number of the teachers and support staff that we inteviewed reported the idea of enhancing self-esteem and cultural pride as a tool to raise academic achievement as the primary goal of the African American Immersion School. As one teacher put it, "We will provide an African centric [sic] curriculum to motivate self-esteem and high academic achievement at [the African American Immersion elementary] school." It seemed that teachers became more convinced that there were close links between knowledge of one's culture and academic achievement as time passed. For example, in the fifth year of implementation, a primary teacher with over 20 years of experience at the school, described the goals in the following manner:

> I still think they're pretty much what they were to begin with, which is trying to bring history into children's lives, making it a meaningful part of their lives and also, hopefully, using it as a tool to motivate children. The main goal is raising academic achievement, so anything that we can do, and this is the goal of doing those other things, is to promote academic achievement.

Another respondent, a support staff member, also made note of the continuity of the school's goals over time. This respondent said:

> After five years, well, I think they pretty much started off with the idea of trying to immerse the kids in African American culture in order to promote a better self-esteem and, naturally, increase their academic achievement. I think that's been the goal of the school all along, but it's been fine-tuned along the way.

The pervasiveness of this theme among the staff was illustrated by the response of a teacher who came to the school in the fourth year that it operated as an African American Immersion School. This teacher indicated that the goal of the school was "[t]o help the students we have to gain an Afrocentric perspective about themselves and get them more culturally aware of their background, and to hopefully, by that, raise their self-esteem and increase their academic achievement." In summary, there was a high level of consensus among the teachers and support staff at the African American Immersion elementary school that the major goals of implementing this African-centered educational model revolved around enhancing self-esteem, cultural pride, and academic achievement. Over time, the staff interviewed reflected a greater sense that the focus on culture was a tool used to help students increase their academic achievement.

It should be noted that most of the teachers interviewed seemed to support the ideas that African American children have low self-esteem and that increasing self-esteem leads to improved academic achievement, even though this idea has not been supported in the literature (Graham, 1994; Irvine, 1990). Yet this remained a firm belief throughout our five-year study.

A second question asked annually of teachers and support staff throughout the five years we conducted the Evaluation Project was, "What can an African American Immersion school accomplish that would not be done by a traditional school?" The responses to this question were quite consistent among the samples of teachers for whom we have interview data in years one, three, and five of our study. Most of the respondents agreed that the distinguishing feature of an African American Immersion School was in the opportunity to focus on the cultural orientation of the African American children it served. This cultural orientation was seen as an important foundation for the development of pride, a sense of identity, and high self-esteem among the children. One teacher's response that typifies this idea is as follows:

> Well, I think the traditional schooling that we have had in the past is more Eurocentric, whereas, with the Immersion school, we are trying to, you know, bring in African American role models from the community for the children. We bring in stories and with African American characters in the story. . . . The similarities in the relationships that the characters are going through are similar to what the children are doing, and they can relate better. I just think we're focusing on the needs of the population that we are teaching.

For some of the teachers, the feature that distinguished the school had important implications for them as well as the children.

At our school, we will accomplish what black African American people are all about. We will learn all about our heritage, how black African American people as a whole have progressed. What we have given to the world. Our kids will learn all about how special they are. As an African American . . . I was not taught this, and I feel with my children here at [the African American Immersion elementary school], it's a learning process to me. I, as the teacher, have learned so much about me that I didn't know with our children. So this will enhance their self-esteem, their self-motivation, the self-worth of the children.

Another teacher voiced a similar response.

Well, in a traditional school, nothing was ever mentioned about our culture and you know that black people had done great things and everything wasn't all bad. I think that is one of the things we are establishing that other schools cannot, because I remember when I was in school, I didn't learn anything about my culture, my history. One class in high school, one in college. Black History Month really didn't go very far as far as helping me learn about my race.

This perspective was pervasive across the school. For instance, one teacher noted:

I am really isolated in my little classroom, but . . . I sense from the kids that I see in the hallway and the art in the hallway . . . just more of an awareness of being African Americans, and a lot of pride and a lot of . . . real concrete knowledge about historical figures that friends of mine who are in other schools, . . . the kids don't. [T]hey have a kind of a general knowledge, but the real specific I see here. . . . [For example,] if you mention someone out of the past, the kids will know who it is and can identify them and tell something about them.

While the three teachers cited had been with the school when it became an African American Immersion School, this theme was also cited by a teacher who in the third year of our study was new to the school: "Well, I guess concentrating on a culture could do that, could raise the self-esteem and, therefore, provide a . . . safer or comfortable school where the kids could learn better, so I see that as being a real strong point." The positive impact of the cultural orientation appeared to have led to some self-reflection for a teacher new to the school in its fifth year as an African American Immersion School:

I think the sense of pride, the sense of history. I can't imagine, you know, growing up as a white girl and learning strictly Asian culture or something that is not relevant to myself. I can see how African American children would get turned off by education. And this just brings it . . . I mean, this . . . we spoil our kids here really. [Because] it's so good here and I think it's so safe.

This idea that the cultural orientation led to a more positive atmosphere in the school was evident in some other teachers' responses. For instance, a teacher who had been at the school for over 20 years noted, "The ideal situation for what we are in here is to provide a family atmosphere which is an extension of the home." Another teacher who came to the school in the third year it was an African American Immersion School expressed similar sentiments: "So I think [it's] the family atmosphere that we have here, and it's because of our curriculum, I think."

An additional theme became evident in the teachers' responses to this question. A number of them described changes they had observed in their students' behavior as well as in their own. For example, in the first year, one teacher said, "I think that the children are excited about coming to school. They feel good about it. They don't have that complex anymore." Another teacher said the following: "I think there is more unity. As the school year has gone on, I have seen fewer fights. And kids are kind of pulling together as a unit, as a group, instead of everybody going their own little way. They have learned to work together for one common cause." By the fifth year, some teachers were describing changes in their behavior as well as that of the students. For example, one teacher stated that this school differed from traditional ones by its level of nurturance.

> I think probably a traditional school spends less time on the nurturing aspect of an education, more on the academics. And the ideal situation for what we are in here is to provide a family atmosphere, which is an extension of the home, or it takes on jobs that maybe the home is not adequately taking on. And, in that role . . . you stimulate children to do better in school.

Our review of the teacher voices at the African American Immersion elementary school revealed two very striking characteristics. First, there appeared to be a very high level of consensus among the faculty about the goals, orientation, and direction of the school. This consensus was evident even the first year the African American Immersion model was implemented. However, it was even stronger in subsequent years. Second, there was remarkable stability in the staff's perceptions of the goals and distinguishing features of the school during the five-year period of the Evaluation Project.

In conclusion, at the African American Immersion elementary school, we have a portrait of a school in which staff developed a relatively clear conception of an African-centered educational model, and they came to this point of view fairly quickly. The foundation on which the staff developed this model was quite stable during the first five years the school operated as an African American Immersion School, although some fine-tuning did occur during this period. It is our view that this perspective was influenced by several facts: First, the school had a strong principal who brought her own clear vision of what this model would be to the outset of the implementation. Second, this principal was buttressed by a staff most of whom had experience with the school prior to the beginning of the experiment and who chose, in large part, to stay at the school and take on this new challenge. This staff was able to socialize new staff to its orientation as they came in during the initial five years the school implemented the African American Immersion model.

— 3 —

A Portrait of the African American Immersion Middle School

When the Task Force recommended that two schools, one elementary and the other a middle school, be re-created as African American Immersion Schools, it was envisioned that the African-centered model would encompass the kindergarten through eighth grade school years. It was expected that most of the students who attended the African American Immersion elementary school would continue on to the African American Immersion middle school. Indeed, it was expected that the middle school would be an attractive alternative for students who had attended the African American Immersion elementary school. Partly in light of this expectation, many of the plans for implementing the two schools were identical, including the requirements for teachers, the procedures for selecting staff for the school, the emphasis on curriculum development, and their inclusion in the documentation and evaluation study. Unfortunately, this expectation did not materialize. Most of the students who graduated from the elementary school did not move on to the African American Immersion middle school. Instead, they went to other middle schools in the city. An analysis of characteristics of the middle school can help to explain why.

THE SETTING

It is early morning and the halls are quiet as teachers prepare their classrooms for the new day. A bell rings and the halls explode with activity as children enter the school. The sounds of lockers opening and closing are mixed with the voices of girls and boys greeting each other and catching up on the latest news. Teachers stand in front of their classroom doors greeting students. Aides move among the students, urging them to get to their classes quickly. After a few minutes, another bell sounds, and adults admonish the stragglers to move along. As suddenly as it began, the noise and movement end, and the halls are quiet again except for the occasional student who is late or running an errand. This scene is repeated seven more times during the day.

The African American Immersion middle school is a large L-shaped brick building, which, along with its parking lot and playground, takes up an entire city block. It is located just about eight blocks from the African American Immersion elementary school. This middle school serves the same community as the elementary school, although its catchment area is larger. The community is generally characterized by poverty, to a large extent the result of the massive deindustrialization the city experienced during the late 1970s and 1980s. However, just a few blocks south of the school, gentrification is proceeding at a rapid pace. One of two middle schools in Milwaukee in which virtually all students are African American, this middle school had a long history of serving African Americans prior to beginning the African-centered experiment. Indeed, many successful African American citizens in this city name this school as their alma mater.

At the time it was named an African American Immersion School in 1991, this middle school's image was such that it was viewed as one of the least desirable middle schools to attend in the city. This reputation had been acquired as a result of two forces. First, this school had been a segregated school. When the school district negotiated desegregation with the federal court, agreement was reached to allow one high school, two middle schools, and approximately 20 elementary schools in the city to remain segregated, neighborhood schools. Other schools took students from throughout the city. This school was one of the predominantly black neighborhood schools. Given the city's racial history, it is probably no accident that these schools were clustered in one of the poorest areas of the city. This leads to the second factor that contributed to the school's reputation: The school's population was not only predominantly African American; it was also overwhelmingly poor. This was the very population that traditional schools had failed to educate successfully locally and nationally.

The failure of the school to serve its clientele effectively was evident in the achievement statistics in 1991–1992, the year before it was officially designated an African American Immersion School. The school's overall grade-point average was 1.70 out of a possible 4.0. The percentage of seventh-grade students scoring at or above the national average on the Iowa Test of Basic Skills was 19 in reading, 17 in language arts, and 12 in math. In addition to these low levels of achievement, the school also had the highest number of students eligible for free or reduced lunch (92 percent) of all middle schools in the district in 1991–1992. Furthermore, its mobility and suspension rates were among the highest among middle schools in the city (Milwaukee Public Schools, 1991–1992). In addition to student achievement, parent participation at the school was low, both with respect to attendance at conferences and participation in the parent–teacher organization.

In summary, the African American Immersion middle school was located in an institution that had developed a negative image with respect to achievement and behavior. Clearly, the school was in dire need of restructuring if it was to improve in its efforts to educate students effectively. Given its student population, the transformation of this school into an African-centered program seemed a logical direction for restructuring to take. Yet this transformation had to occur within the constraints of the middle school.

THE CONTEXT OF MIDDLE SCHOOLS

The idea of establishing schools specifically for early adolescents was advanced at the beginning of the twentieth century in the United States. Psychologists and educators argued that the traditional concept of eight years of elementary school followed by four years of high school did not meet the developmental needs of early adolescence adequately. Neither elementary nor high schools were organized to help these adolescents cope with the major changes they were experiencing in physical, cognitive, emotional, and social development while, at the same time, fostering their academic growth. In the 1920s, junior high schools, usually encompassing grades seven through nine, were established in response to this need. However, by the 1960s, educators and psychologists criticized junior high schools, arguing that they had become miniature high schools, thus subordinating their original goals. The emerging middle concept was explicitly aimed at addressing the developmental needs of early adolescents (Cuban, 1992).

Educators argued that the physical, social, and emotional changes associated with puberty led young adolescents to focus on themselves and their interactions with others more than on academic activities. A number of studies have found that students at this age level often demonstrate a decline in motivation and a disinterest in academic activities along with increased interest in nonacademic concerns (Anderman & Maehr, 1994). A number of researchers, educators, and policy makers have argued that middle schools needed to be organized and staffed to cope with these students' changes in academic engagement (Compton, 1983; Hertzog, 1984; Levy, 1988).

Since the appearance of the middle school concept, there have been continuing attempts to refine it so that it meets its original aims. The latest of these refinements is the Carnegie Council on Adolescent Development report of 1989, published by the National Middle Schools Association (1995). According to this report, which identified best practices and policies at the middle school level, a developmentally appropriate middle school possesses the following qualities:

- Educators who are committed to young adolescents, recognizing them as a specific age group different from either elementary or older adolescent high school students;
- A staff committed to a shared vision of what a middle school should be;
- A community of teachers, parents, and students who hold high expectations for all students;
- An adult who will serve as a mentor and advocate for each student during this period;

- A commitment by middle schools to develop and maintain strong family and community partnerships;
- Creation and maintenance of a positive school climate for all students. (23–27)

In order to develop and maintain a middle school with these qualities, the following programmatic factors were identified: (1) an integrative curriculum that is challenging and supports exploratory learning in students; (2) a staff that is competent in a variety of instructional methods and able to provide varied teaching and learning approaches; (3) assessment and evaluation systems that promote learning; (4) flexible organizational structures; (5) programs and policies that foster health, wellness, and safety; and (6) comprehensive guidance and support services (National Middle Schools Association, 1995).

While all early adolescents must cope with the variety of physical, cognitive, emotional, and social changes characteristic of this period of development, African American adolescents have additional pressures related to their status in the United States. Specifically, with their expanded cognitive abilities, African American adolescents are able to understand and interpret culture and cultural conflict. They become more aware of negative evaluations of African American culture by the dominant European American culture as well as restrictions of opportunities because of their race (Spencer & Dornbusch, 1990). The degree to which African American adolescents are able to cope successfully with these challenges is related to the extent to which they have social support and experiences that allow them to develop a sense of mastery and control with respect to their abilities and the environment (Connell, Spencer, & Aber, 1994; Gordon, 1995).

In a study of African American middle school students, Kester (1994) found that having opportunities to bond with teachers were related to positive school outcomes. Kester also argued that positive school outcomes for these students would be enhanced if more elements of their communities could be incorporated in the school curriculum. The school experiences available to early adolescent African Americans, therefore, can be critical to their personal and cultural as well as academic development. Given the scenarios for early adolescence in general and African American early adolescents, especially, an African-centered middle school model would seem to have significant potential to support academic, social, and personal growth. There is some support for this idea. A study of African American sixth graders compared the social behavior of students holding an Anglocultural orientation and those who had an African-centered cultural orientation. This research found more positive social behavior among the students with the African-centered orientation (Jagers & Mock, 1993).

ISSUES AND CHALLENGES

Unlike the elementary school, the first five years that the middle school operated as an African-centered institution were marked by recurring cycles of change and crisis. These cycles were precipitated at times by internal crises at the school and at other times by external challenges to the school. These crises and challenges, we argue, severely impeded this school's efforts to develop a clear and coherent African-centered educational model. Our observations of this middle school during its initial five years of operation as an African-centered school indicate that these factors were problematic off and on throughout this period. The portrait of this school shows patterns of internal dissension and external assaults that undermined a number of sincere efforts to create a middle school African-centered model.

Internally, issues concerning staff became an ongoing area of contention at the African American Immersion middle school. Specifically, high staff mobility, often accompanied by considerable dissension among staff or between staff and the principal, became a focal point. The announcement that this particular school would become the African American Immersion middle school precipitated a large-scale exodus of staff from this school. In September 1991, the preplanning year before the school was officially opened as an African American Immersion middle school, 66 percent of the teachers and 60 percent of the administrators were new to the school.

During the initial five years that the African American Immersion model was implemented at the middle school, there was a 100 percent turnover in administrators. A new principal was appointed in 1991 when it was announced that the school would be designated the African American Immersion middle school. This principal remained at the school for two years, through the preplanning year (1991–1992) and the first year that the school operated officially as an immersion school (1992–1993). In the early summer of 1993, this principal was suddenly removed from the school. This event created some internal dissension because this principal was well liked by some of the teachers and students at the school. Nevertheless, a new principal was named for the school. This individual remained at the school through the remainder of the period under study.

In addition to the transition of principals, the school experienced a steady turnover in assistant principals during its initial five years as an African American Immersion School. Three assistant principals were assigned to the school. However, in every one of the five years of our study, at least one assistant principal was new to the school.

Similar patterns of high turnover were evident among teachers during this five-year period. Two factors were major contributors to staff mobility. First, in the first three years that the African American Immersion model was implemented, many of the teachers were not permanent staff but, instead, were long-term substitutes. The presence of a large number of substitutes was, in large part, due to the policy of the local teachers' union, described previously, that imposed a quota on the number of African American teachers who could be assigned to any school in the district. This policy limited the number of African American teachers assigned to a building to no more than 5 percent more than the proportion of black teachers in the district. During the period from 1991 to 1994, African American teachers who wanted to be assigned to the African American Immersion middle school were prohibited from doing so. In addition, many white teachers were not interested in coming to the school either because of the negative reputation it had held previously or because they did not choose to become part of this particular restructuring effort. As a result the school had to depend heavily on substitutes. In 1995, when the union policy was discontinued for the African American Immersion Schools, this problem was lessened considerably.

A second factor that contributed to high levels of staff mobility concerned many teachers' failure to complete the requirement of taking 18 college-level credits in African and African American history and culture within the first three years of teaching at the African American Immersion Schools. It must be noted here that the district agreed to reimburse teachers who were at these schools when they began to implement the African-centered model for these 18 credits. However, the district had no such policy for teachers who came to the schools in subsequent years; they had to pay for these courses themselves. This did not seem to be a problem at the elementary school for several reasons. First, the staff was very stable; relatively few teachers came into the school during the five-year period under study. Furthermore, the teachers at the elementary school decided to complete the course requirements as a cohort, thus providing support to each other. Finally, the principal at the elementary school had provided at least partial reimbursement to new teachers coming to the building to facilitate their completion of the course requirement.

At the middle school, however, large numbers of teachers, both African American and white, failed to complete the required 18 credits in African and African American history and culture. As a result, beginning in the third year that this school was an African American Immersion School, this became a reason for the removal of significant numbers of teachers from the school. Furthermore, this pattern continued as teachers continued to fail to take the courses. A number of the teachers we interviewed complained about having to pay for the course requirement. However, we noted that many of these same teachers, again both African Americans and whites, voluntarily pursued graduate-level course work in areas such as educational administration and school counseling. This raises some questions about their commitment to the school's cultural orientation.

The high staff turnover at the African American middle school was sometimes accompanied by internal dissension, among staff or between the staff and the administration. The consistently high turnover of teachers mitigated against the formation of strong bonds across the staff. Rather, at the African American Immersion middle school, the staff tended to be fragmented into smaller groups. However, some larger issues exacerbated underlying tensions among the staff at this school.

One issue that arose in the preplanning year had to do with the question of who should teach in an African-centered school. According to the then-principal, questions were raised about the role of white teachers in an African American Immersion School. In an interview at the end of that year, the principal described the issue in the following manner:

> Again, when I came here, a number of people transferred in with their own ideas on how and what an African American Immersion School should be. And pretty much this was narrow-minded ideas. For example, only black staff could teach black kids.

This is something I was told, and I was told by some white teachers that they were told by some black teachers that they couldn't teach blacks and they were in the wrong place. And, of course, I have been told by black teachers that white teachers have said certain things.

Although these perspectives were not held by all of the teachers in the school, the issue continued to resurface during the first year that this middle school was officially operated as an African American Immersion School. Furthermore, the question of who should teach in an African-centered school was also taken up by individuals outside of the school. In the fall of the first year after the school was opened as an African American Immersion School, the principal reported, "I had community people calling me saying, 'Why do you have white teachers in that building? It's an African American Immersion School. You should have all black staff.' "

This principal made it clear that he did not agree with those calling for an all-black staff at the school. He also was cognizant of the policies that influenced the racial composition of teachers in the district's schools. In an interview conducted with us in the early summer of 1993, when he was being transferred from the school, this principal reflected on this source of underlying tension that persisted during his tenure there and on his response to it: "Due to the fact that this was going to be an African American Immersion School and that we had 70 some percent white staff, the next charge was to allay fears that whites had and that blacks had and get them to work together for the common cause."

The issue became more muted with the arrival of the second principal at the beginning of the second year that this middle school operated as an African American Immersion School. However, it did not disappear entirely. While the first principal seemed willing to work with the existing predominantly white staff, the second one expressed a desire for a larger contingency of African American staff at the school. In an interview, this second principal discussed the most recent memorandum of understanding between the district and the teachers' union that raised the quota on African American teachers at the African American Immersion Schools to 35 percent.

> My honest opinion is that we need to look at that [the 35 percent limit] and why the board is continuing to agree to even 35 percent. Especially for these two schools, because we are attempting to embrace something that is unique, that is very important that we succeed. I think we need to take a closer look at 50 percent at least.

It should be noted that by the fourth and fifth years of this middle school's implementation as an African American Immersion School, the majority of the teachers, about 60 percent, were African American, and the question of who should teach there was not a major issue in our conversations with staff.

A second major area of dissension at this school arose in its third year of operation as an African American Immersion School when it became evident that a significant number of teachers had not fulfilled the requirement to complete 18 university-level credits in African and African American history and culture within the three-year time limit. These teachers were notified in November that they would be transferred out of the school when the academic year ended the following June. Apparently, some of these teachers had not taken this requirement seriously and believed that it would not actually be enforced. Some of the teachers who were to be transferred reacted negatively to this turn of events. Some, in fact, attempted to have the school officially declared "out of control," thereby excusing them from their unmet obligations. While much of their anger was directed toward the principal who supported the requirement, some further dissension was engendered between teachers who had and had not completed this course work.

This middle school began its fourth year as an African American Immersion School (1995–1996) on a high note. For the first time since beginning this experiment, the school opened with a full staff of teachers. Furthermore, with the relaxation of the quota imposed by the teachers' union on the numbers of African American teachers who could work at the school, a significant majority of these staff had requested assignment to the school.

Aware that a considerable proportion of the staff would be new to the school beginning in the fourth year, the administration and some teachers organized an intensive weeklong in-service activity to be implemented just prior to the beginning of the school year. A group of educators from a long-running, successful, independent African-centered school in a nearby larger city led this in-service program. All of the staff at the school participated in the in-service program, which focused on two issues. The first concerned staff team building and cooperative work. Teachers formed small grade-level-based cooperative groups and began to develop activities for the coming academic year. The second issue focused on developing a more pronounced African-centered ethos in the building. For example, to promote a sense of family, the teachers agreed that they would have the students refer to them as "Mama Jones" and "Baba Smith" instead of Mr. and Ms.

In addition to changes in staff, some changes had begun to occur in the student population. In 1994–1995, the third year that this middle school was designated an African American Immersion School, it was also named a citywide specialty school. As a result, the student population was becoming somewhat more diverse with respect to academic background and socioeconomic status.

As a result of the changes in staff, the preparation of staff, and the expansion of the student population, the fourth year began with a sense of euphoria. Teachers seemed eager to get on with the task of building an African-centered educational model. The teachers' enthusiasm appeared to be transferred to the students. Our observations of hallways and classrooms revealed a sense of order and interest was prevalent.

The sense of "new beginnings" at the African American Immersion middle school was severely shaken in October 1995 by a challenge from the district administration. For some time, the School Board had been pressuring the district administration to identify "failing" schools. It was the School Board's intention to force these "failing" schools to suspend their existing practices and reconstitute themselves with new plans aimed, ostensibly, at enhancing the achievement levels of their students. The new plans were to be approved by the School Board. This new policy seemed to be an attempt by the School Board to make individual schools more accountable for the performance of their students. This action was also, in all likelihood, a response by the School Board to increasingly harsh criticisms of the city schools' apparent inability to educate its students effectively.

The district administration included the African American Immersion middle school among its list of failing schools. Although this school had a long history of past failure, it is not clear why it was included on this list at this time. After all, the school was already participating in an experiment aimed at enhancing student performance, the same goal as that sought by the School Board. More important, the district administration's decision came just at the time that the school had finally reached a point where it appeared likely that a viable African-centered educational model could be developed.

Regardless of the factors underlying the decision to declare the African American Immersion School a failing school, the results were profound. Staff morale plummeted. Teachers became distracted from their original task to build a viable African-centered educational program and, instead, turned their energies to a campaign to save the school. This campaign involved rallying support for the school's African American Immersion orientation from parents and community members. It also required staff and students to provide testimony supporting the school at School Board meetings. Finally, it required the staff to spend time preparing rationales and plans justifying the program for the district administration.

The challenge from the district administration also led to increased internal dissension among staff at the school as they sought solutions to their dilemma. One group of staff members, along with the principal, felt that reorganizing the school as a charter school would allow for the maintenance of the existing African American Immersion orientation. Furthermore, this group argued, charter school status would allow the school to become self-governing and would decrease the likelihood of similar challenges from the district administration or the School Board in the future. This idea was initially greeted with widespread acceptance among the staff. However, as details about what was entailed in establishing a charter school emerged, a number of teachers backed away from the idea. At this time, the idea of charter schools was new to this district. While there had been some exploration of the idea, there was considerable resistance to it also. As a result, a number of policies had not been developed. Some of these policies concerned teacher salaries and benefits; others involved other budgetary aspects of school operations. Questions about these issues, which were not easily resolved, led some teachers to be leery of this idea. This flirtation with the charter school idea created dissension within the teaching staff between those in favor and those against the plan. Over time, however, plans to make the African American Immersion middle school a charter school did not materialize. Instead, some staff members at the school spent a considerable amount of time drawing up a plan aimed at removing the school from the list of "failing" schools.

Although the furor over the African American Immersion School's placement on the failing list began to decrease as the academic year 1995–1996 progressed, the external challenges did not. Later in the year, one School Board member mounted a series of attacks against African-centered educational models in general and at this school in particular. These denunciations, which often took the form of bizarre diatribes and unfounded accusations, were reported periodically in the local press.

Despite the internal and external challenges that plagued this middle school throughout its initial five years of existence as an African American Immersion middle school, it retained the mission of achieving educational reform through the implementation of this culturally based orientation. These attempts were mediated by the school's two principals, who brought very different perspectives to the school.

PRINCIPAL VOICES

The first principal at the African American Immersion middle school was new to both the school and the position. Prior to this, he had served as a high school assistant principal for a number of years. The first principal, who led the school in its preplanning year and its first year as an African American Immersion School, held clear goals for the school. He identified these at the end of the preplanning year.

> Our major goal is to provide an educational environment for our children. They are all African American children. So that they can achieve, so that they can meet with success. We know that historically African American children have underachieved, especially African American males. So we are placing emphasis on ways to effectively educate African American children.

An auxiliary goal stated by this principal involved strengthening home and school interactions: "Now, of course, in addition to . . . our first goal, we want to involve parents in the educational process." This principal perceived that the parents of children at this middle school were alienated from the school. "They really haven't seen the school system as a friendly place for themselves or for their children. So we have to reach out to parents." This principal maintained these goals of increasing parent involvement and student achievement throughout his tenure at the school.

Another primary goal for this principal was to socialize the children to behave in an orderly fashion in school. In some ways, this goal was a mandate, for the school had achieved a reputation of being out of order before it was designated an African American Immersion School. In our final interview, just prior to his departure from the school, he indicated the following: "When I first came to the African American Immersion middle school . . . the charge that I saw first and foremost was to establish a kind of discipline that would allow teachers to teach and kids to learn." This principal was fairly successful in achieving this goal by the first year the school officially operated with its African-centered designation. Our observations indicated that order prevailed in the halls and classrooms. In an interview at the end of that year, the principal also made note of this achievement:

> Let me tell you something. Before I came here, I understood that they would not put all grade levels in the auditorium together because the kids would just act out. We

changed that last year. . . . And we will continue to do those things. . . . I want these kids to be able to socialize without problems and appreciate each other.

This principal's primary emphasis was on discipline and student achievement. However, he made little mention of emphasizing the African-centered orientation during the early part of his tenure at the school. In fact, this aspect was articulated only as he was leaving the school.

> The final goal has to be academic achievement. Let's face it, if African Americans, especially African American males, were achieving within expected levels as compared to nonblacks, there wouldn't be an African American Immersion program. So, the bottom line is academic achievement. Now the specialty is to try and get our young people to feel good about themselves, to feel capable, and that . . . is supposed to translate into higher motivation and resulting success. That's the purpose of it.

The man who replaced the first principal at this middle school in the summer before it began its second year as an African American Immersion School was no stranger to this concept. Prior to coming to this school, he had chaired the Task Force and Implementation Committees and served as a middle school principal.

Despite his familiarity with the origins of the African American Immersion School, this second principal did not appear to develop a clear and focused vision of goals for the school. He had numerous ideas and plans that touched on a wide variety of issues. Unfortunately, often these plans and ideas were not enacted. Three themes that seemed to be particularly important to the second principal concerned parent involvement in the school, implementing an African-centered orientation, and a host of staff issues. Underlying many of these issues was a stated need to enhance student achievement.

Shortly after his arrival at the school, this principal talked about plans to increase parent involvement at the school. Early in year two of the program, he said:

> I really want parents to get involved in the educational process, sitting in the classroom and working with the student. Actually, one of the key things to me is that parents are actually being introduced to the curriculum the same way the child is being introduced to the curriculum.

This interest in parent engagement continued. In year three, the principal described the parents in the following manner, "More vocal. More articulate. More willing to critique what we're doing." Later in that same interview he noted that about 10 to 12 parents were involved in writing materials for the school, and said, "They've played a major role. I'm hoping to get a lot more parents like that."

By the fourth year, however, this principal's view on this issue had moved from traditional parent involvement to an emphasis on parent empowerment. When asked to describe changes in parent behavior during that year, he replied:

> Unbelievable. The parents have been unbelievable in terms of their desire to be involved in a day-to-day operation of our school. No bake sales, don't insult me with bake sales.

> Don't insult me with menial kind of things that parents do. I want to be part of the decision making. Who works in this building? Why are you working in this building? You're not doing your job. The decision-making level is what they really want to be involved in. And I've never seen anything like it. And it's been great. That's the difference.

In part, this principal was reacting to the support the parents provided in the fight against the district administration and School Board's identification of the African American Immersion middle school as a "failing" school and the subsequent threat to close it. Parents had supported the school by attending School Board meetings and strongly vocalizing their opposition to this idea. However, it should also be noted that the idea of increased parent empowerment was not uniformly welcomed by staff at the school.

A second area that this principal discussed repeatedly over the years of the Evaluation Project concerned the need to implement an African-centered orientation in the school. When asked about his goals for the school at the end of his first year (and the second year of the African American Immersion emphasis), he responded, "I think the paramount goal right now is to certainly move forward with the whole concept of the immersion school. The uniforms, the curriculum." The principal seemed to feel that implementation of this goal was primarily the responsibility of the teachers.

> I'm putting out a memo reminding the staff that this is a critical year, that you *have* to teach the curriculum that you as a staff have written and that we have to have *full* implementation on everyone's part. Not just fragmented and partial implementation, that everyone must teach the curriculum. Otherwise, we're deceiving parents.

In addition to curriculum development, shortly after arriving at the school, this principal said, "We've got to move on uniforms." In fact, neither of these goals materialized fully during the initial five years the school operated with the African American Immersion focus. Furthermore, in each of our annual interviews with this principal, the inconsistent use of an African-centered curriculum as well as the lack of compliance with the uniform policy was noted.

Finally, our annual interviews with this principal indicated that staff issues were of considerable concern to him. Early in his tenure at the school, this principal stated that "the leadership must come from the teachers, not from the principal." However, in an apparent contradiction of this approach, the following year he reported, "I have announced to the staff that all reading will be taught through the *Great Books* inquiry approach." This pattern of alternation between expectations for staff initiative and actions denoting administrative fiat continued throughout the five-year period of the Evaluation Project. Not surprisingly, this approach led to tensions between the principal and the teachers. In addition, the lack of clear focus by the principal was reflected in staff perspectives.

In summary, the instability caused by the removal of the first principal at the African American Immersion middle school led to tensions during its early years.

This was exacerbated by the very different foci and leadership styles of the two principals. The first principal was primarily concerned with returning order to the school. This individual had a hands-on leadership style and seemed to emphasize positive relations with and among staff.

The second principal's priorities were less clearly defined. Furthermore, this individual had to deal with some difficult issues such as removing staff who failed to meet the educational requirements for teaching at the school. This issue increased tensions among staff. Finally, the second principal's leadership style did little to allay these strains.

TEACHER VOICES

In this section, we turn our attention to the teachers' conceptualizations of this African-centered middle school. The data discussed here came from our annual interviews conducted with staff at the school. As with the elementary school, it is important to note that we were not always able to interview the same teachers in each of the years of our study. However, the teachers who were interviewed in the first four years of our study consisted of a representative sample of those who were assigned to the school in that year. However, in the fifth year we decided to restrict our interviews to two groups of teachers. The first were teachers who had stayed at the school through its initial five years as an African American Immersion middle school. The second group consisted of eighth-grade teachers. These were the teachers of a group of students we had followed longitudinally at the school.

The same set of questions was presented to teachers at both the elementary and middle African American Immersion Schools. As in the case at the elementary school, two sets of questions from the interviews were analyzed here. The first consisted of a series of questions asked only at the beginning of the first year the middle school was officially designated an African American Immersion School. These questions were aimed at understanding teachers' initial conceptualizations of the school. The second set included questions that were asked in end-of-the-year interviews in each of the five years of our study. These questions were aimed at understanding perspectives on the school over time. We begin with a discussion of the questions asked only in our initial interviews with teachers, conducted in the fall of 1992.

Our first question to teachers was, "What is an African American Immersion School?" Many of the responses of the teachers at the middle school were similar to those provided by teachers at the elementary school. A large number of teachers believed the African American Immersion concept was one that builds self-esteem and cultural pride by focusing on information about the children's African and African American cultural heritage. For example, one teacher described the school in the following manner:

> I am going to try to describe what we are doing here. I feel that, first of all, our school
> is predominantly black. And that in itself lets you know that it is an African American

Immersion middle school. . . . We've decided that these students need something different than what has happened in their lives before in middle schools [and] elsewhere. So we try to place the emphasis on building self-esteem. Pride in oneself and knowledge of the contributions that helped come from their ancestors and forefathers and that they do have a purpose in life.

Another theme similar to that found among the teachers at the elementary school linked the themes of enhanced self-esteem and cultural pride to academic achievement explicitly.

I believe that an African American Immersion middle school is a school whereby the children receive instruction as to who they are, who their ancestors are, knowing about their own history, their own culture and hopefully, by being immersed in their own history and culture, that they will get excited about learning and then it will change their attitude about learning.

There was considerable consensus among teachers that an African-centered school was one that encouraged positive self-esteem and cultural pride in African American children. Furthermore, these affective characteristics were linked to student achievement in our respondents' minds. In addition to these perspectives, however, some responses to this question reflected quite disparate points of view among the staff. One area of difference had to do with the idea of who the African American schools were established to serve. Some teachers stated that this was a school specifically for African American students: "It is a school that strives to teach African Americans." Others perceived an even more restricted clientele for the school: "To try to help those who are not succeeding in the public schools."

In contrast, some other staff indicated that an African American Immersion School was not only for African American children. For example, one person said, "An African American Immersion middle school is a school setting where all children are taught about the contributions of African Americans, about the history, the culture and it's not just for African American children." Another teacher said, "I think an African American Immersion middle school is one whose primary focus is on educating not just African Americans but students; educating students from an Afrocentric perspective."

There were interesting differences in staff members' perceptions of the cultural focus of the school also. Some staff took an Afrocentric approach. For example, one teacher said:

I think an African American Immersion School would be a school that would teach students about African culture predominantly. That would teach them about their foreparents, their roots, and where it all started. . . . I think the African American Immersion Schools have really got to focus on African culture first. And then, instead of trying to immerse African culture into American, immerse the American culture into the African culture.

Some other teachers held a perspective that emphasized including information about African Americans into the existing curriculum with little other change. This idea was illustrated by one teacher in the following manner,

> Okay, I view an African American Immersion School as a school that covers the same basic curriculum as all the other . . . schools, but . . . as we go through our textbook, I bring in the roles of African Americans and the importance they played in our society. And show the kids they have self-worth and self-esteem and good role models.

Still other teachers indicated that the cultural orientation served an assimilationist function.

> An African American Immersion middle school, as far as I understand it, is a program that is helping African American youth to find an identity that would give them self-confidence, security, that would help them assimilate or interact with the larger or dominant culture and . . . equipping them to be able to function in the larger culture, but also to value themselves and their heritage.

Finally, in the first year that this school functioned as an African American Immersion School, some teachers expressed resistance to the idea of changing the cultural orientation of the school. One teacher expressed this view in the following response.

> I hear that it is supposed to be pretty much always teaching this immersing as much native African things as you can into the curriculum as possible. I think we do a disservice if that is all we do. I still think we have to teach about living in the United States and 1990s America. . . . You still have to live in this white world we have here. And get along in this white world. So . . . teach the kids as much as they can about their forefathers and things like that, you know, history and that they have contributions to the world; however, you still have to teach them the realities of today.

The responses to this question indicate two perspectives that were prevalent as the African American Immersion middle school began to function. The first was that the students were deficient and in need of intervention to build self-esteem and cultural pride. Beyond this, however, the teachers did not have a shared view of this school model.

A second question in the initial interviews with teachers asked, "What special qualities does it take to be an African American Immersion School?" At the African American Immersion middle school, several themes were evident in their responses.

Several teachers felt that a key quality necessary to the implementation of an African-centered school model was leadership. As one teacher put it, "Number one, you have to have leadership. . . . You have to have someone who is aware of what is going on." Another teacher stated, "It takes an administrator with the vision of what can be done in terms of developing a school of this nature." Finally, one teacher asserted that leadership needed to come not only from administrators at the school but also from the district: "The administrative team has to . . . really believe in this program. And I also think the district owes so much to make this school a success."

Many of the teachers we interviewed identified characteristics of the staff as important ingredients or special qualities that needed to be included in an African American Immersion School. These included personal attributes, knowledge of African and African American history and culture, and levels of commitment to the school and to African American children. In many cases, teachers mentioned a combination of these characteristics.

The perspective that teachers at an African-centered school need to have positive attitudes toward the students and their families and communities was expressed by a number of teachers. For example, one support staff member said:

> I think, first of all, we must have a caring environment here. We have to see the potential in these children. And we have to stop penalizing them for what we see as attitudes or behaviors that are not congruent with . . . our values. . . . I see more counseling services for them. More people from the community coming in and offering support to not only the children but the families.

Another teacher pointed to the importance of not only caring for children but also respecting their culture: "I think you have to have people who really care. Who are really convinced that everybody can learn. And are really convinced that it is important to know people's backgrounds or roots. . . . So that the children know that you are true." The idea of respecting and understanding the cultural backgrounds of the African American children at this middle school was indicated by many teachers as a key quality for an African American Immersion School. For example, one staff member said:

> Number one, I think those people who work in an African American Immersion School must have some background as to who and what African Americans are. They must know something about African American history. They must know something about African American culture. They must believe that all students can learn.

This idea of knowledge of African and African American culture and history was particularly salient for some of the teachers at the school. One such teacher pointed this out.

> The awareness, I think, would be number one. And especially for someone such as myself who is not African American, the awareness of the contributions of the African American people in our society and in our past. And I think it is also allowing the children to begin to explore their past, what they are all about, what their families are all about.

Another teacher argued that the knowledge and acceptance of African and African American culture needed to permeate the school.

In my opinion, it is going to take a person, first of all, that understands the culture of an African American. Secondly, it is going to take a person that truly accepts African Americans and their culture. And thirdly, it is going to have to take a unity among all teachers, whoever is going to be there.

A related issue for many teachers was that teachers had to be dedicated and committed to the concept of an African American Immersion School if it was to be implemented. One staff person addressed this issue in the following manner: "A committed staff. I feel staff that can grow to understand students, that are willing to work with students of various backgrounds." Another teacher said, "I think it needs to be a very dedicated staff, with a willingness to be open to new teaching styles, new learning styles."

In general, there was fairly strong agreement among the staff that knowledge of African and African American history and culture as well as commitment to both the children and the concept of African-centered schooling were important. However, some teachers also identified issues reflecting areas of conflict that would become increasingly salient at this school. One of these issues involved unity among the staff. One teacher was quite pointed about this, saying:

I guess you would need the staff and the school administrators to be all in the same wavelength where they are all kind of whatever you decide what you want your school to be, you all kind of go in the same wavelength. I don't know if we have that right now. I think right now it's still kind of drifting around.

Other teachers seemed more resistant to the African-centered orientation. For example, one teacher said an important quality was "[t]he realization that there are going to be white people that will interact with the black children, and they need to see that now in a positive way." Another indicated that learning African and African American history was positive but cautioned, "I think, you know, that they're living here in the United States of America and they need to know their background, but they also need to be a part of our society. I shouldn't say that because it's just as much their society as it is mine. But just making them aware of that." These comments foreshadowed strains and tensions around race that were present at the school over the initial five years it operated as an African American Immersion School.

A third question asked the teachers, "Why are African American Immersion Schools occurring now in history?" The teachers' responses to these questions fell into four categories. The themes were similar to those mentioned by the staff at the elementary school.

A number of teachers suggested that the African American Immersion Schools arose because African American children were failing in school and society in a variety of ways. However, the specific factors underlying this failure varied. Some teachers argued that the students were failing because of a lack of knowledge of their culture, poor self-esteem, and a lack of positive role models. For example, one teacher noted, "Because of failures. We have found out who is failing. It is the black child. Who doesn't really know himself." Another described "the lack of self-esteem and a lack of pride."

In a somewhat related mode, some teachers pointed to problems beyond the school community as the source of students' school failures. For example, one teacher answered this question in the following manner.

> I don't know if it is necessarily because of education. I think it is because . . . There is a problem in inner-city places. There is too much violence. There are too many things going on. We have to pull the children out of that violence for a while and make them see that to be successful that can't be what happens.

Another teacher responded to this question in a similar vein: "I think, mainly, because of the horrible statistics we are reading, you know, that we are losing, especially the black males, and somebody, thank God, decided that we needed to get these kids back." This same teacher also mentioned, "the pregnancy rate among females" as another impetus for the establishment of these schools.

A number of teachers responded to this question by citing other factors as the impetus for the establishment of the African American Immersion Schools. For example, some teachers saw these schools as a response to the failure of traditional *schools* rather than the failure of the children in them. One teacher noted:

> Somewhere down the line I feel that we have failed to educate . . . the city child or children. And I am not sure, I don't think anyone really knows where we started to fall by the wayside with these students. But I look at our students today, and it is not poverty. Because many of us, myself included, grew up poor. So it's not that. We need this kind of school . . . to take a look at the children, to find out what their strengths are.

Another teacher made a similar comment: "Because our schools are failing so much. I think it has just gotten to a point where people are just saying enough is enough. It's time to change around."

Finally, some of the teachers saw the emergence of the African American Immersion Schools at the beginning of the 1990s as part of a larger social and political movement. These teachers placed these schools in the context of the ongoing struggle by African Americans for parity and equity in schools and in society. For example, one staff member linked these schools to the civil rights movement of the 1960s and to the failure of desegregation to bring about educational equity for African American children.

> I guess change is always gradual. So I guess this is just the culmination of the evolution . . . from the sixties on up. People were able to register to vote. And then they were able to elect people into offices . . . and then when we integrated. I think we have realized that we lost something of ourselves then.

Another teacher voiced similar reasons for the occurrence of the schools.

> I think it has something to do with the movement for black or African American stud-
> ies in the same way there was a movement in the late seventies and eighties for women's
> studies. I think that there is a reaction against the concept of bussing . . . that it is a re-
> action to the fact that integration isn't working out as well as it had hoped.

In a somewhat related fashion, some teachers argued that changing demographics in the city as well as in the nation as a whole undergirded the emergence of these African American Immersion Schools. For example, one teacher stated, "I believe the white aristocracy is not as powerful as it once was—that is one reason. Another reason is the growing numbers of African Americans in this country, and they are having input where they didn't before in politics."

The themes mentioned by teachers at both African American Immersion Schools reflect two quite different perspectives. One, a deficit-oriented perspective, blamed African American children and the African American community for failures in school. This perspective, that is often found in the literature as well as in popular culture, often looks for solutions aimed at "fixing" the deficit child. By contrast, the other themes placed the locus of failure on the schools and on European American domination of the society. These perspectives focused on fixing the institutions and building on the strengths African American children brought to the schools.

As we indicated earlier in this section, the previous questions were asked of the teachers only at the beginning of the first year that the African American Immersion middle school was implemented formally. The remaining questions to be discussed here were asked of the teachers in their annual year-end interviews during the five-year Evaluation Project.

The first of these questions asked, "In your opinion, what are the goals of an African American Immersion School?" A number of the teachers' responses reflected two themes that remained consistent over the initial five years that the school operated as an African American Immersion School.

The first of these themes argued that a major goal of this type of school was to build self-esteem and to help the children develop pride in themselves through knowledge of the positive aspects of their cultural heritage. For examples one teacher described the goals of the school in the following manner:

> I think it is to infuse African American history and culture into the curriculum as well
> as use new learning styles to reach, teaching techniques to reach different learning
> styles, to raise consciousness of African Americans to take pride in the African
> American culture. And to bolster their self-esteem and respect for one another and the
> African American culture.

Common perspectives among many of these teachers was that the students had low self-esteem because they did not know about their heritage or they did not know about the positive contributions of Africans and African Americans. The following response from a teacher is illustrative of that perspective: "[The goal is] to build the self pride, a pride in a heritage, a pride in the individual that hasn't been, well, that hasn't been perceived to be in the African American culture. Especially among the youth."

Another teacher emphasized the need to counter negative images of African Americans:

> I feel the goals should be to educate our students, the African American students, in their heritage and in their culture. Let them know about the contributions of our people and let them know that we're not all dope sellers, drug addicts, pimps and whores as we're depicted.

A closely related theme was expressed by a number of teachers consistently over the five-year period. This theme linked the emphasis on African and African American history and culture explicitly to fostering student achievement. One staff member reflected this theme at the beginning of the first year in the following manner:

> I think the goals are to educate African American children. And . . . I would hope that the goals would be not only to educate African American children but to make them very much aware of who they are, to make them understand that they are valuable to this society, that they are talented. They can aspire to be what they want to be. And that they, by becoming educated and knowing who they are, that they can make choices as they go into the broader society.

This idea, that the African-centered focus of the school could be a tool to enhance student achievement, became more pronounced in the teachers' descriptions of the goals of the school by the end of the first year. Some examples are illustrative. One teacher said:

> [The goal is] to become . . . sensitive to African culture and to decipher from African culture those ingredients or resources or strengths that may be beneficial and therefore help the students to define themselves and re-define where they are going and where they would like to be.

Another teacher reinforced this view.

> I believe the goals are to bring a focus and an emphasis to the heritage that is derived from Africa. I believe if the students realize that, they will have a better understanding of who they are and be better able to function in society. So, I think, a goal would be to inform the students of their heritage and help them to grab it and use it as a power source to carry on in America.

Still another example from the first year was the following.

> The goals of the school. Okay. Well, to raise the academic levels and the performance levels of the students by infusing them with their African American culture. That

would be the main goals and then related with that would be to enhance the students' self-esteem by increasing their knowledge of their own heritage and of their legacy that has been left to them.

It appears evident that by the end of the first year this middle school formally operated as an African American Immersion School, that there was considerable consensus regarding two primary goals of an African-centered model. These were, first, to enhance students' self-esteem and cultural pride and, second, to foster student achievement. Furthermore, these two themes reappeared in subsequent years of our evaluation study.

Some other themes became evident as teachers described their perceptions of the goals of an African American Immersion School. For example, some focused on the goal of raising achievement without including any reference to the cultural focus of the school: "Overall, the goals are, first, to increase student attendance . . . We feel if we get the students here every day, we will be able to teach and thereafter they will be able to achieve in the academics . . . if they desire to." It is interesting to note that this perspective was evident, even in the fourth year that the school operated as an African American Immersion School. This was the year that began on a high note but was rocked by challenges from outside the school. Teachers' perspectives regarding the goals of the school were more divergent during this year. For example, some still did not include the cultural orientation of the school in their descriptions of goals. "The goals are, to me, to improve the students' academic levels in all subject areas."

In a related vein, another teacher appeared to minimize the cultural emphasis.

> I think they [the goals] need to be narrowed and more focused. I can agree with implementing the African American concept into the curriculum, but the bottom line is these kids have to be able to go out and function in the total world. Which means you got to read and . . . be able to do math. . . . So I feel these are the skills that these kids need. They need the basics. You give them the basics, they'll be able to get the other stuff.

A quite divergent point of view was expressed by some other teachers in year four. This year several teachers included a distinct Afrocentric perspective in their description of the goals of an African American Immersion School. For example, one teacher said, "The goals, I believe, are to get our students to see the world from an African perspective." Another teacher stated that the goals of the African American Immersion School "would be the goals of any school. The only difference is that we're meeting these goals by educating children from their own cultural perspective."

Finally, in the fourth year that this middle school operated as an African American Immersion School, some of the teachers expressed frustration that the goals were not being met. Said one teacher, "I think our goals are the same as they were the first year that we started the immersion program. It's just that we haven't achieved a whole lot from year one." Another perceived that the goals were "to make each subject immersed in the program. And I know a lot of times it isn't carried [out]." It should be noted that the teachers expressing this point of view had been at the school since it began as an African American Immersion School. In part, their frustration may have been a result of the repeated challenges that had confronted the school during its first four years as an immersion school.

In the fifth year of our study, we interviewed a restricted sample of teachers. We included only teachers who had remained at the school all five years and eighth-grade teachers. When asked to describe what they perceived as the goals of the school, these teachers returned to one of the primary themes that had been expressed since year one: to build self-esteem and cultural pride. For example, a teacher stated, "The goals of an African American Immersion School are to assist the children in learning about their own culture and history and discovering their own identity through that culture and history." Another teacher said the goals were to "raise the self-esteem of our students by indoctrinating them in their culture and making them proud of their heritage."

Other teachers interviewed in the fifth year repeated the Afrocentric theme that had been mentioned the previous year. For example, one teacher explained this perspective very clearly.

> The goals of an African American Immersion School would be to put African and African American history at the center of the curriculum. Which means we highlight the roles that different Africans and African Americans have played in history. Where there's math, science, social studies, English, etc., Africans are the focal point.

This particular teacher had come to the school the previous year as part of its new beginning. Another teacher who had served the school for five years provided a similar perspective, saying,

> I think, after five years, . . . the goal of an African American school is, first of all, to teach children from their own cultural perspective and as a result of teaching them from this perspective, we hope to help these children become empowered socially, economically, and academically.

In summary, some teachers at the African American middle school held perceptions of the goals of an African American Immersion School that were quite similar to those professed by the teachers at the African American Immersion elementary school. The most commonly perceived goals involved raising self-esteem and increasing cultural knowledge, often, but not always, in the service of obtaining enhanced academic achievement. However, the staff of the middle school also displayed variability in their perception of the goals of the school. For example, differences of opinion about the curricular focus of the school persisted during the first five years. These disparate views may have been a reflection of the lack of unity among the school staff in general.

The final question to be discussed here was intended to understand the staff's conceptualization of this African-centered school experiment, particularly as it differed from traditional school models. This question asked, "What can an African American Immersion School accomplish that would not be done by a traditional school?" This question was also asked at the beginning and end of the first year and annually in each of the subsequent years of the Evaluation Project.

Several themes were voiced consistently across the first five years that the school was formally designated an African American Immersion School. One theme emphasized the cultural orientation of the school as the primary factor distinguishing it from more traditional schools. A number of teachers felt that an African American Immersion middle school could instill a sense of cultural pride and identity and enhance self-esteem among the students. One teacher summed up this theme in the following manner:

> I don't think a traditional middle school would emphasize so much of the African American theme and provide so much information on that. I think that is just the biggest factor. I guess all the other activities go along with that. I mean, they are really broadening the students' awareness of the different accomplishments of African Americans in the history as well as providing a lot of role models from the community, a lot of people coming in and instilling pride in the students.

Another teacher voiced a similar view: "Hopefully it will give them a sense of pride and respect for themselves and for each other." Another teacher argued that this orientation had been absent from traditional schools for a long time by saying, "I guess we are trying to take them back, take the students back to the roots of their heritage and give them the identity that they definitely need. You are not going to get this in our regular schools. They haven't gotten it in the last 30 years."

A large number of the teachers we interviewed felt that this African American Immersion middle school would have a greater impact on student success both in and out of school than more traditional schools because of its African-centered focus. One teacher predicted, "They will learn more about themselves . . . and hopefully . . . will be able to take some of these themes that they are seeing and use [them] later in life." Another teacher articulated, once again, the potential of the emphasis on African and African American history and culture as a tool to motivate students as distinctive for this school:

> Hopefully, as I said it before, we can get our students turned on by education. We can get them to the point where they want to read and learn about their history and their own culture. . . . Once they are motivated and excited about reading and learning, they can make choices as to once they get out in the broader community, they are not limited.

Another teacher hoped that "out of this would come a desire to be educated, to create pride."

In a related vein, several teachers felt that this school would be able to focus on the specific needs of African American children more than traditional schools. There were two aspects to this theme. One perspective was that the students came to school with deficits that had to be fixed. For example, one teacher felt the African American Immersion School would be more effective than traditional schools, "especially with the population we have . . . because there are a lot of needs, individual needs that simply cannot be met with the regular middle school." Another teacher was more explicit.

> According to some research that I read lately, African American students have the highest dropout rates and other statistics we can quote here, and obviously, the report says that something needs to be done. And, ideally, it would change the failure rate, would change the attendance and dropout problems, it would improve skills, it would help children compete in an increasingly competitive world, unfortunately. Hopefully, all those people that haven't been served and all these people's needs that haven't been met would be able, or a large majority of them would be able to be met in a school like this.

A second perspective focused more on building students' strengths. For example, a teacher felt this school would provide a more authentic learning environment for African American students.

> I think it will be a more true schooling in that it will encompass a more well-rounded approach to history and culture. I think it will also serve to raise, bolster, self-esteem in the students. And I think it will also address the different learning styles that students have. And by doing that, it will have a direct effect on their self-esteem in that there will be a lot of positive experiences that the students will have.

Throughout the five years of our study, the teachers voiced the idea that the distinguishing feature of this school was its potential to enhance student self-esteem and academic success. The focus on African and African American culture was the vehicle for realizing this potential. Indeed, this theme was expressed most frequently. For example, a teacher said, "I think there is a much more well-integrated sense of . . . the background of people both as African Americans in this country and also as having a history from Africa and a connection to modern-day Africa." In the third year of this experiment, this same teacher noted this was a school "where students get an opportunity to be more focused in their knowledge" and hoped the emphasis on African and African American culture would "give them an extra advantage in their future lives."

From a different perspective, some teachers thought this school differed from more traditional middle schools in its potential to serve the African American community in the city. For example, one teacher said, "An African American Immersion School will raise the level of consciousness in the community." Another hoped that "in the black community it is a school that they can identify themselves with as being an excellent school that serves the community and serves the kids." And another teacher predicted that "this African American Immersion School can be a unifying force to African Americans in this city. . . . This can be a culture center for African American people."

Finally, a related theme that began to be voiced by some teachers in the third year that this middle school operated as an African American Immersion School suggested that this school, unlike others, had the possibility of empowering students as a result of its cultural orientation. Some examples of this perspective follow.

> I think it will empower them. I think it will give them a sense of mission in terms of what they should be doing for their family, for their friends, for the people that they care about . . . and I think that it can also begin to give them the kind of insight that will make them competitive with the rest of the world.

Another teacher felt this school could "give kids some ownership." Another teacher felt the school could "make the students change agents; they can learn to identify the inequities in society and do something about them." Similarly a teacher said, "I think what it does is help children start finding or start seeking their place in their community as well as the global community."

In summary, the consensus among the teachers we interviewed over the first five years that this middle school operated as an immersion school was that the cultural orientation that distinguished this from other middle schools had the potential to have a more profound impact on students' self-esteem as well as their academic and worldly success. Some teachers felt the cultural focus could encourage students to work for change in society.

There were high levels of optimism regarding the African American Immersion middle school's potential to have a positive impact on students because of its cultural orientation. However, by year three, some teachers began to express frustration that this potential was not being met. For example, one teacher said this school differed from traditional middle schools because

> [i]t is to immerse the school in black culture. I think we at the African American Immersion middle school missed the boat on it though. It certainly is not living up to my expectations. We could do a much better job. I think it still has a chance, but we need teachers who are completely dedicated.

This sense of frustration grew in the following years. Some teachers discussed what could have been done at the school if it "worked properly" or "if it's carried out the way the plan envisioned it." Another teacher lamented, "We have not consistently done anything that people have told us, but make this program slip." Finally, one teacher in responding to this question said, "Well, we could have accomplished a lot if we could have chosen. . . . We could have taught a lot of culture beyond and above what's really permitted to teach in public school." However, this teacher went on to say, "We're very limited in who we had here."

In summary, teachers' responses to this question revealed several themes that were consistent across the initial five years the school operated as an African

American Immersion middle school. One of these themes focused on the school as a special place because of its cultural orientation. A second was that because of this cultural orientation this school would attend more closely to the specific needs of poor African American children. However, a third theme emerged toward the end of this period. This was an increasing sense of frustration that the school was not fulfilling its mission.

SUMMARY

In summary, our portrait of the African American Immersion middle school shows a school where the attempt to implement an African-centered educational model was beset with problems. Some of the challenges originated within the school as a result of tensions between staff and administrators or among staff. Others came from the district administration and the School Board. These problems made it difficult for the school to develop a clear shared vision of what an African-centered model at the middle school level could look like. These issues also prevented the school from successfully establishing some of the foundations necessary to be effective for middle school students generally. Despite these repeated setbacks, however, some teachers expressed optimism for what a school of this type could accomplish. Throughout the initial five years encompassing the period of our study, staff persisted in their belief that an African-centered schooling experience had positive potential for these students.

—— 4 ——

Transformations

By the beginning of the 1990s, school reform issues had become entrenched in school districts nationally. However, some researchers began to criticize these reform movements because of their lack of attention to the cultural dimensions of schooling (Mirel, 1994). This was particularly important when instituting reform efforts in urban communities that are characterized by cultural diversity among students but also by structural factors that affect individual and family functioning (Noguera, 1996; Williams & Newcombe, 1994).

In this chapter, we focus on the efforts made to convert the African American Immersion elementary and middle schools from a traditional to an African-centered educational orientation. As some of the first public schools in the nation to attempt to implement such an orientation on a school-wide basis, these schools could be considered pioneers. There were some models of African-centered schools available in independent schools (Hoover, 1992; Lee, 1992), and individuals working to develop the African American Immersion Schools availed themselves of information about them when possible. However, there was little empirical data available that provided information about the processes of transforming schools into African-centered models of education. Furthermore, as public schools, the African American Immersion Schools did not have the flexibility of independent schools. Many of their policies and procedures were dictated by the district, and they had to incorporate new ways of doing things while continuing to implement these district policies and mandates.

Given this situation, it is important to understand how the schools attempted to transform themselves from entities that were known, although ineffective, into entities that would stress African and African American cultural orientations as foundations for teaching and learning. This chapter focuses on school-level transformations. Specifically, we describe and analyze overall changes that occurred in each school over the five-year study period. In addition, we analyze how teachers', students', and parents'—the major stakeholders in schooling—communication and interaction patterns changed over this period. Finally, we discuss the links that were formed between these schools and the African American communities in the city.

In keeping with the overall focus of the book, we concentrate on teachers' perceptions of these changes. The African American Immersion Schools were launched with several ambitious goals. Among these were to change the cultural orientation of schooling, to enhance student achievement, and to forge closer ties with the African American community. As the primary individuals charged with implementing these goals, it is important to understand how teachers perceived school-level changes, whether they changed the ways they interacted with students and parents and how they viewed student–parent interactions.

The data discussed in this chapter focus on teachers' perceptions of school-level changes over time at the two African American Immersion Schools. Two questions asked in our annual year-end interviews with teachers are analyzed. The first was, "How has this school changed over the year to become an African American Immersion School?" The second area had to do with changes in the interaction patterns among students, teachers, and parents over time. These questions were designed to elicit teachers' evaluations of the kinds of changes they were experiencing as their school was developing its African-centered orientation. The patterns emerging from their responses were important in understanding to what degree and how changes were reshaping the overall climate of the schools. We will discuss the teachers' responses to these questions first at the elementary school, then at the middle school.

TRANSFORMATIONS AT THE ELEMENTARY SCHOOL

As in the previous chapter, we describe information obtained from teachers' interviews in the first (1991–1992), third (1993–1994), and fifth (1995–1996) years of our five-year longitudinal documentation and evaluation study of the school. Because we are interested in change over time, we will discuss the data sequentially for these years. It should be remembered that since we were not able to interview the same teachers repeatedly over the five-year period, the data include a representative sample of teachers for the particular year under discussion. Even though our data do not describe the responses of a longitudinal sample of teachers, they do reflect typical representations of teacher views in any given year.

School-Level Changes

In year one, the teachers' responses to this question could be categorized into three major themes. With respect to the first theme, teachers described a variety of surface-level changes that had taken place in the school. These included such things as the name, the advent of uniforms for students, the physical appearance of the building, and the decision by some staff members to wear African attire. Several teachers felt the physical changes conveyed the orientation of the school quite directly. For instance, one teacher said:

> I think when you walk into the building, it is obvious that you know that this is a school [that's] immersing itself into the African heritage, from the things that you see on the walls, from the displays of the children's work in the hallways. Also from the attire that you see the children and the faculty members wearing. I mean, it is just prevalent everywhere.

Another teacher echoed this view with the following: "Just by looking at bulletin boards and displays all over the school, you can see change as soon as you walk into the building. Because that is the focus."

Some teachers felt these surface changes were most prevalent in the first year the school operated as an African American Immersion School. For example, one teacher said: "The superficial things have changed quite a bit. The name changed. The uniforms have changed. The programs have changed. But I honestly don't see a lot of changes in behavior and that sort of thing, which, to me, is a better judge of what is going on." These initial changes could be viewed as setting the stage for broader restructuring.

The second area of change that was described by some of the teachers in their interviews concerned programmatic and structural characteristics of the school. For example, one teacher focused on the initiation of the family structure in which teachers and their classes were grouped into small groups called families: "With our family focus, you know, you keep, you have the African culture. The family is very important, so we try to bring that into the school system. The kids feel that they belong to a group. That is our family." In this case, the teacher tied the structural change to the cultural orientation of the school. Another teacher described changes in physical appearance but also mentioned structural changes in the school, noting, "I think better committees that are working harder than ever before . . . and of course we have become an SBM [site-based management] school. So we have that going every month. And getting input from people." One substantial programmatic change that had been implemented with the advent of the African-centered model involved the introduction of additional support staff and specialists as described in Chapter 2. One teacher noted, "It is really incredible how having full-time specialists and full-time counselor and social worker makes such a difference. You can see that has improved right there."

By far the most frequently mentioned area where teachers perceived changes in this first year the school operated as an African American Immersion School described changes in the teachers' behavior and outlook. This general theme was discussed in several different but related ways. First, some teachers noted changes in the teachers' interactions with students. For example, one teacher noted, "I do see us taking, in some ways, more time dealing with kids' problems. Now that is a plus." Another teacher mentioned this area of change with the following: "I think that I have seen a lot more of what I spoke of earlier. Where the teacher is taking more time to explain and talk about something that is not right rather than just tell them this is not right and it's not going to happen." In another illustration of the theme of changes in teacher behavior and outlook, some teachers focused on staff interactions among each other. One teacher said, "To me, we are more like a family. We care about one another." Another teacher voiced similar sentiments: "I see the teachers working together more like a family. They seem to be more cooperative." Another teacher noted greater interdependence among the teachers. This teacher said, "I think we, as a staff, got together and we became closer and relied, not relied, but went for help." In all these cases, the teachers appeared to bond more closely as a result of undertaking this experiment.

A third area of change in staff behavior and outlook was related to the teachers' attitudes toward and involvement with the African-centered orientation of the school. For example, one teacher discussed changes in teachers' outlooks as they related to their role as staff in one of the first African-centered educational models that had been implemented in a public school setting.

> For right now I would say, since the beginning of the year, we were all keyed up for the change. Maybe anxious is a better word. And now, I think everybody just sort of takes it in stride. There is not this feeling so much of the fishbowl where we are constantly being watched. We adjusted and adapted to the fact that we are an African American Immersion School, and that's okay and we really don't care about anybody who comes in to observe us as to what they think because our first priority is to meet the needs of our students. If they don't like what we are doing or we don't do a good job on that particular day, that's okay.

This teacher seems to have been reacting to the tremendous amount of publicity, both national and local, that accompanied the opening of the elementary African American Immersion School.

Some of the other teachers reported feeling more comfortable with the concept of building a school culture and curriculum on African and African American culture. One teacher mentioned "the heightened awareness of the African American culture" as an important change in the school during its first year of implementation. Another teacher described the process of her own immersion into an African-centered schooling orientation in the following manner:

> Everybody is more comfortable with it. Everyone is more immersed. It's like when you are just putting one foot in the water and it's cold and you kind of like stick it in real tentatively. I think we were pretty cold in the beginning and the people that were more immersed went in faster. And people that participated in [a professor's] class got big time immersion right off the bat. I mean, they got water splashed right in their face and they said, "Oh, what the heck. Let's go in." And I think we have just moved into getting into the swim of things.

This teacher also described some of the anxiety that was associated with this school's position as one of the first public African-centered efforts. However, this teacher also alluded to the importance of the requirement that teachers take 18 college-level credits in African and African American history and culture to support their efforts to change the school and curriculum.

Another teacher indicated increased comfort with African-centered ideas and, again, related this to the classes staff were required to take.

> Well, I just think as you teach and as you go along, it becomes a more natural thing to incorporate. You know, you are always thinking in the back of your mind, How can I acknowledge the African American contribution in this subject area? And the more classes we take as a staff, the more aware we are where famous people fit into which areas and in the background of Africa in everything.

Many of the teachers noted greater ease with African-centered perspectives in this first year.

While most of the teachers described positive changes such as those mentioned above, a few teachers expressed some disappointment that there had not been as much change in the school as had been envisioned or hoped for. One teacher said, "I guess for myself, I pictured all these things to happen. But it didn't quite get there as I hoped." Another teacher expressed similar views, noting that some had very high expectations when the school year began.

> We had the little in-service in the summer and we got a lot of ideas. We came back to school, and I think everybody wanted to use those ideas right away and make changes, change the whole world. It didn't work out that way. What you have to realize is that this is an ongoing thing. It is not a quick fix. . . . It is something you have to continually work at; it continuously is evolving.

This teacher described the initial reactions of many, both in and outside the African American Immersion Schools. The search for rapid and dramatic changes was most evident among the media and others who were onlookers to this process. This teacher's recognition of the more gradual, evolving nature of change became reflective of the general perspective taken in the African American Immersion elementary school.

By year three, teachers had a better sense of what they were doing in the classroom and were clearly engaged in the process of transforming the school into an African-centered experience for students. It is important to note that by the third year there was evidence of improved academic achievement. That year, 87 percent of the third graders taking the state-level reading test scored at or above the passing level.

Some of the teachers continued to espouse the theme of changes in teacher behavior and attitudes related to greater ease in implementing an African-centered educational orientation. This notion was illustrated by the following response: "Well, I think we are more into what the program is all about, and I think the longer we work in the program . . . the more understanding, like you learn by doing. I think I have a little more understanding about what I am supposed to be doing than I did at first."

Another theme that had been mentioned in the first year was focused on staff re-lationships. For example, in year three, one teacher said the school had changed be-cause "I think the staff has been sharing a lot more." Another reported the following: "Well, I now notice that the grade levels seem to be closer; the teachers in the grade levels seem to be talking more and communicating more about more things and. . . . [T]hey seem to have a unifying effect in their lessons because . . . I see certain things in the same grade levels."

A new theme also became evident in the teachers' responses in the third year, how-ever. This concerned teachers' perceptions of changes in the students' behavior. For example, one teacher said, "Well, I noticed the discipline seems to be a lot better, and I think the uniforms have helped, too. They seem like a closer-knit family." Another teacher felt the children had more positive self-regard as a result of the African-centered orientation of the school. This teacher said the school had changed over the year in terms of "how they [the children] feel within themselves. How good they feel. And I think it has really made a difference with our children."

By the fifth year, many of the teachers had institutionalized a number of changes that now distinguished their conceptualization of an African American Immersion School. This included evidence of African and African American culture in every classroom. In addition, there were school-wide programs such as an active chorus, an annual "African American male teach-in," and a "career day" highlighting the im-portance of positive African American role models. Students were given opportuni-ties to enhance their social development through participation in the student council and peer mediation.

Two themes continued to predominate in the teachers' responses. One was that the teachers continued to feel greater ease and comfort with the focus on African and African American history and culture. For example, one teacher stated, "Well, I think it's stronger. Yeah, for myself, I've had a lot more resources and I feel more com-fortable with the curriculum in integrating the African curriculum with the tradi-tional educational courses that I'm supposed to teach. So, it's just a more cohesive environment."

The other continuing theme was that teachers perceived changes in the students' at-titudes and behavior. In addition to discipline and self-regard, teachers identified other changes they perceived in their students in the fifth year. For instance, one teacher felt the students were becoming more attuned to the African American emphasis of the school. "I think the children have internalized things. . . . We're seeing it in their writ-ing and the way they express themselves when they ask questions about what the African American Immersion School is and what it means to them and how it changes things." Several of the teachers perceived changes in the students' attitudes to school and learning. For example, one teacher said, "The children's attitude toward school has changed. I see more young people coming to school ready to learn and fo-cused on why they are here." Still another teacher mentioned the overall improvement in students' performance on the district's standardized tests as an important change.

In summary, over the five-year period, the teachers perceived a variety of transfor-mations at the school level. In the first year, there was more of an emphasis on more

superficial changes such as changes in the building's appearance, the types of displays, and the attire of students and teachers. In the third and fifth years there was
an increasing focus on more internalized changes, such as changes in teachers' and
students' behaviors and attitudes. Teachers became more comfortable using African
and African American historical and cultural material in their classrooms. In addition, staff interaction became more cooperative. Finally, beginning in year three and
increasing markedly in year five, the teachers focused more on positive changes in the
attitudes and behaviors of their students.

Changes in Interaction Patterns

The second set of questions focused on teachers' perceptions of the interaction
patterns between the major stakeholders in the school: teachers, students, and parents. The first asked if they had seen any changes in teacher–student interactions
over the year.

In general, the elementary teachers' perceptions of teacher–student interaction patterns were consistent over the first-, third- and fifth-year interviews. In general, these
teachers held positive views of their students and saw their interactions improving
over time. One teacher's response in the first year was typical: "I guess I never had a
problem with my rapport with kids." Another staff member, responding to this question in year five, said, "I think . . . [student-teacher interactions have] have always
been pretty positive." These teachers did perceive positive changes in teacher–
student interactions; they often attributed these to changes in the teachers' behavior.
For example, in year one, one teacher said, "I am somewhat warmer than I have been
in other years." In year three, this teacher perceived that the staff as a whole was more
responsive to students, saying, "I see us, within the school building, going to greater
lengths with kids to solve the problems here and to use more resources." In year five,
a teacher described teacher–student interaction in the following words: "We respect
the children and they respect us."

When asked if there had been changes in interaction patterns among students
over the year, the teachers' responses showed a consistent pattern across the first,
third, and fifth years. Teachers described some student-to-student interaction patterns as initially positive and improving, whereas others were problematic. For example, in year one, a teacher said, "I think for some students it has made a difference
in that they feel pride in themselves and they're behaving better. For some of the students, their attitudes haven't changed as much. We have some, particularly males,
who we are concerned with. Who are very angry. Very angry."

By year three, teachers had incorporated the cultural orientation and other resources as tools to support the development of positive behaviors in students. For example, one teacher discussed how she used culture in the classroom:

> With [my] kids, that is always going to be a problem. I mean, it doesn't work; it's not
> magical, but I think there are times that we can use [culture] in the sense that this is
> their common heritage and there is like a sense of unity, and maybe when squabbles

break out or arguments break out, that is something that we can kind of use as a tool in terms of the commonality . . . of things they are up against as opposed to arguing over each other's. So I mean I think it's a tool and in time it will become a bigger tool.

Another factor that was seen as underlying improved student behavior was a peer mediation program that was instituted in the third year. A staff member pointed to this in the following response: "Oh, yes, the peer mediation and the conflict resolution skills. I see students who are more able to restrain themselves and think before they say something bad to somebody who has said something bad to them. Or I've seen other students step in between other students to say, 'Cool off.'" In the fifth year, these tools continued to be seen as a positive influence on students' interactions with each other. While issues around students' behavior continued to exist, staff felt they had resources available to them to help them deal with them. However, a great deal of improvement was seen generally.

Parents are one of the major stakeholders in the schooling process. Yet parents, especially poor, African American parents, are often portrayed as uninterested in their children's school experiences. We were interested in knowing if there were any transformations in teachers' perceptions of parents over the initial five years of the operation of the African American Immersion Schools.

With respect to teacher–parent interactions, two patterns were striking. First, the teachers at the elementary school had very traditional interactions with parents. They tended to judge their interactions with parents according to the degree to which the parents responded to teachers, attended parent conferences, and visited the school. In the first year, most of the teachers visited parents of their students in their homes. Many reported that these visits were successful; however, a number indicated they had trouble connecting with parents. Although home visits were mandated for the African American Immersion Schools, they did not become institutionalized. Second, however, the teachers at this school tended to view the parents with compassion. They recognized that the parents were concerned about their children and understood the struggles that many of these poor families were undergoing. These themes were consistent in data from the annual interviews in the first, third, and fifth years the school was an African American Immersion School.

In general, many of the teachers reported positive interactions with parents. For example, in year one a teacher reported the following:

> I have made lots of contacts with parents. I keep up with them on the phone and with home visits. You have to go on the home visits. I feel that doesn't make you have to keep in contact with the parents; that forces the parents to have to keep in contact with you. I feel you are having constant information being passed back and forth, and with our Merit Cards . . . every Friday they will get a notification of how their child is doing and they have to sign. We get it back Monday. At least we know that an adult at their house has looked at what they have done for the week.

Another teacher described the difficulties parents often have communicating with the school in the following manner. "I have many parents that work full-time. Work double shifts. And as I told [the principal], we keep in close contact on the phone. They are very concerned. It is not that they are not concerned; it is just that they cannot get off work." In general, teachers tended to view parents positively.

Finally, teachers were asked if there had been changes in parent–student interaction patterns over time. Most of the teachers had little to report in response to this question. Most indicated that they had not had opportunities to observe students interacting with their parents. Those who had saw these interactions primarily in the school setting and characterized them as positive. For example, a typical response was the following, made by a teacher in year one: "The interaction that I have always seen is that the parents come in and pick up the kids. That kind of thing. It has been really positive." A similar response came from a teacher in the fifth year: "Basically, I've noticed that at conferences . . . and I would say that the relationship was a warm relationship. It was a caring relationship." Again, parents tended to be seen in a manner that was traditional but compassionate.

School Community Links

At the African American Immersion elementary school, initially there was a great deal of interest in the school from a number of groups in the community. In year one, an ambitious mentoring program was established with groups such as the African American firemen, the African American police group, and various other African American groups in local businesses as well as service organizations. However, this program was not able to be implemented because many of these groups did not follow through on their commitments. Over time, this school's community links became limited to one individual who worked with a number of classes and a couple of African Americans who worked with one of the school's business partners. However, these people maintained continuous relationships with the school that have continued. In addition, the school formalized community involvement through the annual African American male teach-in. This daylong program brings in a variety of African American men from all walks of life. The men visit classes and end the day with a school-wide ceremony in which both students and their visitors are honored. Similarly, career day also highlights various occupations in the Milwaukee community.

During the five-year period there were some significant transformations in terms of the teachers' perceptions of the school climate. To summarize, the teachers seemed to feel that the African-centered orientation had an important impact on the school. This impact was evident, not only in superficial changes in the appearance of the school but also in more profound changes in teachers' attitudes and behaviors that were more internalized. Furthermore, these changes in teachers' attitudes and behaviors became institutionalized as they developed an ethos of cooperation and sharing. This ethos meshed with increasing comfort with African-centered thinking. Over time, these teachers became comfortable with an African-centered orientation, and this perspective seemed to have become normative for them.

On the other hand, there appeared to be little change in how these teachers viewed students and their parents and their interactions with them. In general, these particular teachers tended to have positive and compassionate views of both students and their parents. Most of the teachers seemed aware of the difficulties poor parents were faced with and of the impact of these on their students. Yet their interactions with parents tended to be limited to traditional ones in which parents were expected to respond to the school's parameters for interaction. For example, contacts with parents generally were limited to traditional school events such as conferences, school programs, or other occasions when parents came to the school. Visits by teacher to parents' homes were initially mandated, but they never became fully institutionalized and declined in frequency over time.

TRANSFORMATIONS AT THE MIDDLE SCHOOL

As in Chapter 3, we report here data from four of the five years we studied this school. These are years one (1992–1993), three (1994–1995), four (1995–1996), and five (1996–1997). Year one marked the official opening of this school as an African American Immersion School. Year three was the year of upheaval when many teachers left the school. Year four marked a new beginning; it was the first year the school had a full staff of regular teachers who had chosen to be assigned there. Year five marked the final year of our study. Not surprisingly, the transformations at the middle school were hampered by internal and external factors during this time.

In year one, four major themes emerged from the teachers' response to the question, "How has the middle school changed over the year to become an African American Immersion School?" These themes focused on (1) surface changes, (2) changes in teachers' behaviors and attitudes, (3) changes in students' behaviors and attitudes, and (4) programmatic and curricular changes.

Similar to the teachers at the elementary school, several of the middle school teachers focused on changes in the name of the school and in the school's overall appearance as evidence of a transformation to an African-centered approach. One teacher said, "I can see a change in the appearance and in the aesthetic environment. Teachers are getting into decorating the rooms and halls with ethnic prints and drawings." Another staff member responded in year one by saying, "Well, we had a name change."

In the second theme, also similar to the elementary school, a number of the middle school teachers cited changes in their own attitudes and behavior. One teacher attributed these to changes in personnel, stating, "The type of teacher that has come and the administration, at least the principal, is different and . . . he is trying to get in the discipline for the kids, and they are also looking at the kids' problems more than in the past." Another teacher stated, "I would say we've become more goal oriented. We've become more focused as a faculty. Our students have become more focused as a result."

Other teachers described change on a more personal and individual level. For example, one responded with the following:

> I took part in a class in the first semester that was provided because it was an immersion school. I became aware of African viewpoints, legacy, of one's heritage, and of the think-

ing style that I think has helped me to become more effective as a professional in the
building here and has allowed me to be more effective with the students.

The third theme mentioned by several teachers in year one focused on perceived
changes in the students' attitudes and behaviors. For example, one person said:

> I see a difference in our students. . . . They have begun to take more pride in themselves
> and in their school. More kids are involved in activities, and they are excited about the
> different things that are going on, and they like to compete for going to the dances. . . .
> They don't want to miss those kinds of activities and trips that we take them on.

Another stated, "I think the first thing I see is much improved behavior. . . . The students really seem to be getting a sense of pride in the school, of their special place in
an African American Immersion School."

The fourth area of change described by the middle school teachers emphasized
programmatic aspects of the school. Here teachers focused on the introduction of
African and African American history and culture into the school and the curriculum. One teacher discussed this change in the following manner:

> I think we have seen more things being brought into the school culturally; events, mu-
> sic, and that type of thing. . . . There has been a lot of environmental improvement to
> the building in the direction of the school's emphasis and focus, and I think a lot of
> teachers have made a definite effort to teach their individual curriculums with as much
> as they could bring in.

Another teacher focused on the changes that had been made in the curriculum.

> First of all, we try to revamp the curriculum so that it is more reflective of positive con-
> tributions that African Americans have made in this country, to this society, and also
> to the world . . . and making our students aware of their heritage by going back to the
> great African kingdoms and teaching them about Egypt.

This early emphasis on curriculum change was related to the decision to devote a
large amount of teacher time to curriculum writing during the year and summer before the school was officially opened as an African American Immersion School.

Overwhelmingly, a majority of the teachers at the middle school felt positive
about the changes that they perceived during the first year it implemented the
African American Immersion orientation. However, a very small number of
teachers sounded a negative note. For example, a teacher responded to the question
by saying, "There was a lot of disorganization this year . . . the changeover of the administration. . . . I think it has been a very poor year as far as organization goes."
Although the number of teachers expressing this point of view was small in year
one, it is important to note that this undercurrent was persistent and grew during
the initial five years the school attempted to initiate an African-centered educational model.

The third year that this school operated as an African American Immersion middle school was one of upheaval as many teachers were told that this would be their last year in the school because they had failed to meet the required 18 credits in African and African American history and culture. Because this information became known early in the school year, the atmosphere of the school was marked by tension. This was evident in the teachers' responses to the question of how the school had changed over the year in two ways. First, although some of the same themes identified in the first year were identified again, there was considerably less consensus among teachers around them. Second, more teachers felt that the school had changed for the worse.

One theme that carried over from year one concerned changes in students' attitudes and behaviors. For example, a teacher said, "I, believe it or not, have seen some subtle changes in students' behavior and how they respond to each other. They're gradually becoming more culturally aware. I see a sense of pride in African American children that I don't think existed prior to their becoming a part of this program."

A second theme that carried over from previous years focused on changes in teachers' attitudes as they became more comfortable with the concept of an African-centered orientation. One teacher expressed this theme in the following manner: "I feel like I'm able to have a more integrated curriculum." Another stated that the staff "are becoming a little bit more familiar with the subject matter."

A third theme that carried over focused on more superficial changes. For example, one teacher said there had been more African American speakers at programs. Another stated that more of the students were wearing uniforms.

A fourth theme that persisted from the first year was that the school had changed in a negative manner. However, in year three there was a marked increase in the number of staff who espoused this view. Some teachers expressed frustration over what they saw as a breakdown in staff cooperation on curriculum development. For example, one teacher who had been involved in this said:

> I think it slipped terribly back. I'm very disappointed about that because I thought after the first two years of work we were really on our way to building a curriculum. I mean I worked this summer and I produced some things, but that was more personal . . . and very little was done as a staff. And even things that had already been produced as far as a curriculum . . . have not been added to. In fact, I don't see . . . that the new teachers . . . or even some of the teachers who have been here a bit are using it more.

While several other teachers echoed this idea, another felt they lacked even more basic understandings of an African-centered orientation.

> I think a lot of the people are trying, but I don't think that a lot of them understand the concept of immersion. . . . I don't think that they know . . . or they had not been provided with enough kind of information. . . . They don't really see how a lot of these things tie together in terms of our culture and how we should use it to live our lives.

Still another teacher felt the lack of progress in establishing an African-centered orientation was because "we have so many subs in our building until it's real difficult for them to function within the expectations we have for our program."

In summary, in the third year this middle school operated as an African American Immersion School, teachers felt that little forward progress was made in implementing this model. Some even felt that the advances made toward establishing an African-centered educational model were becoming eroded. These perspectives were expressed amid an increased level of tension at the school. Many of the teachers who knew they would be leaving for failing to meet the educational requirements resented this and expressed ill feelings toward the administrators who were enforcing the policy as well as toward other teachers who were remaining at the school. As a result, staff morale as well as staff cohesion was low throughout the year. The staff upheavals had an impact on the students during that year also. We observed an increase in disruptive behavior among students.

The fourth year at the African American Immersion middle school was one of promise and disappointment. Although the year began with a mostly new and enthusiastic staff, this was also the year that the district administration threatened the school with closure. In addition, the charter school issue divided the staff, and the entire school program was attacked.

It was against this backdrop that we conducted our annual year-end interviews with African American Immersion middle school teachers. Their responses to our question, "How has the school changed over the year to become an African American Immersion School?" reflected this tumultuous year in two themes. One theme focused on the promise of the full staff with a renewed mission. The other focused on the external challenges to the school.

With respect to the first theme, several of the respondents focused on the staff changes in answering the question. Some noted that the majority of the staff were African Americans. One teacher said, "This is the first time I've seen this many African American teachers in one particular building, for one. I think that makes a great impact." Another noted, "We have moved to approximately 60 to 65 percent African American teachers. Teachers who can definitely identify with a number of the backgrounds which these children come from." Some other teachers felt the new staff was more committed to the concept of African-centered schooling. For example, a teacher said, "The biggest change this year has been staffing, trying to get a staff that believes in both the focus and vision of this school."

A related theme that highlighted the renewed sense of optimism at the school focused on redefining the school's original goals. For example, one teacher said, "What is Afrocentricity to you is different to me, and I think [it] needs to be defined more." Another teacher, new to the school that year, said the staff were "getting to know each other and actually defining . . . what the goals are." Still another teacher who had been at the school previously said the school had changed because "I think there is more unity among the teachers."

This sense of optimism was also evident in some teachers' perceptions of positive changes in students' attitudes and behavior. One said, "Our children are starting to take pride in their school and their program and themselves." Another teacher said, "This year, I see the students being more focused on their history and . . . on the culture." Still another teacher said, "I think that the students and parents were a lot more committed to the program this year than what I perceived they were last year."

The other predominant theme teachers mentioned in answering this question focused on the negative impact of the challenges to the school. One teacher summed this perspective up in the following manner.

> I think there have been just many, many horrible negative changes this year about the African American Immersion middle school. And I think we started out the year very strongly, positively. . . . [The] foundation was there with the teachers who stayed. The new blood was coming, stirring things up in a positive way . . . and then the board came along and said we were a closed school. And from then on . . . the students took it very personal that the school would be closed and that was evident in their grades, it was evident in their behavior, it was evident in attendance. I feel the teachers' morale was often low. . . . We simply felt most of the time that we didn't know what was happening and we couldn't even effectively address parent or student questions. . . . And all of these sorts of things affect your day-to-day operation and how you teach and how you facilitate learning in the building.

Another teacher echoed this view with the following observation: "For the last four years things were getting on the right track for [the] Afro American program. But this year, things got totally off track because of the school closing and the Charter petition for this building."

Much of the frustration and disappointment engendered in year four carried over into the fifth year. In this year, we only interviewed teachers who had remained at the school throughout the five-year period and eighth-grade teachers. Several teachers responded to the question about school change by pointing to the erosion of the immersion concept. One teacher described the year as "The worst year as far as African American Immersion." This teacher went on to say that teachers and administrators were not knowledgeable enough to implement a change. Furthermore, this teacher argued the school lacked support, noting, "And you just have something that was a very good idea that people tampered with, threw it out there and decided that okay, it's there, now make it work without the support that we needed." Another teacher voiced similar concerns in responding to the question: "That's kind of difficult for me to answer because I know how we wanted it to change and I don't think we ever evolved. I don't think we really made it to where we had intended to go."

Perhaps in relation to this sense of frustration, some teachers described negative changes in student behavior. These teachers focused on a lack of discipline as underlying this behavior. This may reflect students' reactions to the turmoil the school had experienced during the past year.

Teacher–Student Interactions

As with the elementary school, middle school teachers were asked if they had observed changes in interpersonal interaction patterns at their annual year-end interviews. One question asked if they had seen any changes in the interactions between students and teachers. In the first year of the African American Immersion middle school, the majority of our respondents reported that these interactions had become more positive. Many of the teachers said that there was better rapport between teachers and students. For example, one teacher said, "I have noticed a lot more comfortable atmosphere." Another said, "I believe there is more of a relaxed air with the students. There seems to be less strain." It should be noted that this year was under the tenure of the first principal at the African American Immersion middle school. This principal was working to get students out of the halls and into the classrooms, and the teacher–student interaction patterns may have reflected this emphasis.

Some teachers attributed the improved interactions to their own increased sensitivity resulting from staff development activities aimed at increasing their cultural awareness. For example, one teacher said, "I think through the in-services all the teachers are becoming more understanding of the learning styles of the black student. It just seems to be a more positive attitude around here." Another teacher said, "I see more interaction and I see much more because we've had so many workshops and been told so much that we've got to treat this child with respect, so much more of that is coming out."

By year three, there was a decided change in the teachers' perceptions of teacher–student relationships. While some teachers still saw them as positive, others reported these interactions were more mixed. For example, one teacher described these interactions in the following manner: "I think there's more informal conversation between students and teachers this year, more so than in the past. In some cases, that's good; in some cases, it goes a little too far, and it takes away from the seriousness of what the atmosphere should be." Furthermore, some described teacher–student interactions as more negative in the third year. One teacher said interactions between students and teachers had become "more confrontational." Another said, "It's become increasingly difficult for them to get along and for them to get along with the teachers. I'm not sure why."

It must be remembered that this was a year of upheaval at the middle school. Tensions were high among teachers because of the impending removal of those who had failed to complete the instructional requirement of 18 college-level credits in African and African American history and culture. In addition, there were other signs of deterioration at the school. For example, one teacher reported that there was a decrease in the numbers of students on the honor roll.

> But on our last Honor Roll list there were only 80 students, whereas last year we always averaged about 90 to 91 students. And how come that's happening when we have more students in the building this year? We created these accelerated classes. Why are we getting ten less students on our Honor Roll list?

Furthermore, our observations of the school noted an increase in concerns about disciplining students.

In year four there was still another shift in teachers' perceptions of their interactions with students. There was an increase in the numbers of teachers reporting positive relationships with students. In part, this was attributed to the revitalization of the school with new staff members and a new beginning. For example, one teacher alluded to this with the following response:

> Well, I think at the beginning of our school year, we had an in-service, and the in-service stressed ownership or kinsmanship to students. And so we started calling ourselves "Baba" as male and "Mama" as female. And we kind of developed a little relationship that way, and I think that relationship has strengthened, somewhat, the ties between the teachers and the students.

Another teacher said, "I think the students recognize that these teachers are here for them." Still another teacher pointed to the changes in staff as beneficial for teacher–student interactions with the following statement:

> I think it's been positive interaction between teachers and students. I really do because what I see is that having a new staff, practically a new staff, I think 20 to 22 new teachers coming in. In September we were fired up and ready to go. These teachers were interested in being here. The majority of them asked to come here.

Despite this optimistic perspective, some other teachers felt that teacher–student interactions had become more negative during the year, in part because of the external challenges to the school. When asked to characterize teacher–student interactions during the year, one teacher said:

> I've seen it fluctuate. I think [at] the beginning of the year, a lot of teachers . . . came together as a group. . . . But as agendas and different things came up, we were faced with closing; we were faced with the decision on Charter. No one really knew. I think that had a lot to do with children being disturbed as well as staff.

Another teacher tied the deterioration of teacher–student interactions to the challenges to the school with the following: "Since the closing bomb, I don't know if I can simply put into words the devastating effect that had on this school. I mean morale, attitude, everything."

Finally, a few teachers described teacher–student interaction patterns as generally negative. For example, one said, "I think a lot of our students at this point need to be taught respect."

In 1996-1997, the fifth year the African American Immersion middle school operated, the teachers' descriptions of their interactions with students seemed to continue the trends identified the previous year. Again, there was considerable variation in teachers' perceptions. While some saw their interactions with students as primarily positive, others described these patterns as mixed or negative.

Student–Student Interactions

When asked how they perceived interactions among the students, the teachers' responses at the African American Immersion middle school mirrored the patterns evident in their descriptions of teacher–student interaction. In other words, there were changes in their descriptions of student–student communication that were reflective of the varying situations the school experienced during the five-year period of our study. In year one, for instance, most of the teachers we interviewed perceived that student–student communication had become more positive during the year. For example, one teacher said, "They are starting to respect one another, and the reason why I'm saying this is because rather than fight or strike someone, they are more willing to talk it out." Another staff member noted the students supported each other.

> I've seen a lot of kids who care about each other. You know, if someone is having a problem when they come to you, they don't come by themselves; they come in groups. . . . There is just this one person who has this problem and she . . . or he might say nothing, but the others with them will say [student's name] has something she wants to tell you.

On the other hand, some other teachers tended to see no changes in the ways students interacted with each other. When asked if there had been a change, one teacher responded, "I think that is a little premature."

Of the teachers interviewed in year three, more described the student-to-student communication as negative. For example, one teacher, who had described the students as caring in year one, characterized student-to-student interaction in year three in the following manner: "I am concerned about the level of profanity in our building, the lack of respect for self and others." Another teacher said, "They're treating each other with less respect than I've seen in the four years I've been here." It may be that these perceptions of negative student communication patterns reflected the upheavals and tensions the school was experiencing that year. Indeed, our observations at the school revealed a marked increase in disruptive behavior among students during that year.

It must be noted, however, some teachers did not report such negative student interaction patterns. For example, one teacher responded to this question by stating, "I have a really good group of kids this year, so I'm pretty pleased with their maturation levels." Another teacher commented about this interaction by saying, "I've seen the negative as well as the positive."

Not surprisingly, in year four, when the teachers were highly optimistic about renewing their efforts to implement an African-centered educational model, there was another shift in their perceptions of student communication patterns. In this year most of the teachers we interviewed described these interactions as having become more positive during the year. Several attributed these changes to events that had occurred at the school. One teacher attributed changes in student communication patterns to the renewed efforts to implement an African-centered model: "There's been a lot less fights this year. . . . I think that as we're able to give more of an African-centered way of doing things, that's going to affect the relationships of the children."

Some teachers described negative changes in student-to-student interaction patterns in year four. Others saw more positive changes in student behavior and attributed these to changes in the school. For example, one teacher said:

> I've certainly seen positive student-to-student interaction here. I have not seen the verbal assaults or the physical assaults that we've had in the past few years. But then I think that that's all attributed, number one, to having a full staff. As long as I've been

here, this is my fifth year, this is the very first year that we've had a full staff. And I think that's real positive. And I think children need to understand that this is your teacher and this is the person that's going to be here every day. A lot of substitute teachers and vacancies in the building does not make for a positive situation in any situation, in any building. And our children certainly need that ongoing positive interaction and need the stability of having the same teacher being here every day and being prepared for them.

In the fifth year, the teachers' descriptions of student-to-student interactions essentially carried over from those identified in the fourth year. Although we only interviewed a few teachers at the school, in year five, we found that most teachers tended to describe either positive changes or no changes in student-to-student interactions over the year.

Teacher–Parent Interactions

At the African American Immersion middle school, the teachers' perceptions of their interaction patterns with parents were relatively similar in the first and third years. There was a history of parents not feeling welcome at the school. However, during the first year, parents were more visible. If for no other reason, they were required to sit in classes when their child became disruptive. The teachers tended to describe their interactions with parents primarily in terms of the degree to which the parents responded to them. For example, in year one, many of the teachers we interviewed felt their interactions with parents had become more positive because the parents were responding to the teachers more often. One teacher said, "The parents . . . were behind the teacher. I have not had one parent that did not back me up." Several teachers felt teacher-to-parent interactions had improved because more parents were coming to the school. For example, one teacher said, "I have seen more parents. I can be safe in saying the number of parents that have come into the building this year . . . has . . . increase[d], but we need to see more. That would make a big difference." There was some criticism of parents who were seen as nonresponsive to teachers. However, overall, the perception was that there was a parent presence in the school, although interactions were traditional.

In year four, there was a change in teachers' perceptions of their communications with parents. This seemed to be related to an increased level of activism among a group of parents at the school. A number of parents actively opposed the threatened closing of the school as a "failing school." In addition, a group of parents supported changing the school's status to that of a charter school. This group of parents was instrumental in reorganizing the parent–teacher organization into a "Village Council," and they became a visible presence in the school.

Some of the teachers viewed this increased parent activism positively. For example, one teacher said, "I think the parent has become more visible on the school premises and, as a result, there's greater communication." Another teacher described the parent communication in the following manner.

I'm impressed based on past schools. As far as predominantly African American parents coming out. And, the fact that it's an open policy, which I know is standard, but I mean, they really take advantage of it here. And they come in and you never know when somebody's gonna come in, and I like that personally, because it tells me that the parents are concerned.

On the other hand, the increased activism on the part of parents also created tension for some of the teachers. In some cases, teachers described parent communication patterns in terms of issues over power and control. For instance, one teacher said:

I have seen a lot of parents become more involved, and I wish even more would become involved. And then I have seen parents that, due to influences outside of the parent group, have become quite, um, abrasive, let's say. . . . And I think a lot of it has to do with the way they were talked to and what they talked about, about things with the charter and power, and they perceived they had because some people told them they had power. And when they discovered they didn't necessarily have that kind of power, they were a little taken aback and had a little . . . straightening out.

Another teacher saw parents as misinformed, characterizing communication in this year in the following manner.

I can say that there have been a few parents that are not understanding school policy, not understanding the [union] contract, not understanding, you know, the workings of a school, period. [They] have made it very difficult for some teachers in the building. And I think it's just because they're not aware of school policies and procedures. And I think it has been fueled by administration. The participation is up, but it's not necessarily all positive.

In these examples, teachers reflected broader tensions that had been engendered in the school as a result of differences in support for moving to charter status. These differences sometimes pitted teachers against administrators and other teachers as well as some parents.

In the fifth year that this school operated as an African American Immersion School, these themes continued to be expressed as teachers described their interactions with parents. A small group of parents continued to take an activist posture within the school primarily through the Village Council. Teachers' perceptions of parent communication patterns with them again reflected the degree to which they agreed with these parents' viewpoints.

Student–Parent Interactions

When teachers were asked to describe how students' interactions with their parents changed over the course of the school year, three themes were evident. These three themes remained stable across the five years that we observed these schools.

One theme was that the student–parent interaction patterns were primarily positive. One teacher said in year one, "When we had teachers conferences, they would interact with the parents respectfully." Another teacher, interviewed in year three, said, "I find they're very respectful. . . . They'll just about do anything to please their parents." This theme continued to be expressed in the fifth year as one teacher said, "Most of the students respect their parents because most of these parents have high expectations for the children."

A quite different theme was expressed by some teachers who characterized student-to-parent communication patterns as problematic. Several teachers noted that their observations of student-to-parent interaction were structured by the school situation where the parent is called in because the student has behaved in some manner at odds with school policies or norms. For example, a teacher interviewed in year one said:

> A lot of times if the parents come in, it's to bring the kid back from a suspension or something or the child is in trouble for some reason and the parents are not very happy. And you just see them browbeating their children, putting them down and saying, "You know better than that." . . . And every now and then you'll see one slap a child.

The third theme, which was expressed by most of the teachers we interviewed, was that they had not had opportunities to observe students interacting with their parents. Most often this was because their interactions with parents were limited to traditional school activities such as parent–teacher conferences and school programs. Within these narrow structural constraints, teachers tended to be more interested in the parents' reactions to the teachers' agendas than anything else.

School–Community Links

At the middle school, school–community links occurred in several ways. First, several groups and individuals from the African American community worked with students in extracurricular activities continuously throughout the initial five years the school operated as an African American Immersion School. One, an African American women's group, ran a Saturday morning program for girls. Another man organized an after-school Rites of Passage program for boys. Finally, an individual who worked for a major business group in the city worked closely with parents.

An additional community link at the middle school came through a program through which individuals were "artists in residence" at the school. Many of them were local African American artists who worked with students on a regular basis throughout the school year. Often they worked along with regular teachers at the school. This program has also continued.

CONCLUSIONS

The data from these two schools indicate both differences and similarities in the transformation processes at these two schools. Differences were most evident in the teachers' perceptions of changes at the schools during the five-year period of the study. At the elementary school, the process of transformation appeared to flow rather smoothly and consistently throughout the school. Although different groups of teachers were interviewed from year to year, there was a consistency in the themes of school change that were described. Furthermore, there was an apparent progression in teachers' perceptions of change. Initially, they were concerned with superficial features such as changes in the appearance of the building and attire. However, as time went on, they focused more on internal changes such as alterations in their attitudes and behaviors as well as those of the children.

At the middle school, although some of the same themes were cited by teachers, there was no similar progression and flow. This was most likely because of the instability that existed at the middle school compared to the stability of the elementary school during the initial five years.

With respect to interaction patterns, a most striking similarity at both schools had to do with interactions involving parents. Teachers tended to persistently confine their interactions with parents to traditional school functions. Furthermore, parents were consistently viewed in terms of the degree to which they met the teachers' agendas. There was little attempt by the teachers to assess parents' perceptions.

The data derived from these teacher interviews can be considered in the broader frameworks of school reform in general and African-centered school reform in particular. Pechman and King (1993) described six factors that were critical if long-term reform was to be successful. These were (1) a school environment that was stable with respect to structure, norms, and atmosphere, (2) backing from the district admistration, (3) the constructive participation of teachers in leadership roles, (4) a faculty who coalesced in support of change and who (5) maintained commitment to the change process over time, and (6) a principal who took an active, facilitating role. Boykin (1999) argued that if African-centered school reform is to be successful, African-centered principles must infuse the entire school process. Our data indicate that the critical factors identified by Pechman and King (1993) were more evident at the elementary than at the middle school. We suggest that because these elements occurred at the elementary school, there was greater infusion of African-centered ideas across the school. These ideas included a collectivist sense of family among the staff, high levels of cooperation, and an increasing ease in using African and African American stores of knowledge as foundations for teaching. By contrast, the middle school lacked many of these elements, and the utilization of African-centered ideas and principles became the purview of individual teachers rather than a school-wide effort.

— 5 —

Surface to Deep Transformations

In this chapter we move to a description and analysis of the transformations that occurred on the classroom level in the two African American Immersion Schools. The analysis of classroom transformations in these two schools is derived from two related theoretical orientations. One has to do with distinctions between surface and deep cultural transformations (Boykin, 1994, 1999). The other is related to differences between expert and novice teachers (Sternberg & Horvath, 1995; Westerman, 1991).

Boykin (1994) discussed the distinctions between surface and deep cultural transformations in African-centered schools and classrooms. He described surface cultural infusion as the presentation of important information about African and African American history and culture. This information is conveyed through images, stories, and facts. Deep cultural infusion, on the other hand, involves consideration of the processes and rationales for schooling. It often includes consideration of values underlying teaching and changing the overall ethos or culture of the school or classroom. A number of other writers and researchers have supported this distinction. They have argued that the establishment of an African-centered classroom involves both changes in the information presented and changes in the ways the classroom is organized, in the pedagogical practices used and in teachers' perspectives on students (Allen & Butler, 1996; Bell, 1994; Boykin, 1999; Delpit, 1995; Lee, 1992).

The growing literature on expert and novice teachers also provided a contribution to our analysis of classroom transformations at these two African American Immersion Schools. Several studies have suggested that expert teachers differ from novices in important ways and that these differences may have important implications for student learning (Gormly, McDermott, Rothenberg, & Hammer, 1995;

Sternberg & Horvath, 1995; Westerman, 1991). These researchers have indicated that expert teachers not only have more content knowledge, they also are more efficient in integrating their knowledge and adapting it to meet students' needs. In addition, expert teachers are more efficient and effective problem solvers in planning, executing and evaluating their teaching (Sternberg & Horvath, 1995; Westerman, 1991). In general, expert teachers might be expected to engage problems on a deep rather than a surface level.

The data analyzed in this chapter are derived from three questions asked of teachers in their annual year-end interviews. These questions are as follows: (1) "What kinds of things have you done to infuse your curriculum with the African American Immersion School theme?" (2) "Have there been changes in your effectiveness as a teacher in terms of your work in the African American Immersion School?" (3) "Can you give us some examples of your classroom successes this year?" Each of these questions was aimed at uncovering the levels of transformation that took place in the classrooms at the African American Immersion Schools. The teachers' responses to these questions are supplemented with our school and classroom observations. Each school will be discussed separately. These discussions will be followed with our conclusions regarding the types of transformations that occurred and the contexts that gave rise to them.

THE ELEMENTARY SCHOOL

At the elementary school, there was a clear developmental pattern in the changes that occurred at the classroom level over the initial five years that it operated as an African American Immersion School. Much of this pattern reflected the movement from novice to expert teaching described in the literature (Sternberg & Horvath, 1995; Westerman, 1991). In this case, many of the teachers at the elementary school became increasingly expert in infusing material with African and African American content into their curriculum. In addition, many of these teachers changed their perspectives; some became more reflective about their teaching, whereas others changed their beliefs about the students. The transformations that occurred in these classroom settings had implications for teachers' behaviors, for their perspectives on outcomes for their students, and for the socialization of new teachers to the school. The developmental patterns these transformations took is most evident in a chronological description of classroom activities at the African American Immersion elementary school. As with previous chapters, we will describe teacher responses to our questions in the first, third, and fifth years of the African American Immersion elementary school.

During the first year that the elementary school implemented an African-centered educational model, we observed that a majority of the teachers were very actively engaged in creating change in their classrooms. Some of this change involved changing the physical environment. Maps of Africa and pictures of famous Africans and African Americans were hung on walls. The traditional letters of the alphabet that commonly adorn school walls were replaced with the "Afrobet," pictures associating letters of the alphabet with famous African Americans. In addition, many of the classrooms used African cloths and illustrations of historical and contemporary African and African American life to decorate their rooms.

While many of these artifacts were initially provided by the teachers, as the year progressed, some encouraged their students to contribute these also. Thus children's drawings and constructions were added to the walls and surface tops in the classrooms. For example, one teacher said:

> I've acquired . . . African American prints or I should say art prints of African American artists, contemporary artwork. I had the children look at them. We've talked about it and tried to work the ideas that the artists used in their work into something we could do at our level. I've explored historical references, ancient artwork . . . and again, we have tried to recreate our own version of ancient projects.

These changes in the physical environment of the classrooms were pervasive in the school. By the end of the first year, almost all of the classrooms contained some significant physical manifestations of the cultural orientation of the school.

In addition to changes in the physical environment, the teachers at the African American Immersion elementary school also were actively engaged in changing the curriculum. Almost all of the focus on curriculum change involved infusing the content of the traditional curriculum with African and African American images. For example, one teacher noted, "In social studies, I did a unit on wants and needs, which is part of our social studies curriculum for [my] grade. But instead of doing it from the traditional standpoint, I did it using an African movie on the former pygmy people of Africa, on the Baka."

In some cases, African American content was infused, although a Eurocentric value system was retained. For example, one teacher emphasized the importance of material wealth by giving students information about a wealthy African American entertainer: "I read things to them that they may not know. They did not know that MC Hammer was building a million-dollar home, over a million-dollar home."

Other teachers emphasized the contributions made by African Americans to the general society. For example, one teacher infused the classroom curriculum in the following manner: "I teach black history every day. I bring in different objects that we have talked about, that . . . inventors have done. We have been able to even have a math lesson about the light bulb." Another teacher used "African and African American people and some of their inventions . . . to build my vocabulary lesson." Still another teacher said, "We did kings and queens. We did African American inventors."

In some cases, information about Africans and African Americans was infused into ongoing teaching strategies. For example, one teacher noted, "Because we have had the book, we just continued to teach our reading strategies. We now have African materials to use to do that." In other cases, however, teachers reported some restructuring of their teaching strategies as a result of considering the infusion of

African and African American materials into their curriculums. For example, one teacher changed the atmosphere in the classroom:

> Well, I noticed that this year . . . during work time, I feel like I have a more relaxed atmosphere. It doesn't always have to be rigid where they can't talk, sit straight in their seats, but I do have an area, a reading corner where I bought a piece of carpet and a bean bag chair and there are some stuffed animals. The kids love to go over, even during work time, like they're doing spelling or whatever. They like to go over and lay on the carpet and do it.

Another teacher was able to establish continuity between home and school learning through the use of proverbs.

> One of my parents came up to me during a parent conference, and she said that her son had mentioned a proverb to her . . . "Do not say the first thing that comes to your mind." It was from Kenya. Because her husband had said something and he started spouting off all these proverbs and explaining to his father what they meant. She said her son not only has knowledge of what these things are, but he has wisdom because he can use them in the right time and the right places. She came and thanked me for giving him wisdom.

For some of the teachers, the required course work served as an impetus to change some of their teaching strategies. For example, one teacher noted the following: "I am taking a course now in learning styles, and now I am starting to change my instruction based on that. Students I couldn't reach before, now I understand why. And I am setting up different approaches, and I tried quite a few of the ideas. It's true. They work." Another teacher took advantage of the course work related to this experiment in establishing an African-centered educational model to try out some new teaching strategies.

> I have done a lot of new things that I had never done before. With my background reading as well as some of the classes that I am taking. One of my successes is the sense of working with groups and allowing them to kind of create a sense of group within the classroom, be at a table; four or five students.

Finally, during this first year at the African American Immersion elementary school, a few teachers reported changes in their views of themselves and their students as a result of their need to change their classroom orientations. For one teacher this change took the form of some self-reflection. When asked if there had been changes in teaching effectiveness, this teacher responded in the following manner:

> Probably in some ways there has been. I think looking at myself, my classroom a little bit differently than I have. Some of this has to do with some of the course work that I have been taking too. . . . [B]eing forced to go back to school, I think maybe I am making an effort to be more nurturing than I was before.

Another teacher noted that the classes in African and African American history required of teachers at these schools had affected the ways she worked with students.

> I think that because of the classes that I am taking outside of school. . . . [O]ne was just learning about African Americans and why they are the way they are. That made me more aware so I can deal with the children in a better way. I am also taking this course about different learning styles, which means then we can change our angle as far as we teach kids.

Another teacher felt that the first year of work at the African American Immersion School had had an impact on her work. "I'm becoming more sensitive to the differences, in terms of working with African American children and their families and learning ways that I can more effectively work with them."

Finally, one teacher reported a change in the way she viewed the students in her class. This teacher indicated that she was able to break down some stereotypes she held about African American students' behavior. This teacher described how she changed her interpretation of disruptive behavior among her students.

> Maybe it doesn't have anything to do with the immersion part of the program, but I looked at our kids and I said, "These are all okay kids. These are all normal kids." And then I said . . . [that] this . . . didn't have anything to do with . . . being rooted in Africa. It just had to do with bizarre behavior. I wasn't afraid to identify it.

In summary, then, during the first year at the African American Immersion elementary school, teachers were actively engaged in changing their classrooms. Much of this change occurred on the surface level of transformation. Content about Africans and African Americans was substituted for content about Europeans and European Americans. Furthermore, much of the infusion of content into the curriculum focused on kings and queens of Africa and the contributions of famous African Americans to society.

However, there were some signs of transformations at a deeper level, also. Some of the teachers were beginning to reflect on and change some of their classroom teaching strategies or their perceptions of students. It is important to note that the course work required of teachers to remain in the school was an important impetus to these deeper-level classroom changes.

During the third year that the elementary school implemented the African-centered model, many of the trends regarding the transformations that occurred on the classroom level continued from the first year. Some teachers continued to substitute African American content for European and European American content in their curriculums. For example, one teacher said, "When I was in Africa, I brought back a lot of dashikis, and so the group of the week gets to wear the dashikis, take them home. . . . In my room, I have a lot of African American things up; whenever in reading I can tie them in, we always tie it in."

On the other hand, several of the teachers described themselves in ways that suggested increasing levels of expertise and accompanying ease in infusing their curriculums with information about African and African American history and culture. For example, one teacher described efforts to infuse the curriculum in the following manner:

> I have tried to incorporate into my social studies curriculum the geography of Africa and the particular emphasis is on . . . Kenya and the Masai people, so we have studied that. We also put in an element of the Bacca people of Cameroon. When I do science, I try to relate it to rain forests or savannahs or things that are in Africa, not necessarily just that are here. The more I work at this, the more the infusion becomes sort of a natural part of the day. You don't have to think about doing it; it's just when you do something you automatically think about its connection with Africa and/or with Black America. So it's not quite as chopped up as it was the first year we started at this.

Several other teachers indicated that they found it easier to infuse their curriculums with African and African American history and culture. For example, one teacher said, "Oh, I think I 'm more comfortable with it, just because I know some of the materials that are available." Another described movement from novice to expert in implementing this particular African-centered model by saying, "I think that I have tried to infuse a little more because . . . you know, every year you get new resources, new ideas."

By the third year this school operated as an African American Immersion School, some teachers were becoming more reflective about their own teaching. This has also been acknowledged as one aspect of the progress from novices to experts. For example, when asked to comment about perceived effectiveness with respect to work at the African American Immersion School, one teacher stated the following:

> I'm not sure that I am any more or less reflective. I am more aware of my own deficiencies when I see other people that are very good at, something that I am not so good at, and that shows up very much. . . . So I guess maybe I don't feel I am doing things any worse than I did, but I am more aware of things I could be doing better.

Another teacher was similarly self-reflective when asked about effectiveness during the third year this school operated as an African American Immersion School. "I think things are, a roller coaster is almost too fast of a medium to call it, but there are hills and valleys; it's more like a walk in the park, but the park has a lot to it." This teacher also reflected upon the importance of this particular African-centered educational model beyond the classroom.

> My expectations are high, and these are only small human beings, not even fully developed, but at the same time, I feel a certain critical need to see some fruition because of the factors that are coming into the program . . . and the community . . . with violence and drugs, and we don't have the time we need to incorporate these lessons and use them immediately. . . . We don't have five years to have them nurture the seed and see it grow. And that is my personal opinion, but so be it.

A theme that began to emerge more frequently in the third year at the African American Immersion elementary school was that some teachers began to describe efforts to restructure their classrooms and change their teaching strategies. For example, one teacher incorporated aspects of African American culture into the ongoing organizational structure of the classroom: "We do things with [historically black college] names such as Tennessee State. [The] five tables in my room have a predominantly Black college or university name, and little things like that I think would give them incentive."

Another teacher described her classroom in the following manner: "Mainly, our room is divided into reading centers, so we try and make sure the kids see themselves portrayed in the different [areas]." In this case, African and African American images permeated the classroom. This teacher went on to point out that these images were in posters, books, decorations, music, or "just the general layout of the room."

In summary, by the third year the elementary school operated as an African American Immersion School, teachers were beginning to demonstrate expertise in integrating African and African American history and culture into their curriculums. This increased work with a new orientation to knowledge led some of the teachers to be more reflective about their pedagogy. Furthermore, some of them were altering their classrooms in ways to incorporate African and African American content as permanent aspects of organizational patterns.

During year five, many of the themes identified in earlier years were continued. An increasing number of teachers indicated they were becoming more expert at infusing their curriculums with knowledge based on African and African American history and culture. One teacher said, "I think the longer you're in the immersion program, it just becomes second nature to you. . . . You just become more familiar with this so . . . you infuse more and more as the program goes on." Another teacher described how the reading program in his classroom had become more infused: "I've tried to join the things that are required in reading; for instance, we have a Basal series here. [I've] tried to not just supplement, but [I'm] trying to bring in African American–centered themes and African American–centered literature as an integral part of the reading program." In other words. this teacher had moved from an "add-on" approach to one that incorporated African-centered concepts into the basic structure of the curriculum.

Two new themes also emerged in the fifth year at the African American Immersion elementary school. One concerned the socialization of teachers who were new to the school. Although teacher stability was generally high at the elementary school, some mobility was inevitable during the five-year period under study. Given that, an important issue concerned how new teachers were socialized into the ongoing school vision. This issue was particularly important because of the high level of cooperation and consensus that had already been built among the teachers in this school. However, the consensus about the vision as well as the sense of cooperation among the staff seemed to have supported the socialization of new teachers in this setting. For example, one teacher found formal support through the classes and a mentor.

Well, this is all new to me. I mean, all new knowledge and I got books. I actually started reading more on the culture. I have a class right now, "Working Effectively with Black Families," and it's very interesting. So I really try. I've read . . . two or three books on the culture to understand that. And I have a mentor teacher who is a black woman and she's really good and she's helped me. She's taken me to the Baptist Church. You know, she's got me involved, so I understand.

Another teacher who was new to the school received formal support from other teachers: "I co-teach a lot with another teacher, which is really nice. We've done a lot of hands-on things—cooking with the children, we've made quilts, we've learned songs. Just a wide variety of things with them." This teacher also was supported informally by the general orientation of cooperation that had been built up in the school during its initial five years as an African American Immersion School.

I came here last year. It was new to me and it was just an adjustment. This year I believe I worked much harder to define what it is I'm supposed to accomplish, and I consciously put the efforts to do that. And I sought out help, much more help from others. And I've gotten a lot of help and a lot of good suggestions. And I think that's made a big difference.

Clearly, formal and informal supports to socialize new teachers were in place at this school.

The second theme that emerged in year five at the elementary school had to do with teachers' interest in the outcomes of this model for students. A number of the teachers described more positive student outcomes as a result of the implementation of this particular model. Furthermore, the teachers conceptualized these outcomes as occurring in personal, academic, and social skills areas. For example, one teacher stressed her students' personal growth when she said:

When they came in September, basically, they felt like they couldn't, they couldn't do some of the things that second graders are supposed to do. So it was like a little struggle, but very rarely now do I find a child say they can't. They do try, and I think that from what I've seen, I think that they believe in themselves and their self-esteem is growing a lot over this past year.

Some of the other teachers talked about student outcomes in terms of academic improvement. For example, one teacher noted that at the beginning of the year "[t]hey came and they couldn't hold a pencil. And they're reading. I mean, they're reading and I don't have three or four of them reading. I have fifteen of them reading." Another teacher noted, "In reading, some of our students were doing so well that we moved them above grade level." For many of the teachers in this building, academic improvement, especially in reading, was significant. One of the teachers tied reading success in an African-centered schooling context to long-term success.

I have about eight former students come back to see me. And they walk in and go, "Hi." And they were the lousiest, awful boys that I had the first year I was here. And they're coming back to report that they're in alternative schools, but they're still there and they're making it and they're doing it. And they learned to read on their tummies right here in the little elementary building on a different Afrocentric literature.

Finally, some of the teachers talked about student outcomes in terms of improvements in social skills. For example, one teacher said of the students in her classroom, "They're just learning how to get along, learning not to hit, learning to share." Another teacher said a major success for the year was "[r]eaching kids who were considered unreachable. I guess . . . just people who I saw their attitudes at the beginning of the year and see how they changed towards the end of the year." One teacher talked about a strategy he had used to help students improve their social skills.

> I've done so much as far as rap sessions where we discuss what the problem is. I've even videotaped them doing a rap session because, a lot of times, it's one way of doing that. But what I did was watch a rap session and I taped it. And they got to see themselves like I see them. And I think that woke them up too. I mean, it was amazing; it was like, "Wow, I do that?" I'm like, "Yeah, boy, you do that." . . . So I think the class from where I got them in September to now, and they motivate each other, you know.

In summary, during the initial five years that the elementary school implemented this particular African American Immersion model, teachers' perceptions of classroom formations followed a developmental path. Initially, the teachers were primarily concerned with infusing their curriculums with historical and contemporary information about African and African American people. During the five-year period that we studied the school, the teachers gradually moved from novices to experts in implementing this infusion process. One way this expertise was demonstrated was that they became increasingly comfortable with the information and were better able to gain access to it. Another illustration of this expertise was evident among those teachers who were able to integrate this information into the curriculum rather than use it simply as an add-on to already existing materials and lessons.

As a corollary to this increasing expertise, many of the teachers began to alter their classroom pedagogical and organizational strategies to incorporate African-centered themes into their ongoing instructional activities. This not only helped integrate an African-centered orientation in these classrooms, but it made it a more permanent fixture there.

As further illustration of the developmental tendency of staff in this school during the initial year period, we observed that teachers gradually moved from a focus on their activities in the classroom to an increased interest in the impact of these activities on students. By the fifth year, many of the teachers talked about classroom transformations in terms of the outcomes they observed in students. This shift from a teacher focus to a student focus has been seen as another aspect of increasing expertise among teachers.

As has been mentioned in previous chapters, the African American Immersion elementary school was characterized by a high level of consensus and cooperation among the staff. This cohesiveness was encouraged by the building principal who stressed team building as strongly as cultural change. This atmosphere of staff cooperation tended to serve as an important basis of support for teachers who were new to the school during the five-year period of our study.

THE MIDDLE SCHOOL

During the initial five years that the middle school was designated an African American Immersion School, we did not observe a developmental pattern in the implementation of African-centered activities on the classroom level. Instead, the efforts to transform the school from a traditional to an African-centered focus seemed to occur in fits and starts among individuals and various groups of teachers. Overall, the attempts at transformation on the classroom level occurred in relatively short cycles. From a school-wide perspective, these efforts tended to be fragmented and disjointed. Despite this overall tendency, however, there were a number of promising beginnings of activities aimed at creating an African-centered educational environment for middle school students. In addition, there were some instances where African-centered curricular activities were designed, implemented, and carried through to fruition.

Because the events that occurred at the middle school did not follow a clear developmental path over time, our analysis of this aspect of the middle school does not follow a chronological order. Instead, we begin our discussion of classroom-level transformations at the middle school with an analysis of the many efforts at transformation that began but were not fully implemented during our five-year study. Then we will describe some attempts at curricular and environmental transformation that were more successful, and we will speculate about the factors underlying these successes.

CURRICULUM AND CLASSROOM ENVIRONMENT

At the African American Immersion middle school there were numerous beginnings as staff members tried to transform the curriculum and classroom environment from a traditional to an African-centered perspective. In some cases, these beginnings were related to the various cycles of initial years, upheaval, and new beginning the school experienced during its initial five years as an African American Immersion School. In other cases, however, individuals and small groups of teachers began new initiatives related to African-centered schooling that were not connected to these broad school-level changes.

School-Wide Themes

The attempts to transform the curriculum in the classrooms at the African American Immersion middle school were initially supported by the development of school-wide themes. These themes, identified earlier in Chapter 3, were initially aimed at supporting a cohesive transformative perspective. Developed under the auspices of the first principal at the African American Immersion middle school, these themes were initially embraced enthusiastically, albeit superficially, by some of the teachers. For example, one teacher described how she attempted to change her curriculum in the following manner in the first year of this experiment:

> Well, the way we were set up this year, we had different themes. So I used those themes and tried to relate them to the kids' lives. They talk about themselves and we talk about African Americans. And I had to do a lot of studying about African American scientists myself so that I could find where they would fit in.

Another teacher said:

> I tried to keep up with the themes that we had for every report card period. . . . At the beginning of the year and through most of the year until I had the student teacher, I would put up for a week . . . one African American person, and I would put up sort of a flimsy drawing of something that person did and then we would discuss it.

Another teacher described the infusion process in the classroom primarily in terms of incorporating the themes in the first year:

> I am trying to think of the last thing we focused on. I can't come up with anything specific right now, but if there was something, if it was working with entrepreneurship, the last theme, we worked a lot with going out, taking the students into the community, and seeing different businesses and seeing different positions there, and . . . that helped [the students] see African Americans in the community and get to know more about the jobs that are available.

Although the school-wide themes continued to be identified as an important component of this school, they were used less and less frequently over time.

Individual and Small-Group Efforts to Develop an African-Centered Curriculum

In addition to the school-wide themes, we observed throughout the initial five years at the African American Immersion middle school that teachers initiated a variety of activities aimed at transforming their classrooms from a traditional to an African-centered focus. Some of these efforts were small-group activities, supported by the school administration and intended for implementation across classrooms. Others were activities initiated by individual classrooms for their sole use. It is important to note that many of these efforts did not come to fruition over time. Instead, they were initiated and disappeared; then new efforts began in subsequent years.

One small-group activity that was initiated even before the school was officially opened as an African American Immersion middle school involved the establishment of curriculum writing teams. These groups were to work cooperatively to develop African-centered materials in the various subject areas mandated in this district's middle school curriculum. These teams created the school-wide themes and were to help teachers translate them into classroom activities. One teacher illustrated this in the following response to a question about classroom activities during the first year of the middle school's existence.

> Well, I was on a curriculum committee this summer and helped design the lesson plans for History to work with our different themes. . . . [I]n the beginning of the year, I used a lot of the lesson plans that we had designed as far as the shields, and the name and exploring things like that. Myself and [another teacher] were instrumental in getting the African American textbook that we use as supplementary to our—I don't want to say "regular" history—to our other history book.

This curriculum committee had begun to develop activities that could be used across classrooms to implement the school-wide themes described in earlier chapters. One activitiy that was designed to accompany the theme "Who Am I?" asked each student to design a shield that was reflective of his or her conception of self and the contexts within which the self was embedded. These shields were displayed in each classroom during the school year.

Another curriculum team worked on infusing African and African American content into the middle school science curriculum content. For example, one teacher noted the following:

> I worked on the science curriculum because it is my background, and we followed the curriculum as it was; and if they were talking about blood types, then we'd bring in Dr. Drew; and if they were talking about space exploration, then we bring in . . . you know, different African Americans who excelled in those areas.

Some of the curriculum writing efforts were focused on specific events. For example, during the first year, a series of events were scheduled around the birthdate of the school's namesake. One of the teachers discussed how this was integrated into the curriculum: "I was in charge of writing all the curriculum for Malcolm X week, so I wrote 12 different lessons for reading and English and social studies . . . and they're using those for the whole school for everybody." It should be noted that although this work was intended to have an impact in classrooms across disciplines in the school, there was little evidence of a cooperative effort among teachers.

The emphasis on curriculum writing by the staff at the African American Immersion middle school continued into the third year that it implemented an African American Immersion model. However, these efforts were no longer as widespread as they had been in previous years. Some of the teachers continued to work cooperatively and refine their efforts, however. One teacher discussed a cross-disciplinary effort that had been under way since the school had been designated an African American Immersion School.

> We teach Social Studies and English together. Since we do a lot of planning together, daily planning and planning beforehand, some things we've been doing all along

and some things we've improved upon, fine-tuned, and some things we've added. For instance, in History we use the African American experience textbook along with the regular, ah, recommended textbook, and this summer we went through it and wrote up exactly where they infused together . . . and we went through the AV [audiovisual] materials we have in the building and where they fit in. . . . In English, on a daily basis we do a DOL [Daily Oral Language]. We start the class with that. We've gone through over the last several years and written one for every day of the school year. . . . And we've made all the subject matter African American so every day they not only get a language activity, [but] they learn something about their history and culture.

In addition to developing curricular materials that infused African American history and culture into their specific class curriculum, these particular teachers also attempted to integrate the school-wide themes into their work.

And we've taken our whole list of free write topics and . . . we've gone through and put them in so they fit with our school African American themes. So like right now we're in "Rites of Passage," and the last part of the year we're moving into "Entrepreneurship" . . . responsibility, and so they're all about those kinds of things. . . . So we've developed all of those, and we use those on a daily basis.

These teachers had infused the content of the curriculum extensively, bringing African American content into spelling and reading and even developing "a whole African American poetry unit." This work was to have been copied and made accessible to other teachers in the building. Unfortunately, however, this did not happen. This teacher and the colleague left the school at the end of the third year because they had not completed the 18 college credits in African and African American history and culture required to remain on the staff at the African American Immersion Schools within the allotted three-year limit. When they left, their work on curriculum development was not carried on. In fact, the materials they developed were soon lost; thus other teachers were not able to build upon this beginning effort.

Another promising beginning in the area of curriculum development concerned the establishment of a Science Fair at this middle school. The Science Fair was implemented first in 1992–1993, the first year the school was officially operated as an African American Immersion middle school. The Science Fair was organized and implemented largely by one teacher. During the weeks and days before the Science Fair was to take place, it appeared as though it would not be implemented successfully. Yet at almost the last minute, things fell into place, and students were able to set up and display their exhibits in the school cafeteria. The teacher who coordinated this effort felt this was one of the highlights of the academic year.

I think pulling off this Science Fair thing yesterday was probably the biggest [success] this year. I didn't think it was gonna go, up to the last second. The kids presented the projects in class to each other; they didn't make displays; they didn't bring things; they stood up there and giggled and didn't know what to say. I thought, "This isn't going to

be good," but they set it up downstairs yesterday, and many of them had gotten themselves together and finished their projects because I talked to them and told them how
disappointed I was, and it came together.

Despite the last-minute rush to pull this program together, it was a successful event
in the school. Unfortunately, however, the Science Fair did not become institutionalized. The teacher who coordinated it initially left the school at the end of the first
year. The Science Fair was implemented again during the second year that the middle
school operated as an African American Immersion School; however, it did not have
the scope or enthusiasm exhibited the previous year. After that, the Science Fair was
not presented again during the five years we conducted our study of the school.

During the first three years at the African American Immersion middle school,
many of the individual teachers were actively involved in efforts to infuse information
about African American and African history and culture into their curriculums.
Many of these efforts seemed to involve simply adding African and African American
information on to the existing curriculum. One example of this add-on activity was
discussed by a teacher in year one. When asked how he had infused his curriculum,
he responded in the following manner:

> I'll go back to the pre-Revolutionary War, and in there, I have all my students research
> what the time period was like. We watched a couple of movies; then we discussed why
> we didn't see in our history books African Americans . . . "What do you think they
> were doing at that time?" and "How many of them do you think there were?" And then
> we went into a time period where I just taught maybe 10 more years of regular text-
> book, and then . . . around the 1820s or so, we talked about, "What do you think life
> would have been like for an African American in the South? in the North? in the
> West?" And they had to, after getting into three . . . groups, just talk about it—what
> part of the country you'd want to live in, what would have been the best area to live in,
> what the problems were, the economics, the cultural, the social problems, the dis-
> crimination. We went through all of that. And we just kept going; about every 20 years,
> we'd stop and add it.

As is evident from this teacher's description, the material about African American
history and culture, although included, was not integrated into the ongoing curriculum. Rather, African Americans were discussed tangentially. In addition, African
Americans were still treated as objects of study rather than as central to the students'
learning experiences.

During year one, another teacher attempted to use information about Africa to correct prevailing stereotypes. However, this information was still treated as an add-on
to the traditional curriculum.

> Some of the things that I have done was to take [it] a step further using other materials
> to talk about African Americans but yet not take away from talking about the subject
> matter at hand. So this gives them a broader insight. For example, for so many years,

Egypt has been taught in isolation from Africa. We began talking about Egypt and telling them some things that Egypt was rich in and tied in Africa with Egypt. They began to have a different view of Egypt, different from what was taught to them in the past, so this was an awakening.

In year three, a teacher indicated, "I always focus on the contributions of African Americans." This emphasis on African American contributions was echoed by a number of teachers. For example, in the interviews we conducted with teachers in year four, one teacher stated:

> We made African American science books where we took a lot of things from the past and I instructed them and showed them how the things have helped America in so many different ways. . . . [In] math I told them about Benjamin Banneker, who was a black mathematician . . . and also in social studies, how Matthew Henson went to the North Pole . . . and other people that had a lot to do with education and other historical events.

This theme continued into the fifth year, when, for example, a teacher noted, "I just finished a unit on Jackie Robinson because of his 50th year anniversary. . . . I did something with Tiger Woods." This teacher went on to say, "I kind of listen to what's going on and bring in current events as much as I can."

Some of the teachers attempted to move beyond the level of presenting these middle school students with information about the contributions of African Americans or facts about African and African American history. For example, in year four, one teacher, who had been at the school for several years, used the contributions approach as only one way to infuse her curriculum with African-centered themes.

> I work with a particular reading group, and all of our focus has been on looking at the contributions of African Americans, be it through reading, be it through poems, plays, skits, whatever I'm involved with, with the students, and I was involved with the [name of a television show] know your history quiz. But a little more than that. I've also been involved in trying to create an aesthetically enhancing or supportive atmosphere here at this school. I've been involved in getting role models to come into the school. I've been involved in setting up programs that spoke to our history and our culture. I've been involved in planning field trips that spoke to our history and culture.

Although there were consistent efforts by individual teachers to infuse African and African American history and culture into their classroom curriculums throughout the initial five years at the African American Immersion middle school, these tended to be isolated and sporadic. Our classroom observations at the school revealed a wide range with respect to the degree that teachers established African-centered themes in their classrooms. While some tried to do so, others continued to use the traditional materials available to them. Perhaps as a result, many of these efforts remained on the surface level of presenting factual knowledge about African Americans to students.

It is important to ask why this pattern of repeated beginnings became so prevalent at the African American Immersion middle school. Our analyses suggest several possible explanations. Some of the underlying factors have been discussed in previous chapters. These include the high rates of teacher mobility during the period under study as well as the lack of leadership from the school administration. As a result, when teachers left the school, many of their efforts, such as cooperative curriculum writing, were not preserved. Several other factors seemed to contribute to the difficulties many of these teachers had in developing sustained African-centered curriculums.

One factor had to do with the teachers' own lack of a firm knowledge base to build a curriculum on. As we have indicated in earlier chapters, many of the teachers at this school did not obtain the required 18 college-level credits in African and African American history and culture during the time they were assigned to the African American Immersion middle school. Furthermore, most had not had this kind of background knowledge in their own academic studies. Related to this, the year before it was designated an African American Immersion middle school, there was a professional relationship with a local university. As a part of this relationship, a faculty person from the university was assigned to work with the teachers. When the school took on its African-centered mission, this university faculty member provided course work related to this mission and was available to work with individual teachers in the area of curriculum development. Unfortunately, however, this person left the university, and no one took on this function at the middle school. Thus, teachers lost one source of support.

Another factor limiting these teachers' efforts to develop an in-depth, long-term African-centered curriculum concerned the lack of coordination among the staff at the African American Immersion middle school. Teachers at this middle school did not spend much planning time together. This was not because such time was not available to them. Indeed, teachers were required to be at the school one half hour before the students arrived each morning. This time was designated as staff planning time. However, there often was no consistent coordination of these teacher meetings. As a result, many of the teachers were left to use this time as they saw fit. While some groups used this time for group planning, others conducted a variety of other activities. In addition, there was a lack of coordination between outcomes from these meetings and their impact on the overall development of the African American Immersion School program.

A third factor that appeared to limit the level of transformations in many of the classrooms at this middle school had to do with the role taken by staff who were assigned to support teachers' development. Similar to most of the middle schools in this district, the African American Immersion middle school was assigned an implementor and a learning coordinator. One of the primary roles of these staff persons was to help teachers develop and implement an African-centered curriculum. During the initial five years at the African American Immersion middle school, a succession of individuals filled these staff positions. Two different individuals served as implementors during this time. The first was assigned to this position during the year before the school was officially opened as an African American Immersion School and also served during the initial year this model was implemented. This individual had little input into curriculum development. The second person began serving as implementor on a part-time basis during the second year the school was an African American Immersion School and held this position through the fourth year. However, this individual was often given other administrative tasks as well as teaching tasks and, therefore, had relatively little time to work on curriculum development with the teachers. During the fifth year, no one was assigned to the implementor position at the school.

Three different individuals served as learning coordinators during the first five years that this school attempted to implement an African-centered model. The first, who had been at the school prior to its becoming an African American Immersion School and who remained there through the beginning of the fourth year of this experiment, was not committed to the cultural orientation inherent in this type of educational model and thus provided little input into curriculum development in this regard. The second was assigned this task after the fourth school year had begun and expressed some frustration about this, noting in an interview, "Not starting off in the beginning of the year . . . I couldn't do some of the things I would like to have done." This individual also expressed frustration about the role in the following manner:

> You can see my pet peeves are more that we don't have a way of supporting whatever curriculum we come up with in a way that's likely to make it work. In terms of a learning coordinator, some of the traditional things of learning coordinator have not been passed on to me. In other words, [the] learning coordinator in the past . . . had a lot to do with coordinating the curriculum, purchasing the materials, choosing in-services, staff development, and so forth. And I really haven't had much of a play in, been asked to play those goals, so my thing has been just directing and supporting whatever goals we develop because we can't coordinate it overall.

This individual left the school at the end of the year, and in the fifth year, a third learning coordinator was designated. This individual never seemed to be able to provide teachers with support during the one year that this position was held. Overall, teachers received little support in curriculum development and implementation from either inside or outside the school.

FOCUS ON THE STUDENTS

A second major theme that became evident at this middle school concerned the teachers' focus on the students. This focus had two aspects. Some of the teachers perceived the students as causing or having problems. Furthermore, these problems were often seen as interfering with both the teachers' instructional activities and the children's learning capacities. This theme was pervasive throughout the initial five years that this school operated as an African American Immersion School.

In part, the perception that the students who attended the African American Immersion middle school were troubled was related to not-uncommon views of poor African Americans. For example, at the end of the first year, one teacher described his students using frequently held stereotypes of this population.

> Well, of course, it is very demanding and working . . . with ex ed kids, and of course that is very demanding. And working with the implementation of a new program, that is an additional demand. And the kids, I think, are becoming a lot more hyper and a lot of the basic values, in a lot of cases, kids don't come with. They come with a lot of things that are detrimental to their development emotionally and otherwise, which impedes their progress.

This teacher began describing problems attributed to the students' label of exceptional but quickly moved to attributions about the students' values. In that same year, another teacher complained that she could not be effective because "I have had more students that were disruptive this year." Still another stated, "I know the majority of these kids are very lazy, but I know they can do work."

In some cases, teachers expressed concern about the educational levels of the students at the school. For example, in the fourth year that this school operated as an African American Immersion School, a teacher noted the following:

> It appears to me that we're getting just many, many, many more children that are coming into this building that are not readers and who can't do simple tasks that we're asking them to do. And, you know, I know there has to be a place in this city where we send children with problems, with all kinds of problems, and I don't have a problem with this building being such a place where you can send these children for help. However, we're not given the tools we need to do this.

This teacher went on to describe the situation in her class: "I have a class that's about twenty-six, twenty-seven kids and I adore them. And I work very hard for them. But I have not made, I've made little or no gains with these children because they all have such needs that they're not able to assist each other."

On the other hand, some of the teachers were more concerned with attempting to establish positive relationships with the students. In fact, some of these teachers judged their success in terms of the degree to which they were able to establish such relationships with students. For example, in the first year, one teacher described changes in his effectiveness in this manner: "I am relatively young at the profession, so the changes that have been made are mainly through the respect that I have gained from the students, the understanding of how to work with the students."

Another teacher, interviewed in the fourth year of the implementation of the African American Immersion orientation, discussed how in-service workshops had supported an improvement in relationships with students: "You know, they have come in here and done in-services, and basically, what we have to do and . . . understand is that all students learn differently, and we have to try and find out how to bring out the best in these children." Later in this conversation, the teacher mentioned that some of the students were troubled: "But it does help to understand that these students do come from, some of them do come from disadvantaged backgrounds, and anything could be going on at home."

In part, the focus on students could have been related to the fact that these are early adolescents, and at this age students do tend to demand increased attention from those around them. However, in many cases, it seemed that this focus tended to overshadow efforts to establish an African-centered orientation in many of the classrooms at this middle school.

SUCCESS STORIES

Despite the numerous curriculum efforts that were begun but not carried to fruition, and despite the tendency of some of the teachers to allow their focus on the students to overshadow efforts to establish an African-centered orientation in their classrooms, there were some limited instances of successful transformations at the African American Immersion middle school.

One particularly successful initiative involved a group of teachers who worked co-operatively across their disciplines. For two successive years, this group of about six teachers developed a series of learning experiences for their students that culminated in a school-wide activity. In the first two years, the event was Market Day. For several weeks, one group of sixth graders worked cooperatively using social studies, language arts, math, art, and home economics to prepare a simulation of a traditional African marketplace. The students used social studies and language arts to obtain information and write about African market traditions. Math was used when the students learned to convert African currencies into American ones. Art was the foundation for the preparation of the goods for sale in the marketplace as well as advertising for the Market Day. These activities culminated in a Market Day event when students set up a market and sold goods they had made. In the first year, the Market Day event was rather small; it was held inside the school. However, the students repeated this activity the next year, when they were seventh graders. This time, the Market Day culminating event was expanded to the school playground, and members of the community were invited to participate.

The following year, when these students were eighth graders, they and their teachers completed another interdisciplinary project entitled "The Harlem Renaissance." Students studied about the period of the Harlem Renaissance and created a series of artifacts and skits that simulated that period.

The efforts of this particular group of students and their teachers reflected a sustained African-centered curriculum design. Furthermore, these events incorporated an interdisciplinary orientation, cooperative learning activities, and opportunities for students to be actively engaged in meaningful academic tasks. This group of students worked closely with the same small group of teachers over time. Finally, the students were able to display the fruits of their labor, thus receiving positive reinforcement from others for their work. In other words, the Market Day and the Harlem Renaissance activities not only provided evidence of an African-centered educational activity; they also met many of the criteria for best practices at the middle school level.

Because the Market Days and Harlem Renaissance activities stood out as some of the few activities that were completed successfully during the period we observed this school, it is important to analyze the factors underlying these accomplishments. We suggest that three components were particularly supportive of these curricular transformations.

One component had to do with the nature of the students who participated in these activities. Initially, when in sixth grade, these were students who were placed in a group labeled "academically talented." As such, they were perceived as having higher status than other students in the school.

A second component had to do with the nature of the teachers. These teachers had developed a cooperative relationship that continued during the three-year period. Furthermore, most of these teachers moved with their students through sixth, seventh, and eighth grades. As a result, they were able to develop and maintain close working relationships with their students as well as with each other.

A third component underlying the success of the Market Days and Harlem Renaissance activities was that this group had external support. Specifically, the teachers participated in a project funded through a local university. As such, they worked with a faculty member from the university to develop curriculum and pedagogical strategies cooperatively.

These three factors provided an important backdrop of support that was not available to other teachers at the African American Immersion middle school. This support may have allowed this group of teachers to transcend some of the problems that pervaded this school and hampered the development of African-centered curricular activities among so many others. Some of the teachers who participated in these activities also appeared to develop a deeper sense of an African-centered orientation in their own classrooms. For example, one teacher described her classroom activities in the following manner.

> I don't even feel like I start with [the school district's] curriculum. I feel like I start with an Afrocentric curriculum. And I infuse [the school district's] curriculum. I guess from me, a lot of it comes down to helping the students create their own identity. . . . I guess my goal was to make what I did more thoughtful and more related to them, so they would start to develop a philosophy.

Another teacher talked about the potential influence of the Market Day on children.

> With the Market Day coming, I think that's going to be my biggest success. . . . And the reason why I say that is . . . I still believe . . . we have to make our students producers. You know, right now they're just basically consumers. And [we have to] show them that they can produce things, and we'll get them much further, I think, in control of their lives.

Both of these teachers illustrate movement beyond simply adding African and African American history and culture to the existing curriculum. Instead, they referred to a paradigm shift in their perceptions of what the curriculum should offer African American students. Unfortunately, activities like Market Days and the Harlem Renaissance did not continue at the middle school because this group of teachers left the school. However, it should be noted that they moved as a group to another school.

In summary, at the middle school, we did not observe a consistent developmental pattern in the ways in which teachers attempted to transform their classrooms from a traditional Eurocentric- to an African-centered orientation. Rather, we observed many beginning attempts at transformation either that were short-circuited when teachers left the school or that seemed to lose momentum and peter out. Because these attempts at classroom transformation could not be followed through, we saw little evidence of movement from surface to deep levels in instructional practice. To a large extent, we attribute this lack of movement to larger organizational problems that existed within the school as well as to the external challenges the school faced. These problems and challenges were detailed in previous chapters.

It should be noted that although the aforementioned description was characteristic of most of the classrooms at the African American Immersion middle school, there were isolated examples of transformations that did occur and that appeared to move from surface toward deep levels of classroom functioning. Furthermore, we observed the development of expertise among some of the teachers at the middle school. It appeared that these "success stories" were able to be implemented because the teachers were able to transcend the ongoing issues confronting the school and staff.

CONCLUSIONS

The data from the teacher interviews and our classroom observations suggest that the possibility of deep cultural transformation was present but difficult to attain in these particular experiments in African-centered education in a public school setting. However, we did see movement toward deeper levels of classroom change as teachers developed greater expertise in integrating knowledge about African and African American history and culture into their curriculums. As teachers became knowledgeable about and comfortable with information about Africa and African Americans, they also demonstrated increased reflection about their teaching as well as more insightful perspectives about their students. Certain school-level features were important for these transformations to occur, however. These included support from the school administrators, efforts to maintain stability among the staff, and encouragement of cooperation among the teachers. These elements were present at the elementary school. Unfortunately, the absence of these features at the middle school, along with the demands made on the school by the district administration and School Board, constrained efforts to inculcate an African-centered ethos in classrooms.

—— 6 ——

Lessons Learned

The African American Immersion Schools were originally established in response to this urban school district's failure to educate African American children effectively. In 1990, faced with abundant evidence that African American children, particularly those in poverty, were faring poorly, the School Board accepted a number of recommendations from the Task Force on African American Males aimed at reversing this trend. By far, the most controversial of these recommendations was to establish the two African-centered schools that have been the subject of this book. Recognizing the unique nature of this attempt to establish African-centered school models in public school settings, our research study aimed to document their implementation and assess the outcomes for children over the initial five-year period that the schools operated. In this chapter, we discuss these student outcomes and the lessons learned from this study about key issues underlying African-centered schooling in the public setting.

STUDENT OUTCOMES

Given that the primary purpose underlying the establishment of these schools was to have a positive impact on African American students' school achievement and behavior, we will begin with a discussion of outcomes for students during the five-year period of the research. In this publication, school-level performance, rather than individual student outcomes, is the focus of analysis. We will begin with a discussion of these outcomes for the elementary school and follow with our findings for the middle school. The data for these discussions were derived from an annual report published by the school district. This report provides school-by-school profiles of student performance on measures of academic achievement adopted by the district. In addition, this report summarizes several indices of student behavior.

The Elementary School

Three areas of academic performance were assessed at the elementary level in this school district. These included reading, writing, and math. Reading achievement is assessed by means of a statewide test that is administered to third graders. At the school level, achievement is determined by the number of students scoring at or above the statewide average in any given year. Overall, during the period 1991–1992 through 1995–1996, the initial five-years that the elementary school implemented its African-centered model, there was a marked increase in the number of students achieving criterion on the third-grade reading test. Specifically, during the first year the program was implemented, 73 percent of the children scored at or above the state average. In the second year, the number of students meeting the criterion dipped to 30 percent. However, in year three, 87 percent of the third graders scored at or above the state average, and by the fifth year of our study, 92 percent of the third-grade students met this criterion. By the fifth year, third-grade students were among the highest scorers in the city on this measure of reading.

With respect to math, the school district assessed achievement by means of the Iowa Test of Basic Skills during the period of our study. This test was administered to fifth-grade students. Here a more mixed pattern was evident over the five- year period. The criterion used by the school district was the number of students scoring at or above the 50th percentile nationally. Overall, there was a net increase in the number of students meeting this criterion, from 20 percent in the year the school began implementing an African-centered model to 39 percent in the fifth year this model was executed. During the years between these two end points, however, student performance was inconsistent, ranging from a high of 47 percent of fifth graders scoring at or above the 50th percentile in year two to a low of 15 percent meeting this criterion in year four.

Student performance in writing was assessed by tests developed within the district. A writing test was administered to fourth-grade students in each of the initial five years the school implemented its African-centered educational model. Beginning in the second year, a locally developed writing test was also given to fifth graders. Student performance on the fourth-grade writing test was variable, with an annual pattern similar to that shown in the math assessment. Although there was an overall net increase from 67 percent of fourth-grade students scoring above the district average in the first year the school was an African American Immersion School to 91 percent meeting this criterion in the fifth year, there was considerable variation during the intervening years. In year two, 78 percent of the students met the district criterion; in the following year, only 47 percent did, and in year four, the number of fourth graders scoring at or above the district average again climbed to 77 percent. The four years of data on the fifth-grade writing test showed a more consistent trend.

In the second year that the elementary school operated as an African-centered model, 63 percent of the fifth graders scored at or above the district average. The percentage of students meeting this criterion steadily increased in each subsequent year to 98 percent in year five.

Overall, these data suggest a general improvement in academic performance during the initial five years that the elementary school implemented its African-centered educational model.

We also gathered data on several indices of student behavior at the elementary African American Immersion School. These data also were taken from the annual report compiled by the school district. The data available for elementary schools included attendance, mobility, and suspensions. During the initial five years that this school was designated an African American Immersion School, attendance remained fairly constant at 90 to 91 percent. During that same period, student mobility increased from 23 to 38 percent in the first four years. In the fifth year, mobility decreased to 29 percent. Finally, suspensions were a rare occurrence at this school; during the entire five-year period, only one suspension was reported, and this occurred in year two. Serious behavioral issues were handled in the elementary school with a series of interventions that were quite effective.

The Middle School

At the African American Immersion middle school, student achievement was determined by both standardized tests and grade-point average. Unfortunately, we were not able to track student performance on standardized tests over time at the school because the district made numerous changes in the types of assessments it administered to students during the initial five years that this school was designated an African American Immersion School. These changes were associated with a district policy decision to change from nationally based to locally based assessment. As a result, no standardized tests were administered to middle school students consistently during this time period. Therefore, we will use school-level grade-point averages as our source of data for academic outcomes at the African American Immersion middle school.

During the initial five-year period, this middle school's grade-point average profile hovered around the 2.0 mark. In year one, the grade-point average for the school was 1.89. During the subsequent four years the grade-point average for the entire school population was 1.95, 1.87, 2.23, and 2.13, respectively. Over time, there was a slight increase in school-level grade-point average, although this was not a consistent pattern. Beginning in year two, the district began to report school-level grade-point averages for those students with 90 percent attendance. At the African American Immersion middle school, these students obtained slightly higher grade-point averages than the general population. However, the same type of variation was evident. Grade-point averages for students with 90 percent attendance during this period were 2.51, 2.34, 2.55, and 2.56 for each of the four years from year two to year five.

We conclude from these data that academic performance, as measured by grade-point average, improved only slightly overall during the initial five years that this school attempted to implement an African-centered educational model.

In addition to academic performance, we analyzed data on several indices of student behavior at the middle school. These included data about mobility, attendance, suspensions, and truancy among students. These data were also taken from the district's annual report.

The data indicated that student mobility was quite high at the African American Immersion middle school. During the first four years that the school operated as an African American Immersion School, student mobility was at or above 50 percent. In the fifth year, it dropped to 34 percent. Beginning in the third year that this school was designated an African American Immersion middle school, the district began to report average mobility for all of its schools. This provides an interesting anchor for interpreting the mobility rates at this middle school. In each of the years for which these data were available, the African American Immersion School's student mobility rate was considerably higher than the district average. In year three the district's mobility rate was 25 percent, whereas the African American Immersion middle school's was 50 percent; in the following two years the district's average mobility rate was 24 percent and 23 percent, whereas the African American Immersion middle school's was 50 percent and 34 percent, respectively. The much higher-than-average rate of student turnover at the African American Immersion middle school has important implications for student outcomes. Clearly, if students do not remain at the school, they are unlikely to benefit from whatever programs it offers. On the other hand, however, this raises the question, Why do so many students leave the school annually? We are not able to address that question within the scope of this volume. It should be pointed out, however, that student mobility is frequently cited as an issue in schools serving poor urban children.

A second behavioral measure related to student academic performance is school attendance. Using data reported annually by the school district, we analyzed student attendance patterns at the African American Immersion middle school during its initial five years. Student attendance was highly variable during that period. In 1992–1993, the first year of this experiment, overall student attendance was 83 percent. In year two, attendance declined to 78 percent. During the next three years, the attendance rate gradually increased to 79 percent in year three, 81 percent in year four, and 83 percent in year five. Thus, overall, there was no net change in attendance at this school during the period under study. It should be noted, however, that the African American Immersion middle school's attendance rate was close to the attendance average for middle schools in the district, which was 85 to 86 percent in year five.

The third area of student behavior that we assessed at the middle school level concerned student suspensions and habitual truancy rates. The data, compiled and reported annually by the school district, showed that during the initial five-year period the suspension rate at the African American Immersion middle school declined steadily from 80 percent in the first year to 32 percent in year five. During the third, fourth, and fifth years, the suspension rate at this middle school was below the average suspension rate for middle schools in the district. Specifically, the comparative figures were as follows: In year three the average suspension rate for middle schools in the district was 41 percent, whereas at the African American Immersion middle school, it was 39 percent; in year four the district average was 43 percent, and the African American Immersion School's remained at 39 percent; and in year five the district average was 43 percent again, and the African American Immersion middle school's was 32 percent.

With respect to truancy, a more uneven picture emerged at this middle school during the five-year period. Beginning with a 49 percent habitual truancy rate in 1992–1993, the first year this school was officially designated an African American Immersion School, there was an increase to 65 percent in year three. The habitual truancy rate then declined during the following two years to 45 percent in year five. No district-wide figures on habitual truancy were available for comparison.

In summary, student outcomes at the middle school were somewhat uneven during the initial five years that it was designated to implement an African-centered model. Overall, there was a slight improvement in academic achievement as measured by student grade-point averages. With respect to behavioral indices, the picture is mixed. There were improvements in mobility and suspension patterns; however, attendance and truancy rates changed little.

The data on student outcomes at these two schools must be interpreted with caution. First, direct comparisons of student academic performance at these two schools is not possible because of the different measures used. Second, some of the findings can be attributed to the age differences in the students. Decreases in academic performance and increases in problem behaviors have been associated with the transition to middle school (Anderman & Maehr, 1994). Although we cannot make attributions of cause and effect, we note that, at the elementary school, the dramatic improvement in student performance on the third-grade reading test coincided with teachers' completion of the 18-credit education requirement and the school-wide accomplishment of a clearly infused curricular focus in classrooms.

Despite these cautionary notes, we are still left with the fundamental presupposition underlying the establishment of African-centered educational models in this public school district: that an African-centered educational model would provide a more supportive learning environment for African American children than the more traditional Eurocentric schooling milieu. Implicit in this assumption was the idea this model would lead to more positive student outcomes. There is a considerable amount of theoretical support for this presupposition (Asante, 1991, 1991–1992, 1992; Bell, 1994; Eyo, 1991). However, evidence supporting it has been limited to experimental research (Allen & Boykin, 1992; Allen & Butler, 1996; Jagers & Mock, 1993) and applications in independent black schools (Hoover, 1992; Lee, 1992; Lomotey, 1992). The two African American Immersion Schools that are the focus of this volume were among the first to be implemented in a public school system and, to our knowledge, were the first to be studied systematically as they attempted to establish themselves.

KEY ISSUES UNDERLYING AFRICAN-CENTERED SCHOOLING IN THE PUBLIC SETTING

Given the unique situation of these schools, it became apparent to us early in our study that there was an even more fundamental issue that needed to be addressed. This was whether or not a viable African-centered educational model could be established and flourish within a large public school setting. Our observations and data suggest that there are certain variables that are key to the successful implementation of African-centered educational models in the public school arena. These variables include district support, school leadership, and the knowledge and orientation of the staff.

District Support

Our analysis of the events and activities in and surrounding these two African American Immersion Schools indicates that support from administrators and policy makers in the wider school district is an essential ingredient for success. In this particular school district, there were major changes in personnel both on the School Board and within the district administration during the initial five years that these schools were implemented. These changes were associated with differences in levels of support for both the idea of African-centered education in general and these particular schools. For example, the idea of African-centered schooling was strongly supported by some of the School Board members and district administrators who were in place in 1990 and 1991 when these schools were initially conceived and established. However, as personnel changes occurred, we observed less clearly discernible support on this level.

The elementary school opened as an African American Immersion School during the period of strongest support. When it opened, the elementary school received a onetime allocation of funds that were used to institutionalize important structural changes that supported program development. Later, this school was able to maintain its strength even as support for African-centered schooling waned at the district level. However, the middle school was clearly undermined by the decline in support for this concept. First, it did not receive additional funds at start-up. Second, in the fourth year, the school was placed on a list of "failing schools" and required to reconstitute its mission just at the time it was finally fully staffed and beginning to coalesce around an African-centered focus. This action by the school district and School Board had the effect of distracting the school from its primary focus and lowering staff morale.

District support for innovative school reforms may be a function of particular policies that may mitigate against the implementation of new models. For example, the successful implementation of an African-centered model in a school requires that personnel not only accept but are committed to the concept. Yet district and teachers' union policies regarding teacher assignment and placement thwarted this goal during the initial years the schools were implemented. It was only in the fourth and fifth years that these schools were implemented that teacher assignment policies were changed so that teachers who wanted to be in these schools could be placed there.

School Leadership

Given the uncertain support from the district level, the role of the school principal became particularly significant in influencing the successful implementation of an African-centered educational model. There were several ways in that leadership was important here. First and foremost, the principal of such a school must be able to articulate a clear vision of an African-centered educational model. Furthermore, the principal needs to share this vision with staff and accept their input. Then the administrators and staff can work collaboratively to develop and shape a curriculum and school environment over time. Without a clearly articulated and shared vision, however, the school and the staff flounder and become more vulnerable to pressures from those with alternative agendas.

Another important role for the school principal or leader in an African-centered setting is to assist teachers in curriculum development and in developing pedagogical strategies. This can be accomplished by working with staff in classrooms. Here the principal can serve as a model and mentor, observing and commenting on teacher activities as well as demonstrating alternative practices. This type of role also fosters cooperation among staff members. In addition to working with teachers, the principal needs to be flexible—willing to shift programs and policies to accommodate the needs of students as well as staff.

Finally, school principals often serve as the primary conduit by which new programmatic initiatives are introduced to the school. The principal also serves as a sieve, because in some cases, this individual has the option of deciding what programs or initiatives will be pursued. Given this role, it is important that the principal of an African-centered school is selective, supporting external additions that build on the priorities targeting the school's orientation rather than operating on the principle of "more is better."

Our observations and interviews at the two African American Immersion Schools found that there were important differences in the degree to which the principals at the two schools embodied these characteristics. At the elementary school, there was a stable school leader who, together with the staff, developed a vision of an African-centered model that was implemented collaboratively. The principal supported and encouraged staff development and was flexible in modifying school operations to meet staff needs. At the middle school, however, this type of leadership pattern was lacking.

Characteristics of the Staff

A third key element necessary for the successful implementation of an African-centered school model concerns the knowledge and attitudes of the staff, in particular the teachers and support staff. As those on the "front lines," the teachers are the primary models of African-centered concepts; these are the individuals students observe and can, if they choose, emulate. Furthermore, these are the individuals who will interpret African and African American history and culture for children.

First and foremost, teachers need to obtain accurate knowledge of African and African American history and culture. Teachers cannot teach what they do not know. Unfortunately, most contemporary in-service as well as preservice teachers do not know very much about African and African American culture. As a result, teachers who want to work in African-centered settings will have to engage in additional learning experiences in order to acquire the knowledge necessary to develop and implement an African-centered curriculum. As has been noted earlier in this volume, teachers at the African American Immersion Schools were required to complete 18 college-level credits in African and African American history as a condition of remaining at the schools. We observed the benefits of this requirement at the elementary school where teachers completed the requirement quickly. These teachers engaged in ongoing curriculum work with continuous refinements and updates. By contrast, at the middle school, many teachers did not complete the education requirements. This not only led to a high level of teacher mobility; we also observed incomplete and inconsistent curriculum development.

Second, teachers in an African-centered educational setting, as in all settings, need to hold positive attitudes about their students and about teaching. We observed that the teachers at both schools who bought into the African-centered orientation had to revisit their conceptions about the goals of teaching as well as the strategies they were utilizing in their classrooms. This reflection often led teachers to move along the continuum from novice toward expert in incorporating an African-centered ethos in the curriculum and the classroom.

We also observed that the more successful teachers in these schools were those who cooperated closely with their peers to develop and execute curriculums and programs. These cooperative efforts occurred both within and across subject matters and grades. The benefits of teacher cooperation were twofold. First, teachers provided support and assistance to one another as they developed curriculum and tried out new pedagogical strategies in their classrooms. Second, group cooperation provided an important model to students—one that, in fact, supported the communal aspects of an African-centered orientation.

CONCLUSIONS

The announcement that this large urban school district would establish two African American Immersion Schools was greeted with a great deal of attention and considerable controversy. In part, this was because this idea challenged the traditional orthodoxy of public schools in the United States. In addition, however, there was a recognition that this district was similar to many other urban school districts. Serving an increasingly diverse population, schools were finding that their traditional orientations and perspectives were failing to educate large numbers of students effectively. Thus, an African-centered model was considered a viable alternative conceptual framework.

Our research project was aimed at describing and understanding the implementation processes and outcomes during the initial five years that these two public schools attempted to incorporate an African-centered orientation into the curriculum and overall school milieu. We asked if a viable African-centered educational model could be executed within a public school setting. Based on the lessons learned from our extensive observations and conversations with the major stakeholders in this innovative enterprise, we answer with a qualified yes. Our response is qualified because our data indicate that the schools we studied were constrained by a lack of control over external and internal factors that are inevitable within a public school context.

We found that policies and procedures, along with political issues, may either support or complicate efforts to change the cultural milieu of individual buildings within the wider context of a large school district. More important, however, we found that attitudinal factors play a large part in determining the viability of implementing an African-centered educational model in the public school setting. Two attitudinal issues are particularly salient. First, policy makers and practitioners alike must see that there is value in educating African American students, generally, and poor African American children particularly, effectively. Second, educators as well as the broader community must understand the value of an African-centered orientation in curriculum, pedagogy, and policy. This means they recognize the inherent value of African and African American history and culture and the contributions Africans and African Americans have made to the world.

Shortly after the first African American Immersion School opened, we were besieged with callers who asked, "Is it working?" Some of those callers viewed an African-centered educational orientation as a panacea that would ameliorate the negative circumstances many African American students faced in contemporary public schools. Others saw this cultural orientation as a threat and predicted its downfall. Our longitudinal research suggests that neither of these stances was the case. We found that African-centered educational perspectives could be implemented both successfully and poorly. We discovered that although most of those who were active participants in these two school experiments had good intentions, these could not substitute for good teaching. We determined that the establishment of an African-centered model was a dynamic process that took time as well as effort and was subject to a myriad of factors. Despite all this, we still conclude that an African-centered educational perspective has considerable promise when implemented in a nurturing and supportive environment.

References

Academy for Educational Development, Inc. (1967). *Quality education in Milwaukee's future.* New York: Author.

Adeleke, T. (1994). Martin R. Delany's philosophy of education: A neglected aspect of African American liberation thought. *Journal of Negro Education, 63,* 2, 22 1–236.

Akoto, A. (1994). Notes on an Afrikan centered pedagogy. In Shujaa, M. J. (Ed.), *Too much schooling, too little education: The paradox of black life in white societies.* Trenton, NJ: Africa World Press.

Allen, B. A., & Boykin, A. W. (1992). African American children and the educational process: Alleviating cultural discontinuity through prescriptive pedagogy. *School Psychology Review, 21,* 4, 586–596.

Allen, B. A., & Butler, L. (1996). The effects of music and movement opportunity on the analogical reasoning performance of African American and white school children: A preliminary study. *Journal of Black Psychology, 22,* 3, 316–328.

Allen, W. R., & Jewell, J. O. (1995). African American education since *An American dilemma. Daedalus, 124,* 1, 77–100.

Anderman, E. M., & Maehr, M. L. (1994). Motivation and schooling in the middle grades. *Review of Educational Research, 64,* 2, 287–309.

Anderson, J. D. (1988). *The education of blacks in the South, 1860–1935.* Chapel Hill: University of North Carolina Press.

Asante, M. K. (1991). The Afrocentric idea in education. *Journal of Negro Education, 60,* 7, 170–179.

Asante, M. K. (1991–1992, December–January). Afrocentric curriculum. *Educational Leadership,* 28–31.

Asante, M. K. (1992, September). Learning about Africa. *The Executive Educator,* 21–23.

Asante, M. K. (1993). *Malcolm X as cultural hero and other Afrocentric essays.* Trenton, NJ: Africa World Press.

Bell, Y. R. (1994). A culturally sensitive analysis of black learning styles. *Journal of Black Psychology, 20*, 1, 47–61.

Berliner, D. C., & Biddle, B. J. (1995). *The manufactured crisis: Myths, fraud and the attack on America's public schools.* Reading, MA: Addison-Wesley.

Bernstein, B. (1977). *Class, Codes and Controls, Vols. I and II.* London: Routledge & Kegan Paul.

Bourdieu, P. (Ed.) (1973).Reproduction in education, society, and culture. *Sage Studies in Social and Educational Change,* Vol 5. Beverly Hills, CA: Sage.

Bowles, D. R. (1997). *Effective elementary school administration.* New York: Parker.

Boykin, A. W. (1994, September). Surface and deep levels of cultural analysis. In Pollard, D. S., & Ajirotutu, C. S. (Chairs), *Documenting the African American Immersion Schools: A work in progress.* Symposium conducted at the University of Wisconsin–Milwaukee.

Boykin, A. W. (1999, April 19–23). *Theoretical conceptualizations of African centered principles.* Presentation at the annual meeting of the American Educational Research Association, Montreal.

Brown, K. (1993). Do African Americans need immersion schools? The paradoxes created by legal conceptualizations of race and public education. *Iowa Law Review, 78*, 813–881.

Cibulka, J. G., & Olson, F. I. (1993). The organization and politics of the Milwaukee Public Schools: 1920–1986. In Rury, J. L., & Cassell, F. A. (Eds.), *Seeds of crisis: Public schooling in Milwaukee since 1920.* Madison: University of Wisconsin Press. 73–109.

Clark, D. N., & Clark, S. N. (1996). Better preparation of educational leaders. *Educational Researcher, 25*, 8, 18–20.

Compact for Educational Opportunity. (1993). *Perspectives on the Chapter 220 Interdistrict Student Transfer Program: What have we achieved?* Milwaukee, WI: Author.

Compton, M. F. (1983, May). The middle school curriculum: A new approach. *NASSP Bulletin, 67*, 39–44.

Connell, J. P., Spencer, M. B., & Aber, J. L. (1994). Educational risk and resilience in African American youth: Context, self, actions and outcomes in school. *Child Development, 65*, 493–506.

Cuban, L. (1992). What happens to reforms that last? The case of the junior high school. *American Educational Research Journal, 29*, 2, 227–251.

Dalke, W. (1990). *The black educational reform movement, Milwaukee 1963–1975.* Unpublished master's thesis, University of Wisconsin, Milwaukee.

Dawkins, M. P., & Braddock II, J. H. (1994). The continuing significance of desegregation: School racial composition and African American inclusion in American society. *Journal of Negro Education, 63*, 3, 394–405.

Delpit, L. (1995). *Other people's children: Cultural conflict in the classroom.* New York: New Press.

Eyo, B. A. (1991, April 11–14). *Intercultural communication education: An Afrocentric perspective.* Paper presented at the annual meeting of the Central States Communication Association, Chicago, IL.

Frierson, H. T. (1990). The situation of black educational researchers: Continuation of a crisis. *Educational Researcher, 19*, 2, 12–17.

Giroux, H. L., & McLaren, P. L. (1989). *Critical pedagogy: The stage and culture struggle.* Albany, NY: State University of New York Press.

Gordon, K. A. (1995). Self concept and motivational patterns of resilient African American high school students. *Journal of Black Psychology, 21*, 3, 239–255.

Gormly, K., McDermoff, P., Rothenberg, J., & Hammer, J. (1995, April 18–22) *Expert and novice teachers' beliefs about culturally responsive pedagogy.* Paper presented at the annual meeting of the American Educational Research Association, San Francisco.

Graham, S. (1994). Motivation in African Americans. *Review of Educational Research, 64, 1,* 55–117.

Hacker, A. (1992). *Two nations: Black and white, separate, hostile, unequal.* New York: Macmillan.

Harris, N. (1992). A philosophical basis for an Afrocentric orientation. *Western Journal of Black Studies, 16, 3,* 154–159.

Hertzog, C. J. (1984, May). Middle school today: Are programs up to date? *NASSP Bulletin,* 108–110.

Holmes, C. L. (1993). *New visions of a liberated future: Afrocentric paradigms, literature and a curriculum for survival and beyond.* Unpublished doctoral dissertation, Temple University.

Hoover, M.E.R. (1992). The Nairobi Day School: An African American independent school, 1966–1984. *Journal of Negro Education, 61, 2,* 201–210.

Irvine, J. J. (1990). *Black students and school failure: Policies, practices and prescriptions.* New York: Greenwood.

Jackson, C. C. (1994). The feasibility of an Afrocentric curriculum. *Southern Social Studies Journal, 20, 1,* 60–74.

Jacob, J. E. (1991). Black America, 1990: An overview. In Dewart, J. (Ed.), *The state of black America, 1991.* New York: National Urban League. 1–8.

Jagers, R. J., & Mock, L. O. (1993). Culture and social outcomes among African American children: An afrographic exploration. *Journal of Black Psychology, 19, 4,* 391–405.

Jones-Wilson, F. C. (1991). School improvement among blacks: Implications for excellence and equity. In Willie, C., Garibaldi, A. M., & Reed, W. L. (Eds.), *The education of African Americans.* New York: Auburn House. 72–78.

Kester, V. M. (1994). Factors that affect African American students' bonding to middle school. *Elementary School Journal, 95, 1,* 63–73.

King, S. H. (1993). The limited presence of African American teachers. *Review of Educational Research, 63,* 115–149.

Lamers, W. M. (1974). *Our roots grow deep, 1836–1967.* (2nd ed.). Milwaukee, WI: Milwaukee Public Schools.

Lee, C. D. (1992). Profile of an independent black institution: African-centered education at work. *Journal of Negro Education, 61, 2,* 160–177.

Levine, M. C., & Zipp, J. F. (1993). A city at risk: The changing social and economic context of public schooling in Milwaukee. In Rury, J. L., & Cassell, F. A. (Eds.), *Seeds of crisis: Public schooling in Milwaukee since 1920.* Madison: University of Wisconsin Press 42–72.

Levinson, B. A., & Holland, D. (1996). The cultural production of the educated person. In Levinson, B. A., Foley, D. E., & Holland, D. (Eds.), *The cultural production of the educated person: Critical ethnographies of schooling and local practices.* Albany, NY: State University of New York Press. 1–54.

Levy, T. (1988). Making a difference in the middle. *Social Education, 52, 2,* 104–106.

Lomotey, K. (1992). Independent black institutions: African centered education models. *Journal of Negro Education, 61, 4,* 455–462.

McKenzie, F. D. (1991). Education strategies for the 90s. In Dewart, J. (Ed.), *The state of black America, 1991.* New York: National Urban League. 95–109.

McNeely, R. L., & Kinlow, M. R. (1987). *Milwaukee today: A racial gap study.* Milwaukee, WI: Milwaukee Urban League.

Merelman, R. M. (1994). Racial conflict and cultural politics in the United States. *The Journal of Politics, 56, 1,* 1–20.

Milwaukee Creating 2 Schools for Black Boys. (1990, September 30). *New York Times,* 1, 26.

Milwaukee Public Schools. (1990). *Educating African American Males: A Dream Deferred.* African American Male Task Force. Milwaukee, WI: Milwaukee Public Schools.

Milwaukee Public Schools Report Card. District Report. (1991–1992). Milwaukee, WI: Author.

Milwaukee Public Schools Report Card. District Report. (1992–1993). Milwaukee, WI: Author.

Milwaukee Public Schools Report Card. District Report. (1993–1994). Milwaukee, WI: Author.

Milwaukee Public Schools Report Card. District Report. (1994–1995). Milwaukee, WI: Author.

Milwaukee Public Schools Report Card. District Report. (1995–1996). Milwaukee, WI: Author.

Milwaukee Public Schools Report Card. District Report. (1996–1997). Milwaukee, WI: Author.

Milwaukee School Plan Needs Support. (1990, November 6). *New York Times*, A22.

Milwaukee Urban League. (1919–1979). UWM Manuscript Collection 20. Golda Meir Library. Milwaukee, WI: University of Wisconsin–Milwaukee.

Mirel, J. (1994). School reform unplugged: The Bensenville New American School project 1991–1993. *American Educational Research Journal, 31,* 3, 481–518.

Moody, C. D., Sr., & Moody, C. D. (1989). Elements of effective black schools. In Smith, W. D., & Chunn, E. W. (Eds.), *Black education: A quest for equity and excellence.* New Brunswick, NJ: Transaction Publishers.

Motivate, Don't Isolate Black Students. (1990, November 5). *New York Times*, A20.

Murrell, P. C., Jr. (1996, April 8–12). *Beyond multicultural education: African critical pedagogy in curriculum reform for African American children in urban elementary schools.* Paper presented at the annual meeting of the American Educational Research Association, New York.

Narine, M. L. (1992). *Single-sex single race public schools: A solution to the problems plaguing the black community.* Washington, DC: U.S. Department of Education, Office of Educational Research and Improvement. (ERIC Document Reproduction Service No. 348 423)

National Association for the Advancement of Colored People. (1917–1970). UWM Manuscript Collection EP. Golda Meir Library. Milwaukee, WI: University of Wisconsin–Milwaukee.

National Commission on Excellence in Education. (1983). *A nation at risk: Imperatives for educational reform.* Washington, DC: U.S. Department of Education.

National Middle Schools Association. (1995). *This we believe: Developmentally responsive middle schools.* Columbus, OH: National Middle Schools Association.

Noguera, P. A. (1996). Confronting the urban in urban school reform. *The Urban Review, 28,* 1, 1–9.

O'Daniel, R. M. (1994, March 26). *Empowering issues of an Afrocentric perspective: Disempowering racism in American education.* Paper presented at the National Conference on Blacks in Higher Education.

Pechman, E. M., & King, J. A. (1993). *Obstacles to restructuring experiences of six middle grades schools.* New York: Columbia University Teachers College National Center for Restructuring Education, Schools, and Teaching.

Pollard, D. S. (1997). Race, gender and educational leadership: Perspectives from African American principals. *Educational Policy, 11,* 3, 355–374.

Ratteray, J. D. (1992). Independent neighborhood schools: A framework for the education of African Americans. *Journal of Negro Education, 61*, 2, 138-147.

Ratteray, J. D. (1994). The search for access and content in the education of African Americans. In Shujaa, M. J. (Ed.), *Too much schooling, too little education: The paradox of black life in white societies.* Trenton, NJ: Africa World Press. 123-141.

Rury, J. L. (1993). The changing social context of urban education. In Rury, J. L., & Cassell, F. A. (Eds.), *Seeds of crisis: Public schooling in Milwaukee since 1920.* Madison: University of Wisconsin Press. 10-41.

Smylie, M. A. (1996). From bureaucratic control to building human capital: The importance of teacher learning in educational reform. *Educational Researcher, 25*, 9, 9-11.

Spencer, M. B., & Dornbusch, S. M. (1990). Challenges in studying minority youth. In Feldman, S. S., & Elliott, G. R. (Eds.), *At the threshold: The developing adolescent.* Cambridge, MA: Harvard University Press. 123-146.

Sternberg, R. J., & Horvath, J. A. (1995). A prototype view of expert teaching. *Educational Researcher, 24*, 6, 9-17.

Stolee, M. (1993). The Milwaukee desegregation case. In Rury, J. L., & Cassell, F. A. (Eds.), *Seeds of crisis: Public schooling in Milwaukee since 1920.* Madison: University of Wisconsin Press. 229-268.

Taylor, D. L., & Teddlie, C. (1992, April). *Restructuring without changing: Constancy in the class-room in a restructured district.* Paper presented at the annual meeting of the American Educational Research Association, San Francisco.

Trotter, J. W., Jr. (1985). *Black Milwaukee: The making of an industrial proletariat. 1915-1945.* Urbana: University of Illinois Press.

Useem, E., Christman, J. B., Gold, E., & Simon, E. (1996). *Reforming Alone: Barriers to orga-nizational learning in urban school change initiatives.* Paper presented at the Annual Meeting of the American Educational Research Association. New York. April 8-12.

Wehlage, G., Smith, G., & Lipman, P. (1992). Restructuring urban schools: The New Futures experience. *American Educational Research Journal, 29*, 1, 51-93.

Westerman, D. A. (1991). Expert and novice teacher decision making. *Journal of Teacher Education, 42*, 4, 292-305.

Wieder, A. (1992). Afrocentrisms: Capitalist, democratic and liberationist portraits. *Educational Foundations, 6*, 2, 33-43.

Williams, B., & Newcombe, E. (1994). Building on the strengths of urban learners. *Educational Leadership, 51*, 8, 75-78.

Willis, P. E. (1981). *Learning to labor: How working class kids get working class jobs.* New York: Columbia University Press.

Willis, P. E. (1983). Cultural production and theories of reproduction. In Barton, L., & Walker, S. (Eds.), *Race, class and education.* London: Croom Helm. 107-138.

Wilson, W. J. (1987). *The truly disadvantaged: The inner city, the underclass and public policy.* Chicago: University of Chicago Press.

Wilson, W. J. (1996). *When work disappears: The world of the new urban poor.* New York: Knopf.

—— PART II ——

ISSUES IN AFRICAN-CENTERED SCHOOLING

Talent Development, Cultural Deep Structure, and School Reform: Implications for African Immersion Initiatives

A. Wade Boykin

One of the most dogged challenges that continues to plague African American communities in particular and American society in general is how to do a more effective job of educating the masses of African American students from low-income backgrounds. For from many circles, the same conclusion is drawn. By and large, African American children have not been well served by our nation's public schools. Surely the push for African-centered infusions into public schools represents still another attempt to rectify this troubling situation. The major thesis of this chapter is that while there is wisdom and heuristic value in African-centered initiatives, such efforts must involve broader school reform. That is, fully comprehensive transformations are needed that pierce to the core of the schooling process, impacting on the full range of daily activities, outlooks, structures, and outcomes of the schooling process. The core assumptions, functions, and practices of schooling must change (Elmore, 1996; Goodman, 1995). Furthermore, this must be coupled with an understanding of the historical purposes that public schools have served in the American social order, the foundational problematics of formal education, and, in turn, appreciation for the complexities and challenges of school reform (Boykin, 1994, 1996).

In this chapter, salient aspects of African-centered initiatives will first be identified. The larger questions of school reform will then be visited, leading to a plea for an alternative comprehensive model of schooling. A case will then be made that this talent development model of schooling can be successfully fused with African-centered initiatives, particularly the processes of transforming the cultural deep structure of schooling, building on the cultural assets African American children bring with them to school, and ultimately fostering positive life transformations for black children through cultural empowerment. Research consistent with these claims then will be presented. The chapter concludes with a distillation and summary of the line of argument that is advanced.

AFRICAN-CENTERED INITIATIVES

In gleaning the noteworthy scholarship on African-centered educational efforts, certain key aspects merit illumination (Asante, 1987; Hilliard, 1995; Shujaa, 1994; Tedla, 1995). I offer the following rendition. One ingredient is that such efforts typically strive to make salient, if not authenticate, canons and understandings that are African in origin and make these central to curriculum formulations. As Lee (1994) has persuasively argued, the goal is to legitimate "African stores of knowledge" (297). African-centered infusion initiatives also tend to be transformative and "efficacy oriented" (B. Gordon, 1994; King, 1994). They operationalize "liberatory pedagogy" (B. Gordon, 1997) in that through the schooling process African American students are empowered to overcome the impediments of oppression, racism, low status, inadequate material resources, and marginalization that have plagued African Americans for centuries and to which we all too often fall prey. The formal education of African Americans is to be geared toward helping black people overcome the obstacles society has put in our way.

Further, the goal is to enable our children to have hope and to act to change their circumstances beneficially, to transform their lives and those of significant others, and to impact positively on their community as well as the wider society. Education should provide beacons toward bright futures. This concern resonates well with one offered by Carter G. Woodson over 60 years ago in his immortal work *The Miseducation of the Negro* (1933) when he stated, "The mere imparting of information is not education" (x). In a related vein, African-centered infusion initiatives would be geared toward rectifying the enduring impact of slavery's legacy on the lives of African Americans and American society at large. Defining people as property and treating people as though they were property are profoundly dehumanizing acts. An effort to dehumanize others is itself dehumanizing for those who engage in it and for a society that condones it. The humanity of this society cannot be completely restored until African Americans are fully participating partners in it. A people's humanity is effectively conveyed through their fundamental cultural expressions (Boykin, 1998).

The traditional cultural voice of African America was officially silenced through the institution of slavery, as this was a key mechanism in the effort to strip away their humanity (Akbar, 1985). Black Americans' participation in American society since the demise of slavery has been predicated upon embracing Anglo-EuroAmerican worldviews, values, and expressions. Yet the "unofficial" original cultural voice of African Americans was never fully silenced. African Americans as a whole, of course, with several individual exceptions, have never abandoned their cultural ties to their African past. They have just sought (even if tacitly) unofficial vehicles for its expression, even if such expression has not been officially sanctioned in mainstream attainment institutions such as public schools (Boykin, 1986; Boykin & Ellison, 1995).

When the traditional cultural voice of African Americans is heard and authenticated via this society's institutions, then the humanity of America at large will be more fully realized, the legacy of slavery will be more likely to be put to rest (none of this precludes the expression of other cultural voices by black people or otherwise), and black people will gain even greater access to their own humanity. African-centered infusion initiatives, by promoting and authenticating the traditional cultural expressions of African American people, provide a path for such realizations.

The transformations identified with African-centered approaches have merit in light of the historical and current circumstances in which African Americans find themselves. They suggest clear strategies and direction for school reform. But there are other, broader school reform considerations as well that must be considered if school reform is to be substantially effective. Indeed, I argue that no effort at school reform will meet substantially with success unless it is sufficiently appreciative of and responsive to several considerations. It must appreciate the historical purposes that schools have served in the American social order and the corresponding foundational assumptions upon which the schooling process is built. In doing this, it must address the full problematics of schooling. It must provide change that is comprehensive, coordinated, and sustained. It must yield an assemblage of activities that permeate the many reaches of the schooling enterprise and do so in a conceptually coordinated, internally consistent fashion.

So what purposes have American public schools served? What is the historical context for current-day practices? These issues have been addressed persuasively by several authors (Goodman, 1995; Plank, Scotch, & Gamble, 1996; Tyack, 1974). Mass public education was established in the first two decades of the twentieth century in response to a convergence of cultural, economic, political, demographic, and social trends of the time period. This resulted in some strikingly consistent functions and operational modes for public schools that have persisted to the present day.

THE TRADITIONAL FUNCTIONS OF AMERICAN PUBLIC SCHOOLS

Perhaps most fundamentally, public education in America has performed a talent sorting and selection function. This was readily apparent as far back as the late eighteenth century when Thomas Jefferson, arguing for public funding for "grammar schools," stated that their purpose should be to identify the few geniuses who "will be raked from the rubbish" (Spring, 1994). In this way, a "natural aristocracy" would emerge composed of only the best and brightest students, who would then lead and direct this nation. This premise has guided and informed educational policies and practices ever since. Traditionally, schools have played a gatekeeping role for society. They sort and weed out. They assess students for purposes of classifying and arraying them along a vertical pecking order from the most able to the least able, from the few who are deemed legitimately talented to the bulk who are average, to the ones who are construed as intellectually handicapped. During the inception of the mass public education movement in the early twentieth century, the talent sorting paradigm was augmented by other crucial principles and assumptions about the functions and purposes of public schools. Several references have documented and elucidated this formative process (Borrowman, 1965; Callahan, 1962; Cubberly, 1916; Curti, 1959; Karier, 1975; Lukes, 1973; Persell, 1977; Spring, 1994; Tyack, 1974).

One such additional function for mass public schooling was to perform a mainstream acculturation function in order to bring the values and behaviors of immigrant children from southern and eastern European nations into conformity with Anglocultural ideals—for example, to get them to appropriate such cultural themes as materialism, emotional containment, providence, competition, and particularly individualism in its many forms. As such, schools were conceived to perform an homogenization function, indeed, a cultural socialization function, that was officially and sharply at odds with principles of pluralism or diversity.

Public schools were also conceived to operate consistent with certain ways of capturing learning and the learner arising from the emerging discipline of psychology. It is well documented that the functionalist principles espoused by William James, the behaviorist principles of John Watson, and especially the stimulus-response connectionist and law of effect principles of Edward Thorndike drove practices of pedagogy in this period (Borrowman, 1965; Goodman, 1995). Consequently, the learner is passive, and learning is to be imposed from outside the person and driven by external motivation, in the form of rewards, incentives, and punishments. Schools were places where drill, repetition, and rote memorization prevailed and where an information accumulation approach to knowledge acquisition was promoted. The "proper" knowledge is gained in a piecemeal fashion, disconnected, largely formalized, and abstracted from real life (Everhart, 1983; Lave, 1996; Rogoff, 1990).

Then, too, the objective of this model was to socialize a labor force to meet the manpower needs of a heavily industrializing society based on a factory work, manufacturing-driven economy. Consider that in a highly influential book written during this era for teacher training, (William Chandler Bagley's *Classroom Management*, 1925) it was advocated that the chief purpose of schooling was to build habits of the kind needed to properly work on the assembly line. Students so trained would have the capacity to work long hours on repetitive, tedious tasks often unrelated to personal motives, interests, or desires. They would be punctual, do drill work, follow commands without hesitation, and generally conform to "company" rules.

Schools were also conceived to fit with the prevailing corporate-industrial model for institutional operation and to serve as bureaucratic institutions. Over time the preservation of the bureaucracy becomes an end unto itself and thus a purpose for schooling. As bureaucratic institutions, schools are characterized by centralization of authority, highly formalized organizational structure, and rule-governed social interactions, with authority residing in roles. Schools would be affect-neutral sites. There would be standardization of procedures and practices. Further, there is a paramount concern with efficiency of institutional operation linked to an insistent preoccupation with quality control (Cubberly, 1916). Students who did not fit this mold were seen as threats to the system's efficiency; hence the "problematics" of education came to be located essentially inside students, inside their immediate family, or the proximal community context. Thus, when things go wrong at school, it is attributed to students themselves who have learning problems, adjustment problems, behavior problems, or family problems, any or all of which would "naturally" impede the learning process (Karier, 1975; Spring, 1994, chs. 9–10).

All in all, it can be argued persuasively that public education still operates largely according to these same premises today. These premises and functions have receded from the spotlight of educational discussion and have been substantially blended into the ordinary, everyday routines of schooling where, all too often, they are unchallenged. They are simply accepted as how schooling is supposed to be implemented. Unless a school reform initiative addresses these premises and purposes, then reform cannot be fully responsive to the foundational problematics of public schooling.

There is a need to change profoundly the way we school in America. Schools most surely need to be socially reconstructed. Schools must be reculturalized. The purposes and functions schools serve need to be redirected and reframed. A different set of operating assumptions for schooling is needed. This is so for several related reasons. These are discussed below.

THE PROBLEMATICS OF TRADITIONAL
SCHOOLING APPROACHES

A talent sorting, weeding-out approach to schooling may have outlived its usefulness. Considerable evidence supports this view (Boykin, 1994). Entry-level skills needed for employment have escalated. The cognitive and ethical demands for normal living and decision making are rising. The world is shrinking and global interdependence is increasing. The labor pool, and indeed society at large, will increasingly rely on school graduates from groups that have had the most problematic schooling experiences. Resources are dwindling in our society. As a result of these changes, we will need substantially changed educational practices in order to educate a substantially greater proportion of our student population.

There may be many reasons why children fail to perform well in school. It may be that some are performing in a problematic manner that requires direct corrective intervention. But to reduce all the problems to this source and to invoke this single remedy is a narrow and myopic strategy. Surely, there might be multiple reasons why children fare poorly, and there may be multiple pathways that can lead to school success (Boykin, 1996).

There is real and profound pluralism in our society that should not be swept under the proverbial rug, cast in negative terms, or squashed by cultural imposition (Banks & Banks, 1995; Nieto, 1993). Schools are not culturally neutral terrains. A mainstream cultural socialization agenda still forms the backbone for the hidden curriculum of schooling (Carlson, 1982). As we have become more enlightened on the workings of culture, it is abundantly evident that the cultural terrain of schooling should be expanded. Concerted efforts must be made to become more inclusive and to take into account the experiences of domestic cultural groups whose origins are not European. In doing so, we can take fuller advantage of diverse cultural expressions in the promotion of widespread talent.

In a related manner, different types of learners and learning are demanded for the twenty-first century (Brooks & Brooks, 1993; E. Gordon, 1995; Wilson & Peterson, 1997). The learner must be active. Learning more so must be construed as a socially interactive process. Moreover, what is learned in school should also change. Especially for children from marginalized domestic cultural groups in this society, learning cannot consist of the accumulation and regurgitation of preprocessed facts or piecemeal, disconnected abstractions. Education should not be a passive experience in which students are taught to merely accept things as they are. Instead, it should be made meaningful to their lives, challenging them to be innovative about building a better tomorrow for themselves and others.

Schooling practices should be made more consistent with more recent conceptions offered by the social, behavioral, and human development sciences. In this regard, the importance of the intersection of culture, context, and cognition needs to be operationalized in schooling practices (Rogoff & Chavajay, 1995; Tharp & Gallimore, 1988). Ecological considerations need to be acknowledged as important. Moreover, greater focus should be on how a person can gain enjoyment and stimulation from interaction with the environment intrinsically (Deci, 1975; Hunt, 1965; Raffini, 1995). Finally, traditional conceptions of school learning did not address human development issues sufficiently.

The economic order in our society has changed significantly since the inception of the traditionally dominant model of public schooling (Kearns & Doyle, 1991). We are living in what has been described as a post (manufacturing) industrial era. Today, low-wage factory work forms a fairly small share of the available workforce options. More jobs are now available in the service sector. These new jobs require particular focus on interpersonal and communication skills. We live in an era where information creation, management, analysis, utilization, and transmission are economic commodities, underscoring the importance of communication skills. There also is a premium on high levels of information technology. Fluency and competence with state-of-the-art electronic mechanisms and devices will be an increasingly common expectation in order to function in twenty-first-century workplaces.

To improve the quality of life in schools for students and teachers alike may require less reliance on a strictly bureaucratic, early twentieth-century corporate model of systems operation. Strict adherence to impersonal guidelines for interpersonal exchanges, and casting students and their backgrounds in pejorative terms, may not create a socially conducive atmosphere for learning and for the nurturance of students' potential (Fine, 1994). Teachers who serve as rule enforcers and guideline implementers, who put meeting curricular datelines over genuine learning, and who feel little creative generative voice in the process can feel devalued and depersonalized in the process of teaching (Giroux & McLaren, 1986). While evaluation and assessment of students should no doubt continue, their role in support of a gatekeeping function needs to be reconsidered.

Indeed, an alternative overarching reform philosophy and corresponding model to guide schooling efforts have been formulated (Boykin, 1996). This alternative formulation asserts a different purpose for schooling. It is conceived to be comprehensive, farsighted, proactive, cohesive, and yet responsive to fundamental problematics of formal education. The talent development model of schooling is proposed here. Incorporating this model would change the very core assumptions, functions, practices, schooling attitudes, and the role schools play in society at large. The talent development model starts with the assertion that all students can learn to high standards in a demanding, high expectations academic setting. This lofty goal can be achieved by any school that is committed to providing the appropriate support, assistance, structure, and facilitating conditions. This is a reachable goal for any school that strives to maximize every child's academic development. In the talent development model, authentic academic success in a rigorous curriculum; therefore, it is pervasive rather than within the reach of just a precious few. This then becomes the basis upon which a school and its classrooms are to be judged. *Talent* here refers to high level of competence or performance, based upon an age-appropriate standard of excellence. Virtually any student, it is argued, can attain this standard of performance. *Talent* is not used here to refer to a specialized skill in a particular domain but to general schooling competence and performance. It includes affective and interpersonal concerns, as well as community involvement. *Development* is meant to convey a host of considerations when it comes to talent. It includes identifying, cultivating, refining, sustaining, enhancing, extending talent, providing opportunities for its expression and occurrence, and transferring across different domains and settings, including in and out of school settings.

To fulfill its objectives, the talent development model advocates that a given school provides, simultaneously, multiple determinants for ensuring students' success. This means that the possibility of success for any given child is made redundant by ensuring that each of the major facets of the schooling process is reconstrued as an avenue for success. Specifically, the following steps should be taken. (1) Students should be fortified in those areas where they may be vulnerable to school failure. This would be achieved through providing access to supportive services, be they academic, social, health, and/or mental health; through tutorial assistance as needed; and through fostering a sense of resilience in them. Moreover, as appropriate, enrichment experiences that enhance schooling outcomes should also be provided. (2) Programs and activities should be implemented that ensure that peers, family members, and the local community are functionally supportive of students' success. (3) School personnel must become enabled to serve as advocates rather than adversaries for children. They must come to truly believe and be committed to the proposition that all children can learn, and they must receive sufficient and appropriate professional development activities to support the talent development model. (4) The content of the curriculum, pedagogical techniques, and learning contexts must be challenging, appropriate, effective, engaging, and responsive to the students' interests and needs. (5) Organizationally, the school must be configured and operated to ensure the delivery of successful schooling outcomes. Overall, this model aims to provide appropriate activities and programs that are based on the best available documented evidence that they will lead to enhanced schooling outcomes for the population served by a given school.

The talent development model advocates several themes to inform schooling activities as well. These themes explicitly aim to redress the foundational problematics of schools that have been identified earlier in this chapter, and they are conceived to give substance and focus to the activities that manifest the various successful pathways.

- In order to turn diversity into a strength, the first talent development theme is *building upon the assets that students bring with them to school.* Perhaps all children in America should become fluent in the dictates of mainstream society. Yet the integrity of diverse children's life experiences should be capitalized upon to enhance educational outcomes and facilitate their beneficial participation in the larger society, rather than having legitimate integrity be construed as a roadblock or justification for school failure, as is so often the case via the talent sorting model.

- A second talent development theme is *helping children across key developmental transitions.* Schooling is a dynamic, not a static, process, and there are changing developmental heedings and challenges along the way. From a talent development perspective, it is essential that children's schooling is consistently developmentally appropriate and that children make key transitions as successfully as possible.

- There is the talent development theme of *emphasizing active, constructivist approaches to learning.* There should be a deemphasis on passive rote learning and drill, with an increased concentration on the learner as an active participant in the learning process, with knowledge acquisition viewed as a social construction and with a greater focus on active academic task engagement. Moreover, along with basic skills, there should be greater focus on higher-order thinking skills, critical thinking skills, and creative problem solving. Learning should not be construed as a pouring in and subsequent pouring out process.

- Moreover, what children learn in school at all grade levels should not be so isolated, abstract, piecemeal, formalized, and disconnected. Instead, a fourth talent development theme is the *promotion of meaningful and connected learning.* Knowledge gained should be thematically connected across subject areas. It should be connected to the world outside of school in practical and meaningful ways. A child's formal education should be more greatly situated proactively in children's lived experiences. This should be done to generate greater interest level and also for purposes of cultural empowerment. For example, what a child acquires in school can be put to his or her constructive benefit and to the benefit of his or her family, community, and society at large.

- Still another talent development theme is the *preparation of students for the twenty-first century.* For that matter, the focus should be on helping children to eventually prepare the twenty-first century (Goodman, 1995). Children must be prepared for the information age, where information creation and transmission are major commodity products. They must function in an economy more greatly dominated by the service industries. Schooling experiences must prepare students who can meet the intellectual challenge of high technology in their daily activities. Their world will be more socially and ethically complicated by the fact of global interdependence. Consequently, children must develop full-range communications skills. They must develop interpersonal negotiation skills and conflict resolution skills.

They must have high-level numeracy skills. They certainly must be multiculturally fluent. They must learn to apply the knowledge and information gained in creative and profitable ways. That is, they must become intellectual entrepreneurs.

- Still another talent development theme is the *promotion of school as a community*. Schools should be personal and caring environments. Schools should be places where a sense of belonging is fostered among students and school personnel alike. There should be strong identification with the school. Students should feel they are wanted, desired, and honored in the schools they attend. Their well-being, interests, concerns, and development should be seen as central to the school's mission. Schools can serve as their sanctuaries, as places of hope. In all, schools should function more like small-scaled communities, broken down perhaps figuratively into interconnected families and neighborhoods rather than large, impersonal bureaucratic machines. Efficiency of system operation should not be abandoned; such efficiency should be in the service of the promotion of a sense of community among all school participants.

AFRICAN-CENTERED INFUSIONS AND TALENT DEVELOPMENT

I posit that the thrusts of African-centered infusions are not inconsistent with certain themes of the talent development model. Indeed, manifestations of African-centered infusions can flesh out certain tenets of this reform model. Both African-centered infusions and talent development place premiums on building a sense of community in schools and the development of critical thinking skills, learning processes, and knowledge acquisition all meaningfully connected to children's lives. Both advocate that formal education should serve a transformative function in children's lives and lead to efficacy and empowerment for children, so that they can enhance life conditions for themselves and others. Both advocate building on the assets that children bring with them to school. The African-centered approach more obviously focuses on the factors as they serve to enhance life conditions for people of African descent. The talent development model addresses additional schooling concerns to which African-centered infusion initiatives should pay heed. These would include a focus on human development considerations, especially as they relate to school transitions, skill preparation of students for the twenty-first century, promotion of active academic task engagement, thematic learning across the curriculum, and actualizing a schooling framework that strives to overdetermine success so that virtually no children are left behind in the quest to develop pervasive high levels of performance and competence.

As mentioned above, both approaches promote building on the assets that children bring with them to school, assets that arise proactively out of the children's life experiences. This is a central consideration for reforming schools at the deep structure level. Quite frankly, it sounds laudable to proclaim that all children can learn. It surely seems like the appropriate thing for "concerned and committed" school personnel to advocate. Proclaiming this is one thing, but truly believing it and operating consistent with such a belief are other matters.

The efficacy of building on children's cultural assets is substantiated by the growing body of work examining the interface of cognition and context. It has been demonstrated that the quality of one's thinking in a given situation is tied to the quality of support that situation provides one's thought processes. Further, work on situated cognition reveals that scaffolding on current understanding or competencies leads to better results and produces more positive cognitive change than attempting to add on understanding or pour in competency, assuming a priori that none had existed (Greeno, 1989; Greeno & Middle School Group, 1997).

Moreover, other work suggests that children in school will be quite resistant to changing how they operate and even become alienated from the goals of the change process and those in school who promote it if the children's integrity or current ways of operating are dishonored through the proceedings (Fordham & Ogbu, 1986; Gilmore, 1985; Piestrup, 1973). More concrete elaboration is in order.

In the course of adapting and coping with life circumstances, it can be argued that many black children from low-income backgrounds acquire adaptive competencies that could be capitalized upon in school settings. The adaptive integrity plausibly can be scaffolded for cognitive enhancement and to fulfill a school's socialization agenda (John-Steiner & Mahn, 1996). In recent interviews conducted by a team of researchers here at Howard, we have found that many fourth- and fifth-grade black children have adult-like household responsibilities. They also have day-care responsibilities for their younger siblings or the younger children of their older siblings. These are potentially asset-laden experiences. These experiences have created opportunities for learning and cognitive skill development that are often overlooked by schooling processes. For example, family decision-making experiences promote a maturity in children that is not capitalized on in school settings.

We must also recognize that schools traditionally are not culturally neutral terrains. They were not conceived to be such. Certain cultural themes have come to dominate the extant contexts of schooling. The hidden curriculum is formed by such fundamental cultural themes as rugged or self-contained individualism, competition, and the sanctity of bureaucracy orientation (Howard & Scott, 1981; Lukes, 1973; Sapon-Shevin & Schniedewind, 1991; Spence, 1985). Lack of mastery of this hidden curriculum has been used as a principal basis for weeding out children according to a talent sorting model of schooling (Boykin, 1994). But evidence suggests that if we expand or alter the range of fundamental cultural themes that form the basis of the learning and performance contexts in school, we can capitalize upon the fundamental cultural assets of a wider range of children who participate in a more diverse set of cultural experiences and thereby enhance a larger number of children's learning and performance outcomes (Gay, 1988).

When this scenario plays out for a preponderant number of African American children from low-income backgrounds, it has very direct implications for African-centered infusion efforts. There are Afrocultural themes that permeate the lives of people of African descent throughout the Diaspora. These themes are considered Afrocultural because it is posited that they are rooted in traditional African cultural legacy. These themes are considered fundamental because at base they are rooted in a worldview and belief system that addresses the fundamental philosophical foundations of life's purposes. They, in concert, form a blueprint for living and give substance and texture, indeed meaning, to one's existence. Afrocultural themes include communalism, a movement-expressive-percussive-polyrhythmic orientation, the co-importance and integration of cognition and affect, spirituality, and in the residue of such themes can be derived a premium placed on high levels of sensate stimulation or high psychological verve (Boykin, 1983; Boykin & Ellison, 1995). By infusing such themes where possible into the differing contexts in which schooling gets done, we create changes at the deep structure level of schooling. Making changes at this fundamental level when using African-centered infusion goes literally to the core of the schooling process.

These Afrocultural themes are available to be capitalized upon because they have shaped and informed contexts the children have participated in out of school (Boykin, 1999). Through such participation, the themes get yoked to children's values, perceptions, competencies, and their practice of various skills. These all become more available for constructive expression when schooling contexts are structured and informed by these Afrocultural themes.

A PROGRAM OF RESEARCH

Over the last several years, my colleagues and I have launched a basic (rather than applied) research program aimed at bringing empirical substance, clarity, and verification to these claims with respect to African American children from low-income backgrounds. We have focused in our work on the potential facilitating effects of three postulated Afrocultural themes. These we have labeled *communalism, verve,* and *movement expressiveness.* Communalism denotes the importance of social interdependence, social bonds, mutuality and identity, and duty tied to group membership. Verve refers to a premium placed on receptiveness to relatively high levels of physical stimulation, marked by receptiveness to variability and intensity in stimulation and to multiple sources of stimulation simultaneously present. Movement expressiveness connotes a premium placed on rich, complex, and expansive movement expression as it relates to the amalgamation of syncopation, percussion, music, and polyrhythm.

Since we have postulated that there is a distinctive cultural lens through which many African American children from low-income backgrounds view their schooling experience, we sought to discern the cultural character of their attitudes, preferences, and perceptions and as these may come into disaccord with those prevailing in their schools.

In our work, we have given low-income African American grade school students sets of scenarios depicting high-achieving peers who achieved via differing cultural means. We have found that, on average, these students are quite socially accepting of their peers who would achieve highly via communalism and verve and less accepting or even rejecting of peers who would achieve highly via conformity to mainstream cultural dictates of individualism and competition (Boykin, Bailey, Hurley, Miller, & Albury, 1998; Marryshow, 1995; Martin, 1994). Other work has shown that, on average, African American grade school students indicate high endorsement of learning environments where the academic practices are characterized by communalism and verve and rejection or no endorsement of such environments marked by individualism and competition (Martin, 1997). These results held for black students in virtually all-black inner-city schools and in suburban predominantly white schools. Intriguingly, in a study where grade school teachers of inner-city African American students were given depictions of students who preferred to learn via differing cultural modalities, it was found that the teachers expected children who were more attuned to individualism and competition to be more highly motivated and to attain higher academic levels in their classrooms than students who operated via communalism and verve (T. Walton, 1993). Of course, this is the opposite pattern to what was obtained when assessing the students' perceptions. Surely, this sets up a situation for potential discord in the classroom. This was more directly tested in another investigation (Miller, 1997). It was found that not only did black grade school students on the average prefer academic practices consistent with themes of communalism and verve and reject those consistent with individualism and competition, but they perceived that their teachers preferred individualism and competition and that they would be likely to get into trouble or be punished if they exhibited behaviors consistent with communalism and verve. This occurred even though they further indicated that at home they would be encouraged to learn via communalism and verve and discouraged from learning via competition and individualism.

Taken together, the results from these studies give amplification to children's own voices about their classroom experiences. They seem to indicate that there is a systematic cultural character to the perceptions of at least the children that we have tested. These children display clear cultural preferences, and they seem sensitive to the potential schooling problematics of not embracing Anglocultural themes. These results stand in striking contrast to the claims of Ogbu and others (Fordham & Ogbu, 1986; Ogbu, 1994) that black students simply reject high achievement and their high- achieving peers. Other work has more directly addressed whether African American children would actually perform better and be more motivated in contexts marked by Afrocultural themes.

One study (Albury, 1998) has shown that low-income African American grade school students perform significantly better on a vocabulary test when that test was preceded by a communal learning condition (children worked in groups of three with shared learning material and were prompted to help each other out for the good of the group, with no external incentive) than by conditions marked by individualism (worked alone and offered an external incentive for subsequent high test performance) or interpersonal competition (three children worked at same location under the promise that the one who performs best of the three on the subsequent test would receive a reward). Other studies have examined this communal theme as well.

Dill (1996) examined recall of information from printed text. Children first either worked alone or in dyads to study the text material. The study dyads were of two types. In one, students studied according to an orthodox approach to reciprocal peer tutoring. They took turns playing tutor and tutored and followed a script designed to structure the dyadic interactions. A reward was also offered contingent upon the pair achieving a designated high level of performance. The second peer tutoring condition was communal in nature. Pairs of children were simply told to work together for their mutual benefit, that they should do so because they are from the same community and should help each other out, so they could both do well. Performance on the subsequent recall test was substantially superior for communal peer tutoring in comparison to the other conditions, where performance levels were the same.

In another effort using black grade school children from low-income backgrounds (Coleman, 1996), a communal study (groups of three) condition proved superior to an individual study condition in leading to greater subsequent individual performance on a creative problem-solving task. Students had to generate the number of exemplars that fitted a given concept such as naming reasons one should be proud of a person. Those who had been in the communal condition produced more thoughtful, interesting, and accurate examples than those from the individual condition. Other research has focused on additional Afrocultural themes. Speaking to the theme of verve, several investigations have documented that for low-income black children problem-solving performance is greater when differing types of tasks are presented in varying sequential order regardless of task type, rather than when they are presented in a blocked fashion so that all of one type are first presented followed by all of a second type, followed by all of a third and fourth type (Bailey, 1993; Boykin, 1982; Boykin, Allen, Davis, & Senior, 1997; Tuck & Boykin, 1989; S. Walton, 1994, 1998). This result held even for academically relevant task types such as math, vocabulary, spelling, and logical picture sequencing (Bailey, 1993). Therefore, it proved more efficacious to present the children, for example, with a math, followed by a spelling, followed by a vocabulary, followed by a spelling, and then a picture sequencing than it was to give them first a set of math tasks and then a set of vocabulary, and so on. This effect was boosted when there was background music playing (S. Walton, 1994, 1998).

A series of studies has also been conducted demonstrating that for young black children from low-income backgrounds different forms of learning can be enhanced if the conditions for learning are characterized by opportunities for movement expression that is rhythmically joined to percussive, syncopated music. The beneficial effects of movement expression are also demonstrated when such expression punctuates the imagery of a to-be-recalled story's content. When there is movement imagery in the story and opportunities for movement expression are encouraged in the learning context, the beneficial effects are even more pronounced (Allen & Boykin, 1991; Allen & Butler, 1996; Cunningham, 1997; Mungai, 1997).

To be sure, these studies were essentially done under controlled experimental conditions rather than in actual classrooms. But they do suggest that there are plausible benefits that accrue from the use of Afrocultural themes in learning and performance contexts. Beyond performance enhancement, across the range of these cited studies children also consistently indicated greater preference and expressed more favorable attitudes for the Afrocultural contexts. They also indicated that their home environments are marked by the presence of such themes. Moreover, in general, there were positive intercorrelations among performance and motivation levels in Afrocultural contexts, children's perceptions of how present are Afrocultural themes in their home, and the level of expressed preference for these themes. That there are positive correlations among home perceptions, cultural theme preferences, and context-specific performance and motivational outcomes is consistent with the theoretical position proffered in this chapter on the connections between culture, context, cognition, and motivation.

A central thesis of this chapter is that success in school for poor African American children needs to be more pervasive, more widespread. Our empirical work on Anglocultural versus Afrocultural theme infusion signifies some ways that this can be more greatly accomplished. This line of work does not imply that if we don't teach black children through Afrocultural themes, they cannot otherwise learn. Instead, our work suggests that intellectual competence as well as intrinsic interest in learning school-relevant tasks is potentially there for these children. It implies that academically valuable skills may go undetected or opportunities for the development of potentially valuable skills and competencies for some children may go unrealized in the absence of appropriately facilitating contexts. Moreover, such contexts may lead to children placing greater value on school tasks and to more favorable attitudes toward and investment in school. The implied prescriptions of this work may also reduce negative opinions about these children's academic potential.

REPRISE AND CONCLUSIONS

All in all, African-centered immersion efforts have much to recommend them. These are encouraging undertakings that have considerable potential heuristic value for African American children and communities. It is argued that such efforts should be situated in a somewhat larger analysis and informed by a broader set of concerns dealing with the nature and purposes of American public schooling. Instead, such efforts are encouraged to be talent development oriented. It is urged that such efforts be linked to schooling designed to ensure that all children can learn to high standards in an academically rigorous, high-expectation setting. This entails encompassing a framework where multiple means for ensuring success, covering all major facets of schooling, are present simultaneously. A merger of the tenets of talent development with immersion efforts should not be difficult to accomplish. To be sure, many of the operational themes of talent development such as building on assets, promoting critical thinking and pedagogy, enhancing communication and interpersonal skills, establishing a community of learners, promoting meaningful, connected learning, and striving for empowerment are quite convergent with the stated aims of African immersion initiatives.

Our empirical work on building on assets to change the deep structure of schooling lies squarely at the intersection of a talent development and an African immersion thrust. Additionally, the provision of cultural contexts in school that are linked to Afrocultural themes can make for more meaningful and connected learning experiences for many African American children. Moreover, as the themes are also made part of the content and substance of the curriculum, children further can become more consciously aware of these themes. This can serve as a springboard to critical analyses of the children's challenges in the American social order and thus promote these themes' efficacy in the children's lives. In turn, this can lead to discerning how such cultural themes can be used as vehicles for personal, familial, community, and societal enhancement. Such an enterprise surely can lead as well to a wider purpose for the schooling of African American children and enriches what is to be connoted by school success (Ladson-Billings, 1994).

Schools for black children should be sites for talent development. They should accomplish a range of objectives. They should prepare these children to acquire a broad range of marketable skills but also prepare them to appreciate their cultural legacy and to use it to be proactive contributors to changing their own life circumstances and to enhancing the life quality of others in their community if not in society at large.

NOTE

Preparation of this chapter was supported by a grant from the U.S. Department of Education Office of Educational Research and Improvement (OERI) to the Center for Research on the Education of Students Placed at Risk (Grant Number R117D40005). The views expressed in this chapter are those of the author. No OERI policy should be inferred.

REFERENCES

Akbar, N. (1985). *Chains and images of psychological slavery.* Jersey City, NJ: New Mind Productions.

Albury, A. (1998). *Social orientation, learning condition and learning outcomes among low-income black and white grade school children.* Doctoral dissertation, Howard University, Washington, DC.

Allen, B., & Boykin, A. W. (1991). The influence of contextual factors on Afro-American and Euro-American children's performance: Effects of movement opportunity and music. *International Journal of Psychology, 26,* 373–387.

Allen, B., & Butler, L. (1996). The effects of music and movement opportunity on the analogical reasoning performance of African American and white school children: A preliminary study. *Journal of Black Psychology, 22,* 316–328.

Asante, M. (1987). *The Afrocentric idea.* Philadelphia: Temple University Press.

Bagley, W. (1925) . *Classroom management.* New York: Macmillan.

Bailey, C. (1993). *The influence of cultural attributes and stimulus variability on the academically relevant task performance of African American school children.* Master's thesis, Howard University, Washington, DC.

Banks, J., & Banks, C. (Eds.). (1995). *Handbook of research on multicultural education.* New York: Macmillan.

Borrowman, M. (1965). *Teacher education in America.* New York: Teachers College Press.

Boykin, A. W. (1982). Task variability and the performance of black and white schoolchildren: Vervistic explorations. *Journal of Black Studies, 12,* 469–485.

Boykin, A. W. (1983). The academic performance of AfroAmerican children. In J. Spence (Ed.), *Achievement and achievement motives.* San Francisco: W. Freeman. 322–371.

Boykin, A. W. (1986). The triple quandary and the schooling of Afro-American children. In U. Neisser (Ed.), *The school achievement of minority children.* Hillsdale, NJ: Lawrence Erlbaum. 55–72.

Boykin, A. W. (1994). Harvesting culture and talent: African American children and school reform. In R. Rossi (Ed.), *Schools and students at risk: Context and framework for positive change.* New York: Teachers College Press. 116–138.

Boykin, A. W. (1996, April). *A talent development approach to school reform.* Paper presented at the annual meeting of the American Educational Research Association, New York.

Boykin, A. W. (1999). *Culture matters in the development and schooling of African American children.* Paper submitted for publication.

Boykin, A. W., Allen, B., Davis, L., & Senior, A. M. (1997). Task performance of black and white children across levels of presentation variability. *Journal of Psychology, 131,* 427–437.

Boykin, A. W., Bailey, C., Hurley, E., Miller, O., and Albury, A. (1998). *The influence of culturally distinct learning orientations on the achievement perceptions of African American and European American grade school children.* Paper submitted for publication.

Boykin, A. W., & Ellison, C. (1995). The multiple ecologies of black youth socialization: An Afrographic analysis. In R. Taylor (Ed.), *African American youth: Their social and economic status in the United States.* Westport, CT: Praeger.

Brooks, J., & Brooks, M. (1993). *The case for constructivist classrooms.* Alexandria, VA: Association for Supervision and Curriculum Development.

Callahan, R. (1962). *Education and the cult of efficiency.* Chicago: University of Chicago Press.

Carlson, D. (1982).Updating individualism and the work ethic: Corporate logic in the classroom. *Curriculum Inquiry, 12,* 125–160.

Coleman, K. (1996). *The influence of a communal learning context on African American elementary students' creative problem solving.* Master's thesis, Howard University, Washington, DC.

Cubberly, E. (1916). *Public school administration: A statement of the fundamental principles underlying the organization and administration of public education.* Boston: Houghton Mifflin.

Cunningham, R. (1997). *The effects of contextual differentiation and content imagery on the cognitive task performance of African American and Euro-American working class children: Movement/music explorations.* Doctoral dissertation, Howard University, Washington, DC.

Curti, M. (1959). *The social ideas of American educators.* Patterson, NJ: Pageant Books.

Deci, E. (1975). *Intrinsic motivation.* New York: Plenum.

Dill, E. (1996). *The influence of communal and peer tutoring contexts on the text recall learning of low-income African American students.* Master's thesis, Howard University, Washington, DC.

Elmore, R. (1996). Getting to scale with good educational practice. *Harvard Educational Review, 66,* 1–26.

Everhart, R. (1983). *Reading, writing and resistance.* Boston: Routledge & Kegan Paul.

Fine, M. (1994). Charter(ing) urban school reform. In R. Rossi (Ed.), *Schools and students at risk: Context and framework for positive change.* New York: Teachers College Press. 163–181.

Fordham, S., & Ogbu, J. (1986). Black students' school success: Coping with the burden of "acting white." *Urban Review, 18,* 176-206.

Gay, G. (1988). Designing relevant curricula for diverse learners. *Education and Urban Society 20,* 322-340.

Gilmore, P. (1985). "Gimme room": School resistance, attitude and access to literacy. *Journal of Education, 167,* 111-128.

Giroux, H. ,& McLaren, P. (1986). Teacher education and the politics of engagement: The case for democratic schooling. *Harvard Educational Review, 56,* 213-238.

Goodman, J. (1995). Change without difference: School restructuring in historical perspective. *Harvard Educational Review, 65,* 1-29.

Gordon, B. (1994). African American cultural knowledge and liberatory education: Dilemmas, problems and potentials in postmodern American society. In M. Shujaa (Ed.), *Too much schooling, too little education.* Trenton, NJ: Africa World Press.

Gordon, B. (1997). Curriculum, policy, and African American cultural knowledge: Challenges and possibilities for the year 2000 and beyond. *Educational Policy, 11,* 227-242.

Gordon, E. (1995). Culture and the sciences of pedagogy. *Teachers College Record, 97,* 32-46.

Greeno, J. (1989). A perspective on thinking. *American Psychologist, 44,* 134-141.

Greeno, J., & the Middle School Mathematics through Applications Project Group. (1997). Theories and practices of thinking and learning to think. *American Journal of Education, 106,* 85-126.

Hilliard, A. (1995). *The Maroon within Us.* Baltimore: Black Classic Press.

Howard, A., & Scott, R. (1981). The study of minority groups in complex societies. In R. Munroe & B. Whiting (Eds.), *Handbook of cross cultural human development.* New York: Garland.

Hunt, J. McV. (1965). Intrinsic motivation and its role in psychological development. In D. Levine (Ed.), *Nebraska symposium on motivation.* Lincoln: University of Nebraska Press. 189-282.

John-Steiner, V., & Mahn, H. (1996). Sociocultural approaches to learning and development: A Vygotskian framework. *Educational Psychologist, 31,* 191-206.

Karier, C. (Ed.). (1975). *Shaping the American educational state: 1900 to the present.* New York: Free Press.

Kearns, D., & Doyle, D. (1991). *Winning the brain race: A bold plan to make our schools competitive.* San Francisco: ICS Press.

King, J. (1994). The purpose of schooling for African American children: Including cultural knowledge. In E. Hollins, J. King, & W. Hayman (Eds.), *Teaching diverse populations: Formulating a knowledge base.* Albany: State University of New York Press.

Ladson-Billings, G. (1994). *The dreamkeepers.* San Francisco: Jossey-Bass.

Lave, J. (1996). Teaching, as learning, in practice. *Mind, Culture and Activity, 3,* 149-164.

Lee, C. (1994). African-centered pedagogy: Complexities and possibilities. In M. Shujaa (Ed.), *Too much schooling, too little education.* Trenton, NJ: Africa World Press. 295-318.

Lukes, S. (1973). *Individualism.* New York: Harper.

Marryshow, D. (1995). *Perception of future economic success and the impact of learning orientation on African American students' attitudes toward high achievers.* Doctoral dissertation, Howard University, Washington, DC.

Martin, S. (1994). *Children's attitudes and their parents' and peers' perceived attitudes toward culturally diverse high achievers.* Master's thesis, Howard University, Washington, DC.

Martin, S. (1997). *Students' attitudes toward four distinct learning orientations and classroom environments.* Doctoral dissertation, Howard University, Washington, DC.

Miller, O. (1997). *Cultural influences on the classroom perceptions of African American grade school children.* Master's thesis, Howard University, Washington, DC.

Mungai, M. (1997). *Story-listening and off-task context effects on both the performance and motivation of African American and European American children.* Doctoral dissertation, Howard University, Washington, DC.

Nieto, S. (1993). *Affirming diversity: The sociopolitical context of multicultural education.* New York: Longman.

Ogbu, J. (1994). From cultural frames to differences in cultural frame of reference. In P. Greenfield & R. Cocking (Eds.), *Cross-cultural roots of minority child development.* Hillsdale, NJ: Lawrence Erlbaum Associates. 365–392.

Persell, C. (1977). *Education and inequality: A theoretical and empirical synthesis.* New York: Free Press.

Piestrup, A. (1973). *Black dialect interference and accommodation of reading instruction in first grade* (Monograph No. 4). Berkeley: University of California, Language Behavior Research Laboratory.

Plank, D., Scotch, R., & Gamble, J. (1996). Rethinking progressive school reform: Organizational dynamics and educational change, *American Journal of Education, 104,* 79–104.

Raffini, J. (1995). *150 ways to increase intrinsic motivation in the classroom.* Boston: Allyn & Bacon.

Rogoff, B. (1990). *Apprenticeship in thinking: Cognitive development in social context.* New York: Oxford University Press.

Rogoff, B., & Chavajay, P. (1995). What's become of research on the cultural basis of cognitive development? *American Psychologist, 50,* 859–877.

Sapon-Shevin, M., & Schniedewind, N. (1991). Cooperative learning as empowering pedagogy. In C. Sleeter (Ed.), *Empowerment through multicultural education.* Albany: SUNY Albany Press.

Shujaa, M. (Ed.). (1994). *Too much schooling, too little education.* Trenton, NJ: Africa World Press.

Spence, J. (1985). Achievement American style: The rewards and costs of individualism. *American Psychologist, 40,* 1285–1295.

Spring, J. (1994). *The American school: 1642–1993* (3rd ed.). New York: McGraw-Hill.

Tedla, E. (1995). *Sankofa: African thought and education.* New York: Lang.

Tharp, R., & Gallimore, R. (1988). *Rousing minds to life.* New York: Cambridge University Press.

Tuck, K., & Boykin, A. W. (1989). Task performance and receptiveness to variability in black and white low-income children. In A. Harrison (Ed.), *The eleventh conference on empirical research in black psychology.* Washington, DC: NIMH Publications.

Tyack, D. (1974). *The one best system.* Cambridge, MA: Harvard University Press.

Walton, S. (1994). *The influence of task variability and background stimulation on the task performance of low-income African American children.* Master's thesis, Howard University, Washington, DC.

Walton, S. (1998). *Verve effects: The influence of cultural attributes and two-dimensional physical stimulation on the task performance of African American and European American schoolchildren.* Doctoral dissertation, Howard University, Washington, DC.

Walton, T. (1993). *Teachers' attitudes toward black students who display differing cultural orientations.* Master's thesis, Howard University, Washington, DC.

Wilson, S., & Peterson, P. (1997). *Theories of learning and teaching: What do they mean for educators?* (Blue Ribbon Schools Working Paper). Washington, DC: U.S. Department of Education.

Woodson, C. (1933). *The miseducation of the Negro.* Washington, DC: Associated Publishers.

— 8 —

"Island by Island We Must Go Across": Challenges from Language and Culture among African Americans

Shirley Brice Heath

In 1987, the poet William Meredith wrote a curious set of five verses under the title "Do not embrace your mind's new Negro friend." He urges "atonement first" for those who claim new friendship and are convinced in their minds that they have the "right story" about the history of "Jews or Negroes or some dark thing." Though deceptively simple on the surface, the poem savagely pierces abundant late twentieth-century liberal claims of having no prejudice or having "on good authority" understandings about what is right and good for others. Meredith condemns patronizing claims of brotherhood and urges intense self-examination of motives as well as relentless recovery of stories not told and connections never acknowledged. He calls such a program of self-scrutiny and search for new lessons a "friendless struggle" that will be long, laborious, and painful, but "island by island we must go across."

This chapter represents a small beginning of such crossings. The traveler-as-author here acknowledges a position that carries the label of "outsider." However, even for those who carry the identity of "insider" in studies or approaches they see as centered with an ethnic, national, or racial label, thinking along the lines of Meredith's caution is worthwhile. Examination of motives and degrees of thoroughness in determining stories and not merely the "right story" helps ensure for any ethnic-centered work that it does not fall into patterns of ethnocentrism that have so long marked Eurocentric research and policy.

The broad ranges of music, literature, and religious and political oratory produced by descendants of those who came from Africa have been noted for their influence and creativity throughout American history. Yet the language uses and structures that constitute these cultural forms have been studied and described in selective and insular ways. This chapter urges every educator, and especially those working with African American children, to learn more about the broadly diverse history and evolution of language from throughout the history of Africans in the United States. Moreover, it asks readers to examine motives and consider unintended consequences of claims voiced under pressures of contemporary policy demands and without solid grounding in research.

A further plea here is that late twentieth-century calls for Afrocentric education and acknowledgment of Ebonics lead to deep exploration and abundant illustration of the immense range of variation—regional, historical, and social—within the oral and written language uses of African Americans. This chapter suggests what broadly engaged scholarship on the linguistic, and particularly the literary, accomplishments of African Americans might bring to education, in particular. Exposed here are some of the ways in which studies and promotions of African American life and language have reinforced stereotypes and perpetuated negatives and falsehoods. Some of what has been done—even in the name of Afrocentrism—has been far from centered or balanced in substance and has instead perpetuated notions of African American expressive forms as marginal, dysfunctional, and exotic.

My own position in this chapter is that of long familiarity with black classrooms from the days of segregated schools in the South to current efforts to create Afrocentric schools or African American curricula. From beginnings in Virginia and North Carolina as a rural child with intermittent time in black schools to South Carolina's Penn Center and Mississippi's new freedom schools in the civil rights era, I have maintained involvement. I have played various roles—from visiting teacher to professional development resource to occasional adviser—in a variety of schools for African American students. In the early 1970s as a teacher educator in South Carolina, I guided development of a kit on children's language that was placed in all elementary schools of the state. Grammatical and discourse descriptions, games, and tests covered fundamental knowledge about language as well as specifics on varieties of African American Vernacular English spoken in the state as well as Southern Appalachian and coastal dialects used primarily by whites. Goals of these materials included enabling teachers and students to understand how all speakers play with a range of registers, styles, and dialects to meet their social and instrumental needs. Involving students as early as possible in open exploration of these needs and language resources will enhance reading, writing, and inquiry mode. Children in the early primary grades can carry out rudimentary sociolinguistic analyses and reflect on their own range of uses. In so doing, they develop a grounded feeling for how and when shifts to other portions of their linguistic repertoire may be more appropriate as well as more instrumentally effective (for an example of early primary teachers' work of this type, see Part II of Heath, 1983).

Within the fields of teaching and learning, language forms identified with African Americans have too often been so reduced as to create a sense of limits rather than expanses of narrow marginality and not broad claim to centers. This charge applies particularly to discourse in education and to literary expression, as well as to overdrawn claims about necessary links between particular ways of speaking and matters of identity, adaptation, and choice on the part of African American students. Language varieties along a spectrum termed (dialects of) Black English or African American

Vernacular English carry direct communicational strength and symbolic power. However, any claim that formal learning can and should take place either only or primarily through these varieties shortchanges students' capacities. Such views overlook not only commonsense observations about the ubiquity of numerous varieties of English that every young American hears daily but also basic scientific understandings of the cognitive and linguistic competencies of any neurologically sound speaker. The fundamental issue comes down to respect and knowledge; a primary underpinning of formal education within the United States rests in faith that with knowledge comes respect and understanding. But this process has been painfully slow with regard to African American expressive forms in language and culture. In spite of extensive research, especially since the 1960s, essential linguistic, social, and historical facts have entered neither public understanding nor relevant fields, such as teacher preparation or legal education. Saturation of the media and all levels of education with accurate information needs to continue unremittingly. Public reaction to the Ebonics Resolution of the Oakland, California, School Board revealed just how difficult it is to insert fundamental research findings into debates shaped by abiding racism and refusal to learn that which might dislodge long-held belief systems.[1]

Perhaps most difficult to replace are essentialist positions that assume contiguity of race, language, and culture among African Americans.[2] This position holds dearly to notions of predeterminism or universalism in the direction and nature of lifeways and values of African Americans. Difference and divergence mark the history of Africa as well as Africans in the Americas, but public perception still encircles "blackness" within the fence of homogeneity.[3] Yet any rational examination must acknowledge the range of choice, direction, and purpose that marks individuals, institutions, and belief systems that bear any label denoting African origin.

The same diversity characterizes language structures and uses currently even among groups that may describe themselves as "Afrocentric." From Nation of Islam schools to rural historically vocational campuses dedicated to the schooling of black students, different degrees of exclusivity, attention to religious creed, and projections of future national or Pan African identities enlist different languages (e.g., Arabic, Swahili, Xhosa, English) and their forms and uses. There is no agreed-upon center to Afrocentrism or to the language forms that give its accounts.

The absence of a center speaks to the dynamism of convergences, multiple directions, and selective representation that surrounds the dilemma of what can appropriately be called "African American language and culture." Some of this dynamism depends on historically based connections, others on identity-building visits by individuals to parts of today's Africa, and still others on at-home socially constructed rituals of identity and community. Such shifting patterns of convergence and divergence defy the larger society's penchant for creating and maintaining simplistic, fixed, and artificial categories of distance. Highly selected pushes and pulls that originate within communities of African Americans pose special challenges for those trying to sort out just how language and its related habits and beliefs might fit into formal education. They must untangle the numerous fluctuations in categories of distance that resist accurate portrayals and hard evidence about African American speakers and writers across history. They have to uncover predispositions of spokespersons for African American education that unwittingly endorse Anglo-Saxon or heavily assimilationist presuppositions. Moreover, they have to reveal the ways that current favored choices in literature tend to emphasize damage and victimization. Finally, the complex matter of African American Englishes merits considerable attention.

CATEGORIES OF DISTANCE

It is easy to slip into general statements that equate Africa as continent and source of populations in the United States with nation–states as originating homelands. This slippage has led to easy and often unexplicated generalizations about what is "African" within the African American heritage. This obliteration came first in the Middle Passage, subsequently through slavery in the New World, and finally, through persistent Eurocentric socialization. Lost were the vast differences then and now among regions, tribes, and nations on the African continent. The resulting vacuum in knowledge has no doubt contributed to the persistent lumping of all African Americans as the same in language and culture regardless of region or class (for further discussion of this point, see Mukhopadhyay & Moses, 1997).

Slaves brought to the United States did not come with equal representation from all parts of the continent of Africa. Early scholars such as Melville Herskovitz and Lorenzo Dow Turner made clear the linkage of certain New World traits to particular groups in Africa. The bulk of the slave trade took place in West Africa in areas where slave trading had been established as an integral part of local economic and social structures and as a consequence of conquest. Sharp social divisions, as well as distinct patterns for criticism of leaders, contributed to highly developed forms of "psychological release" through verbal and other art forms within native cultures (Levine, 1977). Europeans through the slave trade greatly and inhumanly escalated the pain, suffering, and death that came with slavery and the shutting down of forms of release and connection. Europeans, both in passage to America and the Caribbean and within distribution of slaves to landholders, generally worked to avoid keeping speakers of the same languages together. They reasoned that if workers on the same plantation came from different language groups, they would be unable to communicate with one another well enough to plot insurrection. Occasionally, however, slave traders kept some groups together, believing them more peaceful and not wanting to risk other more rebellious groups stirring up rebellion or putting in place a pattern of suicide. Nevertheless, the dominant strategies of Europeans worked to stratify and divide slaves, tearing apart West African patterns of social organization.

Throughout the early centuries of U.S. history, enslaved Africans adopted the primary language of the dominant society around them, albeit generally with severe limits on reading and writing. They also adapted its forms and uses to the social needs of their communities. Far better remembered from Africa than intricate grammatical structures or full lexicons were traditions, early socialization habits, and rites of passage and intensification. Thus, naming ceremonies, types of scarification, and rituals associated with birth, death, release, and protection from potential harm by spirits from the unknown world remained long after individuals lost full control of the grammars of the languages of their West African homelands. In those cases in which blacks were severely isolated from others, such as the coastal islands of South Carolina and Georgia, their language variety diverged considerably from others used elsewhere. Gullah, also known as Geechee or Sea Island Creole, is still spoken primarily along the South Carolina coastal islands. Louisiana Creole, also known as Gombo or Negro French, emerged as the language of descendants of slaves brought to southern Louisiana by French colonists, primarily from what is now known as Senegal. Literary artists such as Ambrose Gonzales (1969) and Julia Peterkin (1970) have kept Gullah known to scholars of African American literature, but only a few folktales said to include Gombo survive.[4]

From almost the earliest days of slavery, certain individuals, by dent of particular talents or incidents of chance, won their freedom and slipped away to Canada or to locations in which they existed much more closely with Europeans than did the enslaved majority. These individuals took up the habits of language acquisition that had been well established in West Africa: learning multiple languages whether a trade language such as Bambara and another lingua franca or the language of their neighbors and their employers and coworkers. Thus we have early accounts of bilingual and multilingual Africans in the New World who added French, English, and languages of Native Americans to their rich linguistic repertoire brought from West Africa.

By the early decades of the nineteenth century, thousands of blacks made their way to the northern cities of New York, Philadelphia, Boston, Baltimore, and Washington, D.C., where their free status enabled them to enter a wide range of trades. By 1840, free blacks in cities such as Philadelphia represented nearly 20 percent of the population. William Lloyd Garrison and other leaders of the Abolition movement centered their work among these free blacks and depended on their adeptness in speaking and reading English in a range of registers and genres. The early charters and constitutions of organizations they formed give ample evidence of their high levels of self-education and commitment to community education through the establishment of schools, libraries, literary societies, and newspapers.[5]

The range of variation—regional, institutional, and social—included both oral and written language uses. Yet subsequent versions of "Negro language," Black English, or African American Vernacular English have collapsed these differences and given heavy emphasis to only highly selective "oral" forms—typically those of ritual celebration and often for humorous purposes. Terms such as *oral culture*, *orality*, and *storytellers* appear far more frequently in descriptions of habit of African Americans than *literate behaviors*, *literary*, or *analyst*. Simple folktales (ironically most often as rendered through the words of the white storyteller Joel Chandler Harris) appear in children's reading texts far more frequently than selections from the numerous newspapers, literary journals, diaries, and fictional writings of nineteenth-century African Americans. Brief biographies of orators overlook figures such as Maria Stewart, a black woman who was the first person to address a mixed audience in

American history. Social studies textbooks, when they include primary sources from the past century, rarely portray writings of Ida B. Wells-Barnett and her fellow journalists; accounts of the history of the feminist movement and its close association with women's clubs rarely take note of those clubs led by black women, such as Mary Church Terrell. Particularly notable in their absence from social studies materials are representations of the combined work of black and white women through clubs, publications, and behind-the-scenes political maneuvering. Since the 1980s, numerous collections make available this work in inexpensive and easily accessible form (see, for example, Sterling, 1984; Washington, 1987). Although omission of these key figures characterizes publications written or edited by whites, they receive inadequate attention also in reputedly Afrocentric materials developed for use in secondary schools and in biographies selected as supplementary reading in many elementary schools. In particular, much of this material is biased toward selection of black males—particularly those who as individuals rose from humble beginnings to political and oratorical prominence.

These misrepresentations come along with the prevailing portrayal of African Americans as a group within the seemingly unproblematic division of populations along categorical lines—on the "natural" separation of "races." More recently, social scientists and humanists alike have come to demonstrate the social construction of race, culture, and language and to show how volition, chance, and inequities of access shape individuals and their networks. This work struggles to dislodge premises of cultural entities fixed by either assigned or assumed racial membership and urges rethinking of theories of difference, resistance, and accommodation.

For example, recent work illustrates how representations of the world of individual African Americans as "typical" or symbolic of universal patterns issue directly from either the European and Anglo-Saxon ethos of full-and-free-choice individualism or the tendency to emphasize disempowerment by making overarching claims of group victimization. By the end of the twentieth century, considerable press coverage had gone to images of the "damaged black psyche" and what it has meant for blacks and nonblacks (Scott, 1997). Claims around this concept emphasize a widespread sense of failure among blacks, particularly males, that leads in turn to further incapacity to achieve (see Anderson, 1990, especially chapters 4–7, for ethnographic detail related to this concept). Moreover, contemporary ideas about effects of the "damaged black psyche" relate intimately to long-standing debates among blacks over "uplift ideology." One understanding of uplift speaks to group struggle and carries strong religious ties. A contesting view reflects the push for social mobility, emphasizing self-help, hard work, and class differentiation as signs of "race progress" (Gaines, 1996). Both extremes overclaim, point fingers, and label to publicize their view. Those who promote uplifting the race through celebrating the ideal as high achieving individuals point to low achieving blacks as "making the race look bad." This stance links closely to ideas espoused by those currently labeled as "black conservatives" who argue that many blacks appear to cultivate pity and contempt from nonblacks and to want individual benefits from government handouts and affirmative action as retribution for past group injustices. Such contestations set assimilationist values that favor individualism, competition, and social Darwinism against certain distinctive central values promoted by some institutions characterized as "African American." Prominent among these have been group cohesion for survival, strong-willed faith and optimism, as well as collaborative adaptive strategy-building for seeing through and beyond oppression. Religious groups and certain popular cultural forms have built a strong ethos around these values of cooperation and unity, often in terms that set up an oppositional force against the climate of competition among individuals.

Racism in the unique forms it has taken in the United States is, of course, the major distancing force between blacks and whites. However, the unsatisfyingly broad term of *racism* diverts attention from categorical divisions created and extended within some overtly benign and enlightened moves said to "celebrate" that which is African American. Delineated above have been some of the inaccuracies as well as inadequacies generated by broad terms such as *African, slave, oral,* and *leader* as well as by attribution of only a single trait of greatness to African Americans selected for attention. To be sure, these tendencies mark and mar the history of other groups as well. But for those who would push an Afrocentric perspective, care and concern for accuracy, representation, and context must accompany a desire to reflect not merely individual cases but trends and patterns of group affiliations, many of which have crossed class as well as racial divides.

THE SUBTLE FORCE OF ANGLO-SAXON VALUES

Evident in many Afrocentric materials is celebration of individual achievement, often within metaphors of conquering, overcoming, or overpowering the opposition. Heavy valuation of such individual success lies at the core of Anglo-Saxon and northern European value systems, whereas the normative system surrounding both metaphors and measures of achievement differs greatly throughout West Africa and in the history of adaptations under slavery.

For example, such a basic difference appears between fairytales of northern Europe and folktales of Africa. Here is a case in which comparison provides deep insights into cultural differences. In the former, conflicts occur between individuals (often representing larger forces, such as good or evil, to be sure); resolution comes in many of these fairytales through forcefully subjugating or killing off the enemy. Characters such as the jealous queen of "Sleeping Beauty," the wicked stepmother and stepsisters of "Cinderella," and the child victim of "The Red Shoes" receive such punishments. Authentic West African folktales, on the other hand, are dominated by wily animals who mete out hard moral lessons or manipulate temporary downfalls that result from greed, selfishness, or excessive pride. Similarly, in West African societies, criticism of one's leaders, opponents, or competitors historically came through verbal challenge and not physical harm (see Levine, 1977, especially chapters I and II). In West Africa as well as in early institutional developments under slavery, blacks focused in many ways (though certainly not exclusively) on collaboration and cooperation in groups to promote and reinforce communal values; excessive promotion of single individuals and their achievements surfaced frequently as sinful in black church sermons. The recently frequently quoted "It takes a village to raise a child" reflects (albeit simplistically) this reliance on distributing roles and functions of such important social group needs as child rearing across more than either an individual or even a narrow nuclear unit.

All of these claims to the presence of certain group behaviors should not be interpreted as ruling out the power of individual leadership and achievement. Yet black history in schools and public celebrations of achievement tends to highlight individuals rather than groups or institutions. The power of churches and associated religious groups to promote reading, writing, debate, and artistry and to encourage the rise of leadership by women and men is well documented in archival collections in Boston, New York, Philadelphia, Richmond, Washington, and elsewhere. Numerous biographies and autobiographical accounts attest to strong networks of free blacks who built community resources for educational pursuits by those without sufficient access to formal institutions. The Schomburg collection being republished through the editorial leadership of Henry Louis Gates is bringing back into circulation many of the longer texts written in the contexts of black institutions. In the collection *Early Negro Writing: 1760-1837* (Porter, 1995), most of the entries derived from organizations—constitutions, charters, addresses, letters, orations, and memoirs. This range of genres in which blacks represented themselves almost never enters social studies textbooks or appears in parallel with celebrations of individual blacks. Although the crushing weight of slavery on individuals and families continued for the vast majority of blacks through most of the nineteenth century, the organizational power of free blacks allowed them to create institutional texts, to form organizations and alliances to reshape history, and to prepare to enter the legal and political arenas after the Civil War. These groups merit attention and celebration as much as individual achievers, and the history of oratory as well as of varieties of written genres that go beyond spirituals, work songs, and sermons need to be represented in African American literature of the nineteenth century.

Throughout the nineteenth century, black newspapers and political and literary magazines run by black editors worked as highly effective institutional forces on legal and political matters. In the first decades of the century, black journalists were involved primarily in abolitionism, and journals such as *Freedom's Journal*, published in 1827 in New York City, as well as the much better known *Colored American Magazine* (1837-1841) and *Douglass' Monthly* (1858-1861) established themselves in a tradition of protest. This establishment of the press as an instrument of expression and demonstration of freedom diminished only near the second half of the twentieth century.

Perhaps surprisingly, the continuity of strength of black literary journals sometimes could surpass that of newspapers. From the *Anglo-African Magazine* (1859-1862) through current periodicals that focus on literary contributions of African Americans, these journals have included not only fiction and poetry but also scholarly articles, occasional sketches of paintings, and reviews of gallery shows and musical contributions by African Americans. Many of the names most familiar today to those who study African American literature began in association with one or another of these literary journals—either as staff member or as occasional contributor. Names such as Frederick Douglass, George Vashon, Frances Ellen Watkins Harper, William Wells Brown, and Martin Delany appear in journals well before the literary journals that came to be so strongly linked with the Harlem Renaissance. From Northern cities and often with regional circulation or in association with historically black colleges, such as Howard University, came magazines such as *Stylus*, *Opportunity*, *Crisis*, and *Challenge*—precursors to those that survive today, such as *Phylon*.

But such information rarely reaches public school classrooms of social studies or English—even in units devoted to African American content. Study of individuals and their roles in history predominates over attention to groups or social movements—particularly when these were not associated with a political party. Hence, much of the work of African Americans, who throughout U.S. history have made many of their contributions through group formations, has been neglected. The strong women's club movement of African Americans that grew after the Civil War offers a good example of a critically important contribution overlooked in favor of individual African Americans—particularly males such as Booker T. Washington and W.E.B. Du Bois. Moreover, representations that favor individual achievement of blacks often freeze those whose stories they recount within particular points of time, grand narratives, or fixed worldviews. In addition, a single point of shift (from slave to free, the escape, or the rebellion) is far more frequently recounted in American history than trajectories of change and movement in political and social power in the larger community. For example, Frederick Douglas's story of escape from slavery is much more frequently told than that of his rise to membership in an elite class of Washington, D.C., blacks. Tales of contemporary African Americans generally place them in categories of generalized "service to their people" rather than in specific roles linked to national and international organizations of politics, diplomacy, and commerce.

Even in recent attempts to revise portions of American history to include African Americans, the search for star individuals continues. For example, the history of the American West is now being rewritten to include blacks who were among the explorers, early claimants to landholdings, and frontier men and women. But these come across as individual adventurers who can match the mold of their white counterparts or stand out as singular leaders. For many students, the Underground Railroad too often gets reduced to Harriet Tubman.

Such selective treatment of individuals covers up important knowledge about language uses among African Americans. The Underground Railroad resulted not from the efforts of a single individual but from strategizing and communicational networks from South to North. These depended on stealth, multiple coding of messages, and an array of means of transmitting caches of information linked to geography and seasonal changes that determined just when swamps and rivers were safe to traverse. Many of these efforts succeeded in large part through knowledge gained surreptitiously by house slaves, exposed to intensive and direct oral communication with whites, as well as indirect (and occasionally direct) access to literacy.

The Reconstruction Era and the rise to political prominence of black leaders, a good number of whom were in interracial marriages, brought "aristocrats of color" (Gatewood, 1990) and their habits and values into the halls, chambers, theaters, and pulpits of the nation's capital. Congressional records indicate that the debates of legislative members who were black soared with eloquence: classical references, powerful rhetorical moves, and strong argumentative force—all in variants of regional Standard English indistinguishable from that of their white counterparts. Collections of sermons, drama scripts, and club and society records, as well as legal documents, illustrate amply the extent to which individuals and entire communities in cities such as Philadelphia and Washington, D.C., controlled language forms and uses in a full repertoire from the most formal of the courtroom to the informal of the sitting room chat. Clubs and social groups that operated out of homes, such as that of Georgia Brown in Washington, D.C., studied writings across genres and spawned similar reading groups. Near the end of the nineteenth century, more than 900 Paul Lawrence Dunbar Societies dotted the nation. The extent of continuity from families involved across generations in government and society in cities such as Washington and Philadelphia has come increasingly to be documented in autobiographical accounts (e.g., Haizlip, 1994).

During the early decades of the twentieth century, divergent views over the future course for African Americans came to the fore in the rivalry between W.E.B. Du Bois and Booker T. Washington. They and many of the most elite and powerful of blacks claimed to want more and better educational opportunities for all blacks, while at the same time they debated both the role of concentrated looks back to Africa and possibilities of wider access to a variety of occupations within the United States. Du Bois demanded the right of black men to citizenship and all forms of higher education; industrial education would hold blacks back from the intellectual life to which they could aspire. True freedom had to come, in Du Bois's view, from enlightened knowledge. Political, economic, and moral leadership depended on such breadth and depth of understanding.

Washington promoted education in industrial training programs, maintaining a strict adherence to social discipline and high moral standards and hoping for development of an African American teaching corps. From Tuskegee to Hampton Institute, from 1860 to 1935, Washington promoted educational and economic opportunities that survived political and social oppression. These institutions derived from and sustained a sense of "service" among blacks and questioned little the occupational niches tied to white institutions that resulted for graduates. Many religious organizations led by blacks further promoted the role of service as well as the development of reading and conversation clubs, along with benevolent societies and charity organizations—all of which depended on a range of discursive practices. Private boarding schools and community settlement schools that fostered communities of learning for and by blacks intensified commitment to education and practice in formal discourses—oral and written (see, for example, various accounts in the first decade of the twentieth century in Hampton Institute's publication *The Southern Workman*). Some of these schools, such as the Calhoun Colored School in Alabama, remain today.

Recent research indicates both the attitudinal frame and language used by teachers in historically black schools (Foster, 1997). Clear from this research as well as from arguments put forward by numerous educators concerned about standards of expectation for black children since integration is the fact that expectations mean everything. Historically, teachers in segregated black schools knew not only their children but most of their relatives, and social control and promotion of self-discipline for children drew on a host of supporters. Moreover, black teachers strongly promoted achievement not to set the individual student apart from his or her neighbor or fellow student but to reflect and represent group, family, and race.

With integration, direct connections between schools and family and neighborhood became increasingly difficult to maintain. Teachers rarely lived in neighborhoods of schools in which they taught; social interactions between teachers and students' families and other key institutions, such as the church, became the exception and not the rule. As more and more parents worked outside the household, and the nonschool hours of young people fell to their discretion, peer socialization played an increasingly forceful role. The unity between black teachers and their students in a quest for learning that characterized many segregated schools became much more difficult to achieve.

SELECTIVITY OF WHAT IS "AFRICAN"

The failure to examine presuppositions and what may be out-of-awareness oversights can also extend to endorsements of what is "African." In addition, pressures to exclude moral and religious teachings from public education preclude adequate and accurate coverage. For example, the history of Islam within the United States and its influence on the rise of African presence within American culture during and following the civil rights era rarely enters the curricula of public Afrocentric schools. Yet this history had far-reaching influence on much that is identified as African American within the larger culture, from personal naming practices to celebrations of rites of intensification.

But the language issue goes much deeper and receives relatively little attention. Neither language nor creeds of belief and behavior linked to Islam can claim Africa as spatial origin. Ancient Middle Eastern history has to be considered, along with the history of Islam within the African continent and in the influence of Islamic Africa in the world. Arabic names, formal Standard Arabic, naming practices, and particular discourse forms sit firmly within a religious history and not a purely geographical source (Turner, 1997). Moreover, many attitudes and restrictions imposed by Islamic law differ in fundamental features, if not purpose, from those documented for West African societies—considered recent adoptees of the faith in the long history of Islam. The self-discipline, as well as assertive self-esteem, that marks members of the Nation of Islam urges resistance against moral decline and loss of the sense of identity, family, and history seen as critical to sustaining individual and group within any larger society. Islamic reliance on the law and ancient hierarchical authority structures also differs from organizational forms that characterized West African political systems historically.

Though less integrative, extensive, and tradition-based than Islam's embrace of discipline, pride, and togetherness, the Kwanzaa movement carries some parallels (Karenga, 1977). Highly selective about components it chooses to emphasize, this movement uses terms from Xhosa, a major language in South Africa. Many of the early devotees of Kwanzaa studied Swahili, the lingua franca adopted from a trade language in eastern Africa and the current national language of several East African nations, most notably Tanzania. Important to note here is that this movement puzzles many Africans who see little connection between Kwanzaa practices and any African origins—either religious or cultural. And neither Xhosa nor Swahili would have been among the tongues brought to American shores by slaves from Africa. The use of these languages, as well as cultural practices associated with selected terms, has been a deliberate American choice for purposes of pride, group cohesion, and linkage to newly redefined and intensified values that late twentieth-century African Americans have selected for vitalization. The seven principles of Kwanzaa (unity, self-determination, collective work and responsibility, cooperative economics, creativity, purpose, and faith), resonate strongly with Mao's ideas and also represent the basis of Tanzania's Arusha Declaration in 1964 under President Julius Nyerere who gave many a strong hope for indigenous socialism in Africa. Revisionist histories make evident Kwanzaa's social construction through a convergence of key issues in the 1960s, that are not of the same historical derivation as other long-attested ceremonies, values, and language choices that derive from West Africa.

LITERARY DISTRACTIONS

Literature by and about African Americans merits similar accountability and sensitivity to that urged here for historical, social science, and linguistic representations. The period after the 1980s, when representations of works by African American writers increasingly found their way into K–12 reading and literature classes, stirred not only improved scholarly work but also creative output from contemporary literary artists. This work has only slowly found its way into teachers' manuals or in-service workshops and courses in English teacher education programs. Hence, much of the selection as well as the teaching of African American literature provides only a weak—and often distorted—version of both African American life and the artistic genius of its writers.

For example, choices of nonfiction about African Americans run to works that center on individual success, often through overcoming dissolution within families and communities. Literary autobiographical works, as well as biographies of contemporary heroes, particularly in sports, also promote individual achievements in organizations directed and financed primarily by whites. Rarely do the voices of such individuals speak of values, habits, and beliefs in their lives and communities except to relate these to their individual life course. Almost invariably, the brief biographies written for adolescent readers that narrate the lives of musicians, such as Duke Ellington, neglect their full range of virtuosity, particularly their classical work, and reduce their contributions to only that portion perceived as African American.

These portrayals, generally written with positive intentions, unwittingly support the view that African Americans speak, compose, and perform within only jazz, blues, or gospel traditions.

Missing from school rooms are strong accounts of sustained cohesion and strength across families and various types of memberships within a host of professions, such as teaching, practicing law, or participating in politics or religion. Whereas several decades ago, a legitimate complaint would have been that such works were not available, this is not so in the final decade of the century. For young readers, the *Young Oxford History of African Americans* (Grossman, 1997) in 11 volumes removes this complaint in its emphasis on complexity and difference, collective activity and institutions, and inclusion of groups and types of achievement generally neglected in one-volume works for children and youth. Moreover, adult readers now have numerous choices of biographies that speak to the range and depth of accomplishments of black individuals and, to a lesser extent, of groups. A sampling of such works on African American women might include biographies or accounts of Ida B. Wells (e.g., DeCosta-Willis, 1994; Thompson, 1990) or autobiographies of women in their selected group affiliations (e.g., Andrews, 1986). Contemporary accounts of black professionals serve as essential evidence to students of the extent and variation of career choices blacks have made and how they have found affiliates in their decisions (e.g., Lawrence-Lightfoot, 1988, 1994; see also Streitmatter, 1994, on women journalists). These works illustrate the initiative and creativity of black Americans in educational and business pursuits. Fewer works tell the story of powerful institutional forces, such as the periodical press, religious denominations, and art galleries (for exceptions, see Bullock, 1981, and the Studio Museum in Harlem, 1987/1994).

Until the final decade of the twentieth century, we had few accounts that offered depth on variety or variation among those labeled *slave*, *Negro*, *black*, or *African American*; those termed *mulatto*, *half-breed*, *octoroon*, or *mixed race*; or even those intermittently given classifications as *white*, *native*, *foreigner*, or *immigrant* across American history. It has been so taken for granted that each individual embodies *the* sociocultural history and life ways of any and all members of these groups that terms related to race and culture become routine in phrases such as "African American music, autobiography, literature, etc." Thus just as jazz, blues, and rap get so essentially identified, so do certain types of literary works, such as slave narratives.

Failure in male-female interactions receives much more attention in selections of African music than do musical renderings of commitment to family, work, or tough ethical choices. The story of Harriet Tubman is far more frequently told than that of Francis Harper, Ida B. Wells-Barnett, or Martin Delaney. Preferred works within broad genres of literature, such as novels, become those telling of deceit, illicit sexual desire, and individual escapes. These are often horror-hero stories—tales of horrible circumstances from which a hero emerges. Toni Morrison's *The Bluest Eye*, a frequent selection in secondary English classrooms, represents such an account. Though no one can deny the literary value of this novel, it is nevertheless a tale of interracial desire that can, in insensitive and uninformed classrooms, essentialize blacks as passive, powerless, and if initially resistant, then either compliant or defeated in the end.

Moreover, such choices often implicitly suggest that "blame" in such encounters rests with females. The range of writings by even a single writer, such as Paula Marshall, is often ignored in favor of selections that continue particular themes linked to exploitation toward and within black households and the dangerous ambiguities that result from differential acceptance in the wider society of black women over black men. From the more frequent choice of *Brown Stone Girls* by Marshall to the celebration of Terry MacMillan's *Waiting to Exhale*, the most common fictional works to end up on African American literature reading lists are those that demonstrate wedges—sexual, economic, and regional—among African Americans.

Such assumed isomorphism of race, culture, language, and class results in significant problems, not the least of which is reinforced stereotypes and legitimations of discrimination and prejudice. First, there is the issue of those who inhabit the "narrow strip along steep edges" (Anzaldua, 1987, 3), those who have chosen ways of remaining within their communities and claiming various forms of influence there rather than exiting from their neighborhoods to merge with other escapees from "the past." There is also the issue of those who have moved on elsewhere and chosen to pass as something other than that which their home communities saw them to be. Although this issue as treated in Zora Neale Hurston's classic *Their Eyes Were Watching God* receives some attention, other works that address this point, especially in relation to interracial marriage, enter classrooms far more rarely. Nella Larsen's *Quicksand* and *Passing*, as well as Jean Toomer's *Cane*, are read by African American secondary school students with far less regularity than stories that do not treat the highly complex and politically charged matters of racial mixing, crossing class and racial lines, or regional differences in tolerance or religious fervor. Caribbean literature, rarely treated as "American," contains work by writers such as C.L.R. James, Caryl Phillips, Michelle Cliff, and Jamaica Kincaid that tell of social and geographical movements of identity; yet these receive almost no attention in American literature courses—even at the college or university level. Ultimately, these omissions suggest a failure to acknowledge *who one is* rather than *what one is*. For example, Jessie Faust's works, such as *The Chinaberry Tree*, that celebrate the ability of blacks to become a part of elite American society and to choose a central identity as American rather than African-derived, rarely reach audiences in Afrocentric literature classes.

Language figures centrally in this isomorphism, for it is often the indicator of a presumed necessary connection of race or culture. For example, numerous pieces of literature, such as *Pudd'nhead Wilson* by Mark Twain, initially give no indication of the racial membership of a character except through their speech. The adoption of what is labeled "Black speech" by rap artists across a variety of identities and national origins gestures toward the genesis of this musical form within African American neighborhoods and to its continued commercial success through the efforts of African American promoters. Particular patterns of pronunciation, lexical choices, and syntactic frames trigger recognition of "racial" association with language among audiences of serious and comic theater and among performers from musicians to talk show guests. Crossovers appear in numerous forms in popular culture, and yet any young African American linked to fads and fashions in music at the end of the twentieth century knows well essentialist claims about rap as black. (Many know these claims, while not fully engaging with the heavy commodification of particular forms of "blackness" through the economic engine that drives popular culture, particularly hip hop.) The characteristic "straight talk," multilayered rhetorical patterns, and promotion of strength of the young against authority emerge primarily out of responses to experiences of exclusion, violence, and neglect that other young people now see as marking them as well. What is considered "black talk" marks popular culture from Great Britain to Slovakia.

But there is much more to "talkin' black" than that reflected by the media. Youngsters growing up in neighborhoods, such as the South Bronx, with numerous language groups assume particular voices of "African Americanness" when they want to pass temporarily with age peers and certain interest groups when they travel outside their home neighborhoods (Zentella, 1997). Relationships and partnerships across ethnic and racial lines have not only dramatically increased in the final decades of the twentieth century, but frequent accounts of such families have been published. Joining the increase in interracial marriages has been the phenomenon of serial families; the shift from lifelong monogamy to sequential monogamy has meant that within the same family different individuals carry varying degrees of identification and competence with particular language varieties. In some families, the range may be from a Spanish heavily influenced by local variants of African American Vernacular English to a wide repertoire of types of hyphenated English—Italian American, Chinese American, Vietnamese American—all of which may occasionally be marked by borrowing from "black speech."

AFRICAN AMERICAN ENGLISHES

But what about speech forms attributed to blacks, and how do accounts of such language differ across American history? Early accounts by scholarly observers in the eighteenth and early nineteenth century of language structures and uses by black speakers attest to broad stylistic ranges, rapid generic adaptation, and regional differences.[6] Accounts of slaves in colonial Williamsburg (Tate, 1965) as well as the many advertisements for runaway slaves that appeared well into the second half of the nineteenth century included descriptions of their facility with varieties of English as well as particular habits of speech.

Perhaps best documented have been sermons and other forms of religious oratory used in black churches. The Early American Imprint Series includes collections of such sermons, and since the 1960s, numerous studies, historical and anthropological, have supplemented the writings by W.E.B. Du Bois (1903/1973) that indicated African language uses transformed in black religious speech. Zora Neale Hurston's biographical novel *Jonah's Gourd Vine* (1934) offers a landmark work celebrating a black Baptist preacher. Studies of "slave religion" and the oratory it spawned, as well as the faith in literacy it generated, have given considerable attention to the cognitive and linguistic demands as well as the varieties of preaching styles within black church services (Moss, 1994; Pitts, 1993; Raboteau, 1978; Rosenberg, 1970).

To be sure, these language forms and often the settings that inspired them entered Hollywood films of the 1940s and 1950s, often in minstrel form as parody that demeaned black religious arts of speaking and singing. Close attention to political oratory, especially that of Martin Luther King, Jr., by a few scholars represents what can be only an initial attempt to redress the imbalance of portrayals of blacks not only by Hollywood but also by social scientists. Studies have now begun to document, for example, the range from contemporary Standard English to Jacobean English to varieties of Vernacular Black English within a single political address or church service (Pitts, 1993). Also of note in these studies is emphasis on close listening and attention to nonverbal cues that support the "raising" of hymns as well as the improvisations of jazz.

Well documented elsewhere and in no need of repetition here are accounts of the history and development of particular lexical and grammatical forms that mark varieties of Black English or Ebonics.[7] Treated less frequently is the matter of ways of speaking and the wide variety represented within African American communities across classes. Much of this research has taken place within either lower socioeconomic groups or among teenagers. Rapping, jiving, signifying, and hip-hop language have come to be identified as broadly African American, with essentialist views that would claim these forms represent all black urban youth and the sum total of their male/female, familial, and interracial relationships. Research by both broad-ranging liberals and conservatives has generally failed to consider the commodification and imbalance of power relations that determine selection, marketing, and promotion of only specific kinds of black musical art. The "polemological" (de Certeau, 1984) nature of lyrics receives frequent attention, whereas range, content, and context of art produced and received go unexamined (for further discussion of these points, see Rose, 1994 and Kelley, 1994, esp. chapter 8).

The focus on "counter dominant narratives" (Rose, 1994) of black art results not only in commercial distribution of fodder for racist conclusions about young blacks but also in skewed perceptions of speech events and discourse genres included within the repertoires of African American across class and situations (on this point, see Mahiri, 1998). The bias against studying African American speakers in ordinary interactions, or in highlighting only some interactions as "ordinary," further exoticizes young blacks. Such skewed preferences for objects of study is also reflected in the fact that collections on the language of the professionals, language and the emotions, or the language of different types of work almost never include African Americans. Like southerners, those who may be racially or socially classified as African American are rarely included as Standard English speakers in scholarly research either directly on language or taking language into account indirectly.[8]

Perhaps ironically, elite general interest magazines in the 1990s have gone far in redressing the imbalance of both scholarly representations and those of popular culture's focus on black talk as that of gangsters or hip-hop teenagers. Writing regularly on a broad range of topics in *The New Yorker* as well as other magazines read by numerous professionals have been academics Henry Louis Gates, Cornel West, Patricia Williams, and Robin Kelley, as well as novelists such as John Wideman and Charles

Johnson. In the 1990s, *The New Yorker* profiled numerous African Americans serving in a wide variety of key political, religious, and economic roles and speaking and writing as "AfroSaxons," a term coined by Nathan Hare and extensively used by Harvard University's chaplain Peter Gomes in the mid-1990s.

Considerable redress of past imbalances has also come from African American writers who increasingly refuse to write to public stereotypes and as though black characters have to be marked by their "nonstandard" language, poverty, and victimization. Paula Marshall's *Daughters* (1991) explores the life of a black woman who is a professional. Andrea Lee's *Sarah Phillips* (1984) portrays a daughter of a minister from a middle-class black suburb of Philadelphia. Florence Ladd's *Sarah's Psalm* tells the story of a black Harvard graduate of the 1960s whose return to Africa launches her into a world of Afrocentrism in a second coming of age. Poet Laureate Rita Dove, as well as poets such as Jay Wright, take up topics from around the world and write in highly formal verse forms, as did Robert Hayden, Gwendolyn Brooks, and other African American poets before them. Similarly, much within black music, particularly jazz, goes far beyond the usual heavily commercialized (and often Hollywood-influenced) selections used in classrooms. For example, the many language uses and combinations of sound created by Cecil Taylor and other avant-garde figures are marked by innovative power and imaginative force rarely acknowledged, even among musicians who pride themselves on being linked to the avant-garde. Since the mid-1960s, black jazz and black poetics have come together in new genres highly appropriate for classroom use (Nielsen, 1997).

Neither these works nor their authors receive enough attention in courses centered on the African American experience or reflecting an Afrocentric curriculum. Similarly, those in ethnic studies college classes that focus on African American culture rarely learn about the depth and strength of earlier scholarly work by African American literary scholars, such as Benjamin Brawley (1937). Many in such programs grab recent scholarship and celebrate its originality without knowing well the history of earlier such work. For example, laudable as is the work of current literary scholars, such as Henry Louis Gates, Deborah McDowell, and Houston Baker, rare are those who teach literature today who know the extraordinary contributions of Brawley and Arthur P. Davis, early critics and scholars of African American literature; of Dorothy Porter, former librarian of Howard University; and Alain Locke, English professor at Howard. Neglected are writings portraying the contributions of blacks of all classes to American culture (Butcher, 1956). Collections such as that edited by Porter (1995) also dispel any idea that African Americans held command over only certain genres or styles. Recent American literature anthologies, through both their broad inclusion and their headnote, have also begun to redress past omissions (see, for example, McQuade et al., 1993).

The central point of this chapter has been illustration of the diversity of language uses and language varieties that have marked African Americans since their arrival in the United States. Corollary to this point has been a plea for a much broader representation of the language abilities and language choices of African Americans as actual content matter within all kinds of education. Standard English, with nuances of regional and stylistic differences, comes more easily for many who identify as African American than do forms associated with highly informal, strictly regional, or primarily playful situations and speakers. No neurologically sound speaker of any language controls only a single register, and all speakers develop new language competencies in their lifelong learning. Picking up jargon, new vocabulary, forms of expression, genres, and styles of talking and writing comes with development and assumptions of different identities, roles, and responsibilities.

In spite of these illustrations of the diversity of uses, registers, and styles of language black Americans use, it is important to note that there are certain group-specific features of language that all black Americans will understand, may occasionally use, and acknowledge as indicative of black identity. For example, in the Senate impeachment hearings for President William Jefferson Clinton in 1999, Cheryl Mills, member of the White House defense team and a black female, presented her statement for the defense with no readily discernible patterns of pronunciation, lexical choices, or syntactic frames that could have been identified as "black." However, the organization of the statement punctuated key points with a chorus and response repetition given with a cadence familiar from sermons in many black churches. Sociologist Michael Dyson has described such features as "race specific" rather than "race inclusive" because their use and form link them for all listeners to aspects of black heritage in the United States.

Whereas the bulk of this chapter has focused on content related to language and culture among African Americans, it is important to turn here to pedagogical strategies. Numerous professional development workshops and packets of pedagogical materials have spread ideas that African American students have a primarily "oral" background and need what turns out to be a fairly narrow range of discourse forms in the classroom. Close examination of the full range of uses and genres within the many contexts across which youth move suggests they know these well, at least receptively. To be motivated to produce them will result only when students feel safe and secure stepping into and out of different roles and identities (Fordham, 1996). Necessary therefore in classrooms that purport to have Afrocentric interests at heart will be adequate opportunities for students to play responsible roles within collaborative as well as individual projects, to explore both vicariously and directly the full range of ways of speaking African Americans represent (see, for example, Ladson-Billings, 1994; Lee, 1993; Mahiri, 1998).

But these teaching practices need not be thought of as peculiarly adapted only for the "special needs" of African Americans. No group of students, no matter how they are categorized within the United States today, will reflect a single unified coherent set of specifiable behaviors—linguistic or cultural—exclusive to a single sociocultural unit. Individual, regional, class, and religious preferences will always cut across and into behaviors and values often today too easily termed "cultural." Students' classroom language forms and uses, as well as their ways of behaving, derive now from a much greater range of types of families and neighborhood as well as means of transport than in earlier decades. What results from these changes has been determined by such factors as amount of conversation between adults and children, family adherence to written texts, preferred forms of recreation and practices of discipline, and communal notions of moral and normative codes. It is from subtle daily routines that habits of language use and available structures and discourse forms emerge. These habits, to the extent they become tied to particular identities, then enable individuals to shape and mold the range of identities they wish to play, when they want to shift back and forth, and motivations that prompt them to do so. No youth strongly self-identified as wanna-be disc jockey, fashion modeling executive, or basketball star will substantially shift the language forms he or she links to self-definition, unless there is a significant draw for role change and a sense that there is safety in shifts back and forth.

Teachers therefore have to look with keen sensitivity to classroom strategies advertised as "especially appropriate for African American students" or playing to "cultural differences" or cognitive styles (such as "field dependent"). Delpit (1997) has laid out the perils that come from teaching "other people's children" with curricular materials that fail to consider the subtle ways in which these depend on highly specific background experiences within family structure, class membership, and regional location. Many of such materials also derive from deeply submerged presuppositions about social interfactional patterns dependent on exchange of ideas and information in a debatelike conversation that includes adults and children. Such discourse patterns may include asking clarification questions, referring to particular written genres, and providing argumentative support through a point-counterpoint, individual-against-individual strategy. Extensive practice in these particular discourse forms may be absent from households without sufficient leisure time or joint mealtimes in which to engage in conversations and debate with their children. In addition, the conversational role of children with adults differs markedly across socioeconomic class and regional patterns of African American life as well as that of other sociocultural groups (Heath, 1983). Similar patterns of difference appear also in distribution of roles: Anglo-Saxon or European-derived families in the United States have historically tended to rely on stable role assignments, whereas flexibility and adaptability across a range of roles have traditionally marked many immigrant groups as well as African American communities. Classroom evaluations of effective small-group work today often derive from scoring individual students on their ability to play specific roles (summarizer, recorder, leader, etc.) rather than distributing functions across the group and letting individuals play to group needs out of their particular talents and dispositions. Variation between these two strategies helps ensure that teachers can tap into the preferences and practices of all students—not just those categorically labeled as belonging to one cultural group or another.

The heavy responsibility of being keenly alert to curricular and pedagogical practices tied to "cultural difference" falls especially to those who identify themselves with any form of "centric" education, whether it be Afro, Chicano, Puerto Rican, or Southeast Asian. In each case, educators must also attend to the facts and figures surrounding the education of the particular group of students who form their major concern. For example, in spite of some movement toward equalizing education expenditures in schools and districts heavily populated by African Americans in the 1970s, the final decades of the twentieth century show declines (Irvine, 1990). These schools fall behind most prominently in quality of teacher credentials, experience, and educational background. Facilities, materials, and environmental surroundings similarly do not begin to match those available in the majority of districts that are predominantly white. Such persistent inequities in formal schooling must remain central to actions, rhetoric, and scholarship of those linked to any form of Afrocentric education.

Similarly, these educators—regardless of their location of teaching—must reflect language structures and uses of African Americans fairly. Although it is unrealistic to expect teachers to be trained in linguistics and the history of language structures and uses represented among African Americans, it is imperative that materials and teaching approaches not perpetuate stereotypes or universals associated with particular varieties, such as those of African American Vernacular English. It is also critical that historical representations of communication among African Americans not slip into essentializing and overarching features such as "oral" or styles such as "jiving" or "preaching." These need to be situated within the spectrum of competencies and performances of African Americans, male and female, young and old, southern and northern, eastern and western. The strong tendency to celebrate particular genres, such as playing the dozens, rapping, jiving, or even sermonizing, perpetuates narrow views of interpersonal relations and occupational roles that African Americans choose.

A return to poet Meredith's admonitions is in order here—and, ideally, for perceived insiders and outsiders. Considerable work, as well as extensive discussion of standards and norms of judgment of what is, can be, and has been African within the American context, remains to be done. This call extends to all who see themselves as Afrocentric educators, as well as to others of us whose primary research has been to elucidate specific historical and contemporary niches within language and culture not only among but also about African Americans. Moreover, responsible scholars, journalists, and educators must never let up on the task of historicizing race and its attendant meanings and contexts within the United States. Any effort termed "Afrocentric," whether political, educational, or aesthetic, merits combined and joint work in the spirit of "critical negation, wise preservation and insurgent transformation" (West, 1993, 85). Many islands of belief, entrenched values, and hidden information remain to be informed, negotiated, and traversed.

NOTES

1. Within the first few years after the Ebonics Resolution in Oakland, several volumes appeared. Some address primarily education issues (see especially Perry & Delpit, 1999), whereas others provide a solid grounding in varieties of African American English (e.g., Mufwene, Rickford, Bailey, & Baugh, 1998; Baugh, 1999; Rickford, 1999). An important element of the renewed interest in language issues since the Ebonics Resolution has been attention to avant-garde poets such as Amiri Baraka (Nielsen, 1997). Rickford and Rickford

(forthcoming) treat the theme of Toni Morrison's Nobel Prize speech: "[T]he language . . . it's the thing black people love so much . . . the saying of words, holding them on the tongue, experimenting with them, playing with them."

2. For most of my childhood, I lived in an almost entirely black community, where, aside from the lower Virginia "country" dialect of my grandmother, I learned the local African American Vernaculars. These ranged from the usually highly formal standard variety of black schoolteachers who lived on the farm adjoining my grandmother's to the informal fieldwork talk of those with whom I hired out as a child on local tobacco farms. To these dialects were added those of black communities in the Piedmont Carolinas where I later lived, as well as the Appalachian ways of speaking that white migrants from the mountains brought in their "down-country" move to work in textile mills. Today all these dialects, as well as their social and cultural underpinnings, remain in my linguistic repertoire. In the last decade of the twentieth century, unexpected combinations of dialects, phenotype, and socialization experiences such as those my background provides have multiplied far beyond those of simple black and white crossovers.

3. Perry and Delpit (1999) include numerous discussions of ways in which the media furor around the Oakland Ebonics Resolution not only reinforced stereotypes about blackness but also played up a sense of black shame about varieties of language spoken by African Americans.

4. Extensive work has been done on Gullah, beginning with the work of Turner (1949) and continuing with research by linguists such as Stewart (1967), Nichols (1976), and Joyner (1977). R. Morgan (1975) has been the major scholar working on Louisiana Creole.

5. In intricate detail, these societies stand out in the accounts of McHenry and Heath (1994) and McHenry (1995). Of special interest in these accounts is the strong focus of the societies on the cultivation of rhetorical "genius" as well as literary pursuits among a broad range of types of literature, including the classics. Circulating libraries made available books in science as well as literature to members, and meetings of benevolent and literary societies date back to the eighteenth century. Charters of these organizations illustrate the intimate way in which their drafters knew the Constitution and other documents of the United States. Charters of groups such as the Association of the Free African Society of Philadelphia (1787) gave themselves recognition and authority and conferred similar privileges to those offered in the U.S. Constitution to a segment that then had no legal right to such claims. Hence, these documents may be said to have been written both "to resemble and to menace" (Bhabha, 1994, 86) fundamental documents of freedom and democracy for the United States; they certainly illustrate the depth of knowledge their writers had with key political texts.

6. Early accounts of American Englishes include those spoken by black Americans. John Witherspoon (signer of the Declaration of Independence and early president of Princeton), John Pickering (brother of early diplomat Timothy Pickering), and Frances Lieber (mid-nineteenth-century intellectual) include those observers who have left accounts of such language uses and forms. Many of these have been excerpted and analyzed in volumes of *American Speech*. One of the most valuable of such analyses using primary data is that of Read (1939).

7. For exemplary reviews well informed by both historical study and the sociolinguistic research of the final decades of the twentieth century, see Baugh (1999), Rickford and Green (1997), Rickford (1997), Labov and Harris (1986), and Smitherman (1986). Of particular merit is the review of dialect reading programs provided by Rickford and Rickford (1997).

8. Underrepresentation and misrepresentation of African American language uses and forms have been treated primarily in terms of the general omission of females from studies (M. Morgan, 1994; Smitherman-Donaldson, 1988). Rickford (1997, 171–175) discusses this issue and offers reasons why the misrepresentation might have taken place.

REFERENCES

Anderson, E. (1990). *Streetwise: Race, class, and change in an urban community*. Chicago: University of Chicago Press.

Andrews, W. L. (Ed.). (1986). *Sisters of the spirit: Three black women's autobiographies of the nine-teenth century*. Bloomington: Indiana University Press.

Anzaldua, G. (1987). *Borderlands*. New York: Norton.

Asante, M. K. (1998). *The Afrocentric idea*. (Rev. ed.). Philadelphia, PA: Temple University Press.

Baugh, J. (1999). *Out of the mouths of slaves*. Austin, TX: University of Texas Press.

Bhabha, H. K. (1994). Of mimicry and man: The ambivalence of colonial discourse. In *The location of culture*. London: Routledge.

Brawley, B. (1937). *Negro builders and heroes*. Chapel Hill, NC: University of North Carolina Press.

Bullock, P. L. (1981). *The Afro-American periodical press: 1838–1909*. Baton Rouge: Louisiana State University Press.

Butcher, M. J. (1956). *The Negro in American culture*. New York: New American Library.

Davis, G. L. (1985). *I got the word in me and I can sing it, you know: A study of the performed African-American sermon*. Philadelphia: University of Pennsylvania Press.

de Certeau, M. (1984). *The practice of everyday life* (S. F. Rendall, Trans.). Berkeley: University of California Press.

DeCosta-Willis, M. (1994). *Ida B. Wells: The Memphis diaries*. Boston: Beacon Press.

Delpit, L. (1997). *Other people's children*. New York: New Press.

Du Bois, W.E.B. (1903/1973). *The souls of black folks*. New York: Simon & Schuster.

Fordham, S. (1996). *Blacked out: Dilemmas of race, identity, and success at Capital High*. Chicago: University of Chicago Press.

Foster, M. (1997). *Black teachers on teaching*. New York: Norton.

Gaines, K. (1996). *Uplifting the race: Black leadership, politics, and culture in the 20th century*. Chapel Hill: University of North Carolina Press.

Gatewood, W. B. (1990). *Aristocrats of color: The black elite, 1880–1920*. Bloomington: Indiana University Press.

Gonzalez, A. (1969). *With Aesop along the black border*. New York: Negro Universities Press.

Grossman, J. R. (1997). *Young Oxford history of African Americans*. New York: Oxford University Press.

Haizlip, S. T. (1994). *The sweeter the juice: A family memoir in black and white*. New York: Simon & Schuster.

Heath, S. B. (1983). *Ways with words: Language, life, and work in communities and classrooms*. Cambridge: Cambridge University Press.

Heath, S. B. (1989). Oral and literate traditions among black Americans living in poverty. *American Psychologist, 44*, 2, 1–7.

Irvine, J. J. (1990). *Black students and school failure*. Westport, CT: Greenwood.

Johnson, A. A., & Johnson, R. M. (1979). *Propaganda and aesthetics: The literary politics of African-American magazines in the twentieth century*. Amherst: University of Massachusetts Press.

Joyner, C. (1977). *Slave folklife on the Waccamaw Neck: Antebellum black culture in the South Carolina low country*. Ph.D. dissertation, University of Pennsylvania.

Karenga, M. (1977). *Kwanzaa: Origin, concepts, and practice*. Philadelphia: Kawaida Publications.

Kelley, R. (1994). *Race rebels; Culture, politics, and the black working class*. New York: Free Press.

Labov, W. (1994). "Can reading failure be reversed" A linguistic approach to the question. In V. Gadsden & D. Wagner (Eds.), *Literacy among African-American youth*. Creskill, NJ: Hampton Press.

Labov, W., & Harris, W. A. (1986). De facto segregation of black and white vernaculars. In D. Sankoff (Ed.), *Diversity and Diachrony*. Amsterdam: Benjamins.

Ladson-Billings, G. (1994). *The dreamkeepers: Successful teachers of African American children*. San Francisco: Jossey-Bass.

Lawrence-Lightfoot, S. (1988). *Balm in Gilead: Journey of a healer*. Reading, MA: Addison-Wesley.

Lawrence-Lightfoot, S. (1994). *I've known rivers: Lives of loss and liberation*. New York: Penguin Books.

Lee C. D. (1993). *Scaffold for literary interpretation: The pedagogical implications of an African American discourse genre*. Champaign, IL: NCTE.

Levine, L. W. (1977). *Black culture and black consciousness*. New York: Oxford University Press.

Mahiri, J. (1998). *Shooting for excellence: African American and youth culture in new century schools*. Champaign, IL: NCTE.

McHenry, E. (1995). Dreaded eloquence: The origins and rise of African American literary societies and libraries. *Harvard Library Bulletin, 6*, 2, 32–56.

McHenry, E., & Heath, S. B. (1994). The literate and the literary: African Americans as writers and readers—1830–1940. *Written Communication, 11*, 4, 419–444.

McQuade, D., et al. (1993). *The Harper American Literature* (Vols. 1 & 2). New York: HarperCollins.

Morgan, M. (1994). Theories and politics in African American English. *Annual Review of Anthropology, 23*, 325–345.

Morgan, R., Jr. (1975). Playing dead thrice: Louisiana Creole animal tale. *Revue de Louisiana, 4*, 23–32.

Moss, B. (1994). *Literacy across communities*. Cresskill, NJ: Hampton Press.

Mufwene, S. S., Rickford, J. R., Bailey, G., & Baugh, J. (Eds.). (1998). *African-American English: Structure, history and use*. London: Rutledge.

Mukhopadhyay, C. C., & Moses, Y. T. (1997). Reestablishing "race" in anthropological discourse. *American Anthropologist, 99*, 3, 517–533.

Nichols, P. (1976). *Linguistic change in Gullah: Sex, age, and mobility*. Ph.D. dissertation, Stanford University.

Nichols, P. (1981). Creoles of the USA. In C. A. Ferguson & S. B. Heath (Eds.), *Language in the USA*. Cambridge: Cambridge University Press.

Nielsen, A. L. (1997). *Black chant: Languages of African-American postmodernism*. Cambridge: Cambridge University Press.

Perry, T., & Delpit, L. (1999). *The real Ebonics debate: Power, language, and the education of African-American children*. Boston, MA: Beacon Press.

Peterkin, J. (1970). *Collected short stories* (F. Durham, Ed.). Columbia: University of South Carolina Press.

Pitts, W. (1993). *Old ship of Zion: The Afro-Baptist ritual in the African Diaspora*. New York: Oxford University Press.

Porter, D. (1995). *Early Negro writing: 1760–1837*. [First published, 1971]. Baltimore: Black Classic Press.

Raboteau, A. J. (1978). *Slave religion: The "invisible" institution in the Antebellum South*. New York: Oxford University Press.

Read, A. W. (1939). The speech of Negroes in colonial America. *Journal of Negro History, 24*, 3, 247–258.

Rickford, J. (1997). Unequal partnership: Sociolinguistics and the African American speech community. *Language in Society, 26,* 161–197.

Rickford, J. (1999). *African-American vernacular English.* London: Blackwell.

Rickford, J. R., & Green, L. A. (1997). *African American Vernacular English.* Cambridge: Cambridge University Press.

Rickford, J. R, & Rickford, A. E. (1997). Dialect readers revisited. *Linguistics and Education, 7,* 107–128.

Rose, T. (1994). *Black noise: Rap music and black culture in contemporary America.* Middletown, CT: Wesleyan Press.

Rosenberg, B. (1970). *Art of the American folk preacher.* New York: Oxford University Press.

Scott, D. M. (1997). *Contempt and pity: Social policy and the image of the damaged black psyche 1880–1996.* Chapel Hill: University of North Carolina Press.

Smitherman, G. (1986). *Talkin and testifyin: The language of Black America.* Detroit: Wayne State University Press.

Smitherman-Donaldson, G. (1988). Discriminatory discourse on Afro-American speech. In G. Smitherman-Donaldson & T. van Dijk (Eds.), *Discourse and discrimination.* Detroit: Wayne State University Press. 144–176.

Sterling, D. (1984). *We are your sisters: Black women in the nineteenth century.* New York: Norton.

Stewart, W. A. (1967). Sociolinguistic factors in the history of American Negro dialects. *Florida Foreign Language Reporter, 5,* 11–29.

Streitmatter, R. (1994). *Raising her voice: African-American women journalists who changed history.* Lexington: University Press of Kentucky.

Studio Museum in Harlem. (1987/1994). *Harlem Renaissance art of Black America.* New York: Harry N. Abrams.

Tate, T. (1965). *The Negro in eighteenth-century Williamsburg.* Charlottesville, VA: Colonial Williamsburg Foundation.

Thompson, M. I. (1990). *Ida B. Wells-Barnett: An exploratory study of an American black woman, 1893–1930: Vol. 15, Black women in United States history.* Brooklyn: Carlson Publishing.

Turner, L. D. (1949). *Africanisms in the Gullah dialect.* Chicago: University of Chicago Press.

Turner, R. B. (1997). *Islam in the African American experience.* Bloomington, IN: Indiana University Press.

Walters, K. (1996). Contesting representations of African American language. In R. Ide, R. Parker, & Y. Sunaoshi (Eds.), *SALSA III (1995): Proceedings of the 4th annual symposium about language and society—Austin.* Austin: Department of Linguistics, University of Texas. 137–151.

Washington, M. H. (1987). *Invented lives: Narratives of black women 1860–1960.* New York: Anchor Books.

West, C. (1993). *Keeping faith.* New York: Routledge.

Wolseley, R. E. (1990). *The black press, USA* (2nd ed.). Ames: Iowa State University Press.

Zentella, A. (1997). *Growing up bilingual.* New York: Blackwell.

— 9 —

Culturally Relevant Pedagogy in African-Centered Schools: Possibilities for Progressive Educational Reform

Gloria Ladson-Billings

In the early 1990s there were rumblings in Milwaukee, Wisconsin, about the growing dissatisfaction African American parents and community members were feeling toward the condition of public education for their children. Predictably, solutions from both progressive and reactionary forces were proposed. On what this author terms the progressive side, parents and community members were advocating secession from the system in an attempt to construct a separate school district, free from the antagonism of the central office bureaucrats and beyond the scope of white disinterest. On the reactionary side came a call for public school choice that would support vouchers allowing low-income, urban children to attend private schools. Ultimately, both sides got some, but not all, of what they wanted. The school choice advocates lobbied for and won the only school choice arrangement in the state. The independent district forces won the right to establish two African American Immersion Schools. This chapter focuses on the efforts of the latter and the need to employ a culturally relevant pedagogy (Ladson-Billings, 1994, 1995b) to ensure the success of these schools and similar efforts.

At the time of this writing, the governor of Wisconsin has made Milwaukee Public Schools one of the foci of his education agenda. At the annual State of the State address, Governor Tommy Thompson demanded that Milwaukee Public Schools (MPS) make some dramatic turnarounds or face a state takeover. Briefly, the governor has given MPS two years, until the year 2000, to have at least a 90 percent graduation rate, a 91 percent attendance rate, and a dropout rate no higher than 9 percent. The district's scores on the third-grade reading test also must be at least 90 percent of the statewide average (*Milwaukee Journal Sentinel*, 1998).

The governor's "threat" suggests that Milwaukee Public Schools could do better if someone just made them. However, those of us who have spent considerable time in public schools know that what is wrong in those schools is a much more complicated issue of accountability. This chapter is designed to focus on one aspect of education that may be part of a more dynamic and culture-centered solution.

CULTURE-CENTERED PEDAGOGY

The term *pedagogy* is not often used in preparing teachers. Instead, terms such as *learning* and *instruction* dominate the discourse surrounding teaching and preparing to teach. The use of these terms is not accidental. They represent a more individual-istic psychological orientation to teaching and learning that suggests more prescrip-tive and technical approaches to student achievement. Since the early 1900s psychological theories have been appropriated and applied to education. These the-ories were applied on "scientific" grounds suggesting that statistical methods and standardized testing could provide more accurate information about intelligence and educational achievement (Ryan & Cooper, 1988). Scholars such as Piaget, Bruner, and Skinner have had a profound impact on the way we think about teaching and learning. The curriculum, materials, instruction, and organization all have been in-fluenced by psychological approaches to schooling. Culture, when considered at all, was more of an afterthought.

The primary unit of analysis in psychology is the individual. This focus on the in-dividual is entirely consistent with a Western worldview. Given the U.S. penchant for elevating the individual, for example, "rugged individualism," individual rights, it is easy to see how a psychological view of schooling and education would be deemed a good fit.

Anthropology, as one of the first "colonial" fields, has always been concerned with the group. Of course, Western approaches to anthropology have served to create a di-chotomous "us–them" split. To underscore the "humanity" of Westerners it was im-portant to view Westerners as individuals—to "psychologize" them. Non-Westerners, on the other hand, were not really "human," thus not individuals, and could only be considered as part of some group.

This notion of "group-ness" is not necessarily a negative. Indeed, all human beings have some sense of themselves as members of some group, clan, kin, or cultural group. However, schooling and education have rarely thought to consider students' group status in situations other than the negative, e.g., "ghetto children," "minority students," "Chapter I kids." By the early 1980s, educational anthropologists had be-gun to document the ways in which teachers' understanding of students' cultural group membership and affiliation could help improve their teaching and lead to im-proved learning outcomes.

Sociolinguists such as Au and Jordan (1981), Cazden and Leggett (1981), and Erickson and Mohatt (1982) have examined the nature of the language interactions of teachers and marginalized students. These inquiries have failed to include well-developed discussions of the broader social contexts in which cultural mismatches occur. In response to their "cultural discontinuities" explanations, other anthro-pologists (see, for example, Gibson, 1993; Ogbu, 1993; Suarez-Orozco, 1987) have argued that students of color who, as a group, fail to achieve in schools, form an oppositional culture in a kind of "cultural ecology."

In contrast to both cultural difference and cultural ecological perspectives, African American scholars (see, for example, Irvine, 1990; King, 1991; Ladson-Billings, 1994) have argued for a pedagogical approach that incorporates elements of critical pedagogy (Freire, 1970; Giroux & Simon, 1989). Rather than focusing solely on the microlevel arguments of the sociolinguists or the broad themes of the macroculture outlined by the cultural ecologists, this work has attempted to pull both levels together to develop a theoretical framework of pedagogy that addresses the two levels simultaneously (Ladson-Billings, 1995b). Although this work has been done in public schools that have demonstrated no explicit commitment to African-centered education, I want to argue that this pedagogy is both appropriate and necessary for African-centered education.

In my work with eight exemplary teachers of African American students in a low-income, predominantly African American school, I have been able to deduce a culturally relevant pedagogy that may be important to the success of African-centered schools. From the very beginning of the project, concerns about an Afrocentric approach to research directed this inquiry. I identified the teachers through a process of "community nomination" (Foster, 1989). Parents in local African American churches were willing to recommend teachers they believed were most effective with their children.

Eight of nine recommended teachers agreed to participate in ethnographic interviews (Spradley, 1979). After reading and editing their interviews, the teachers permitted me to observe their classrooms, videotape their practice, and convene a research collective. This research collective employed aspects of African cultural values where teachers demonstrated mutuality, reciprocity, "connectedness," and a sense of "harambee" or pulling together for the sake of the students. This process took almost three years.

None of the teachers in the study worked in what would be termed African-centered schools. Indeed, their schools had poor academic reputations throughout the area. Many families in the neighborhood opted to enroll their children in private schools rather than attend the local public schools. But despite the poor academic reputation of the schools, the teachers in the study developed a pedagogy that supported high academic achievement, cultural competence, and sociopolitical consciousness. I have come to identify these attributes as the criteria for determining culturally relevant pedagogy (Ladson-Billings, 1995b). Below, I will attempt to explain their relationship to African-centered education.

Academic Achievement

No matter what else transpires in schools, parents, teachers, and students themselves expect learning to occur. How that learning is encouraged and measured may vary widely. In Euro-American schooling paradigms, students are expected to master particular sets of knowledge that is legitimated and made official (Apple, 1993). This knowledge may have no relation to students' everyday experiences, but it is deemed appropriate for particular grade levels in particular school subjects. The tests of academic achievement may be narrowly defined pencil-and-paper tasks that assess whether or not students have *remembered* what was supposedly taught.

Culturally relevant teachers have particular dispositions toward knowledge that challenge externally set curricular guides and mandates. They begin with the premise that students come to school knowing something and that it is their responsibility to build the curriculum upon the students' foundational knowledge. I observed an excellent example of this in a colleague's videotape of a fourth-grade teacher who required the students to interview their parents, grandparents, and other family members. She also required the students to bring a "story" from home.

One student lamented that he "did not have any stories." The teacher responded, "If you have lived, you have a story." Over the course of the year, the teacher and students built their curriculum from the family questionnaire responses. One day as the teacher was listing the coming week's spelling words on the chalkboard, a student beamed with recognition and exclaimed, "'Emancipate!' Hey, that was one of the words from my questionnaire." The student's interview with his grandfather had helped him learn about when his great-great-grandfather had been emancipated from slavery.

The teacher deliberately chose words that had meaning and context for the students and ensured that the students would learn to spell more difficult words than those required by the school district. More than spelling "hard" words, the teacher was trying to help students recognize their unlimited intellectual capacities as normal and expected. Her pedagogy was not tied to an external measure of academic success like a normed reference or standardized test. Rather, she wanted students to demand and expect academic excellence of themselves.

Twenty years ago when the public was introduced to the teaching of legendary educator Marva Collins, it was easy to misread her use of a Eurocentric curriculum as a Eurocentric pedagogy. However, a closer reading of Collins's pedagogy (Hollins, 1982) indicates that the *way* she teaches and the kinds of interpersonal relationships she develops are more closely aligned with core values exhibited in African American communities. Marva Collins often employed "call and response," sermonic cadences, extended family, and kinlike social relations to encourage student engagement. In her classes, failure was not an option, and student academic achievement was nonnegotiable.

One of the things that makes this academic achievement possible is the teacher's unwavering belief in the ability of the students to be educated. For want of a better term, I suggest that teachers must believe that students are "educable." Rather than lament that "my students can't learn this or my students can't learn that," culturally relevant teachers perceive students as intelligent and capable of learning whatever school has to offer.

Cultural Competence

Cultural competence represents students' ability to identify positively with African and African Americanness. This aspect of culturally relevant teaching already is a central element of most African-centered schools. By helping to cement their individual and collective cultural identities, the school believes that students will become better students academically. However, in most public schools, students (and some teachers) believe that academic achievement and cultural competence are binary opposites from which students are forced to choose.

This dichotomous representation of academic achievement and cultural competence is reinforced in countless ways throughout the society. For example, when I ask my university students to identify an African American male adolescent academic achiever who appears on regular series television, their most common response is "Steve Urkel." This is the character portrayed by actor Jaleel White on the sit-com *Family Matters*. His character is a stereotype (as is true of most television characters)— a nerd, an egghead, or a "brainiac" who is culturally incompetent.

While it can be argued that the "nerd" image holds for white television characters also, the range and number of white roles makes the nerd just one of a wide array of characters, personalities, and role models for white youngsters. In the case of African Americans, the limited number of available roles magnifies the few characters that appear on the screen. Additionally, the images of African American males who are culturally competent are assigned to those characters whose intellectual capabilities are ignored or downplayed.

For teachers to support the cultural competence of the students, they have to be familiar both with their own culture and with the culture of the students. Culture is a complex phenomenon (Wolcott, 1987). Unfortunately, most white Americans do not understand their own culture and the way their whiteness has afforded them a wide array of privileges and advantages in the society (Wellman, 1977). Thus, most teachers' experiences with "multicultural education" result in a kind of cultural tourism that trivializes the importance of culture in people's daily lives. Instead of really understanding culture, students are led through a series of "exotic" experiences—eating different foods, doing strange dances, and wearing quaint costumes. This approach serves to reinscribe Euro-American culture as normative and natural.

The other problem that many teachers have with understanding culture is the tendency to transmute a social phenomenon into a "cultural" one. For example, a teacher who suggests that "having children out of wedlock is a part of African American culture" has badly misread the social and economic forces that have had an impact on the African American family. Indeed, a look back to a mere 30 years ago will reveal that at that time more than 75 percent of African American children lived in two-parent households.

A welfare system built on dependency, a shortage of jobs, increased incarceration of African American males for what were formerly drug treatment issues, and changes in attitudes toward single parenthood throughout the society all have contributed to the increase in single-parent families. These social forces are not emblematic of African *cultural* tenets.

The job of the culturally relevant teacher is to help students choose academic excellence and cultural excellence. This is most skillfully done when teachers are able to show the relationship between the two. Cultural heroes such as Malcolm X or

Harriet Tubman exemplify both intelligence and cultural competence. Their stories (and many others) should be important aspects of the curriculum.

In my study of successful teachers of African American students, one of the teachers took the students' fascination with contemporary rap music and created a link with poetry. By making a bridge or scaffold from the cultural and popular forms that the students appreciated to a form that is more valued in the dominant society, the teacher was able to show students how what they knew was valuable and transferable. She was able to draw on the reservoir of knowledge that students possessed and extend their learning to the kinds of things that are likely to be tested by standardized measures.

Sociopolitical Consciousness

In addition to developing academic achievement and cultural competence, culturally relevant teachers work to develop a sense of sociopolitical consciousness among students. Beyond helping students to work for individual achievement, culturally relevant teachers work to help students understand the way structural constraints of both schooling and society inhibit the ability of certain groups to advance, no matter how hard they work.

The notion of sociopolitical critique is akin to Freire's (1970) concept of "conscientization" or "critical consciousness" that allows for students to "own" their education and employ the "practice of freedom" rather than the exploitation of others and their environment. The kinds of pedagogy that encourage sociopolitical consciousness may begin with local community issues and expand to regional, national, and/or international ones. Students' learning is meaningful because it is tied to real-life issues that have an impact on them as members of various cultural groups. Thus, students may participate simultaneously in efforts to learn about and protest injustices in their community or anywhere in the world.

In the case of the teachers in my study (Ladson-Billings, 1994), students were encouraged to research the history of their community so that they could raise questions about its current deteriorated condition and land-use policies. Ultimately, they developed a proposal to renovate a burned-out shopping center that had become a magnet for drug dealers, addicts, drunks, and prostitutes. Their proposal was presented to the City Council and received a favorable response. Their work was more than an academic exercise. It was a deliberate move toward sociopolitical consciousness.

In another of the teacher's classrooms the concept of "service learning" was being developed to connect the fourth graders with disabled veterans who were confined to the nearby Veterans' Administration Hospital. The students' responsibilities in this project included helping the veterans negotiate the red tape and bureaucracy of the Veterans' Administration so that they and their families could receive the benefits to which they were entitled. The veterans helped the students better understand the historical context of various wars as well as the role of African Americans in the armed services. The students were able to raise critical questions about the connections between U.S. military and political decisions.

In another example of developing sociopolitical consciousness, Tate (1995) describes the mathematics pedagogy of a teacher he calls Sandra Mason who got her students engaged in real-life problem posing, analyzing, and solving. By looking at the city zoning ordinances the students were able to learn how African American and Latino poor communities were more likely to be zoned "wet," whereas white middle-class communities were more likely to be zoned "dry." This distinction allowed for very dense placement of liquor stores and bars in the African American and Latino working-class and poor communities. The students in Ms. Mason's class began a detailed mathematical and social study of this problem that resulted in communicating their findings to the City Council and a police crackdown on liquor store owners who were in violation of city ordinances.

All three aspects of culturally relevant pedagogy are necessary in an African-centered approach to education. While the academic achievement is the element most on the minds (and lips) of reformers, academic achievement must not come at high psychic and social cost. Fordham and Ogbu (1986) discuss the phenomenon of "acting white" that is attributed to those African American students who are achievers. However, what they do not confront is the social context of schooling that makes high achievement for African American students an aberration. Well-designed and -implemented African-centered schooling makes achievement normative.

In a recent visit to an African-centered school in the East, I was amazed at the sheer number of students in attendance who had previously been identified by traditional public schools as mentally, emotionally, or learning disabled. Of course, in this setting it was virtually impossible to distinguish the formerly "labeled" children because they were performing on par with the other students. The expectation of academic excellence was explicitly stated to students on a consistent and regular basis, and the standards they held for themselves were high.

Cultural competence will require teachers to have in-depth understanding of culture and its role in human cognition. Shujaa (1995) points out that merely providing teachers with African and African American curriculum content will not ensure their internalization of the information and appropriate use of it. Further, white teachers often believe that information about Africans and African Americans is necessary to improve the "self-esteem" of black children (Shujaa, 1995). Rarely do white teachers see this information as a counternarrative to the dominant Eurocentric script (Swartz, 1992) used to provide a more accurate picture of history and social phenomena. The real challenge of most teachers is to recognize authentic expressions of African and African American culture and support them. This can only happen when teachers are open to study and experience African and African American culture.

Third, the incorporation of sociopolitical consciousness requires teachers to take risks that extend learning beyond the classroom. It also requires teachers to examine the social order and point out ongoing and systemic injustices. This kind of social action is rare for most teachers, even in what may be perceived to be "ideal" circumstances (e.g., white middle-class, resource-rich schools), let alone those schools where teachers, parents, administrators, and students are struggling to meet the minimum requirements of a mandated curriculum.

THE DILEMMA OF PREPARING TEACHERS FOR AFRICAN-CENTERED EDUCATION

In the early 1960s, Septima Clark, mother of the modern civil rights movement, began her campaign to improve the literacy of African Americans throughout the rural South. In what were termed "Citizenship schools," Clark and her colleagues taught scores of illiterate sharecroppers how to read and write. Among their "graduates" was Fannie Lou Hamer—an icon of the modern civil rights movement. An interesting aspect of these schools was the fact that Clark refused to use anyone who had been certified as a "teacher."

What Clark and others (see Haberman, 1991) argue is that traditional teacher preparation develops those who are, at best, indifferent to the education of African Americans and, at worst, openly antagonistic toward their educational success. I have suggested that even if we could agree to create community-centered education for all African American students, the daunting task of finding and preparing enough teachers capable of successfully teaching them would still remain (Ladson-Billings, 1994).

Racial similarity does not guarantee successful teaching for African American students. Thus, the issue is not one of racial solidarity but cultural solidarity. Too often, African American teachers have been socialized to dominant culture ways and believe their teaching responsibility is to do the same for African American students. This kind of thinking means that the push to compete on standardized measures and to internalize a Eurocentric curriculum becomes the goal.

When teachers share cultural solidarity with the students they work to help, students become successful in ways consistent with community norms and values. This may include aspects of mainstream success such as high test scores and skill proficiency. However, it also includes a clear sense of cultural pride and a political sensibility.

The current state of teacher education indicates that college and university programs lack a clear vision and sense of mission focused on the success of African American students (Ladson-Billings, 1995a). There is almost no literature focused on preparing teachers to successfully teach African American students. Instead, the literature historically has been encased in a language of pathology that has described African American students as deprived and deficient (see, for example, Hyram, 1972; Ornstein, Doll, & Hawkins, 1971).

Even if we were willing to concede that employing a multicultural paradigm[1] would be an improvement over current practice, we see that teacher education programs have done little to enact such change in the preparation of teachers. Grant and Secada (1990) found that there is a paucity of empirical research to demonstrate that teacher education programs have helped to change prospective teachers' attitudes and dispositions toward teaching those different from themselves.

Zeichner (1992) concluded that "most of our existing knowledge about teacher education for diversity comes from very brief and often vague self-reports about the use of particular teacher education strategies and program structures" (22). Thus, we can say little about the systematic attempt to prepare prospective teachers to teach what Grumet (1988) and Delpit (1988) refer to as "other people's children."

In an attempt to reconcile multicultural education theory and teacher education practice, I investigated multicultural teacher education practice subsequent to the Grant and Secada review to see how closely the literature on practice mirrors the scholarly conceptions.[2] Unfortunately, a search of the literature indicated that few, if any, programs moved past attempting to integrate the content that prospective teachers receive. The literature on the impact of content integration is inconclusive.

One of the best models we have for preparing teachers for diversity is found in the work of the Pacific Oaks College (Pacific Oaks, California). More than two decades ago a group of parents concerned about the preschool experiences of their children developed their own preschool that conformed to their beliefs about nonviolence and social justice. Later, when the parents wondered where their students would attend elementary and secondary schools, they realized that they were in need of a preparatory institution to ensure a ready supply of teachers whose ideology and beliefs were consistent with their own. The resulting institution is Pacific Oaks College, famous for the antibias curriculum (Derman-Sparks, 1989).

Of course, African American teacher educators and community activists also have developed models of teacher preparation. However, most of their efforts have gone unwritten or unread. Lee (1994) points out that from African American free schools during Reconstruction to the Freedom Schools of the 1960s to the community-based schools of the 1970s, effective pedagogical strategies for African Americans have been a central concern of African American communities. However, Lee questions the viability of African-centered pedagogy in public schools that owe allegiances to the state and other constituencies not all supportive of African American learners.

Fortunately, there are movements throughout the nation to support and sustain teachers committed to African-centered education. In San Francisco, the Center for Applied Cultural Studies and Educational Achievement (CACSEA) has made a determined effort to encourage public school teachers who want to teach African American students in an African-centered framework. This work is built upon cultural precepts of consubstantiation, interdependence, egalitarianism, collectivism, transformation, cooperation, humanness, and synergism. The Afrocentric (Asante, 1987) tenets of Maat (truth, justice, balance, righteousness, harmony, propriety, and order) undergird the work of the center. Each summer since 1994, teachers, administrators, community members, and researchers have come together for a week to share teaching strategies, lesson ideas, and the latest research related to African American learners.

One Filipina teacher begins her language and literacy class by proclaiming, "We are all Africans" to help students understand Africa as the home of all humanity. She has each student participate in a ceremony with a partner where each child places a kente colored scarf around his or her partner's neck. As the shawl is draped the partner recites an affirmation about how magnificent she or he is. The classroom covenants urge the students to do their best to help each other to achieve their goals; demonstrate respect for themselves and respect for the property of others; never say negative or discouraging things to each other; and maintain a passion for excellence in what they do.

Another teacher used the jazz of Wynton Marsalis to help his third-grade students sharpen their reading skills. Rather than give in to the students' reluctance to write, the teacher found a novel way to motivate and reassure the students that they possessed the skills to write well. Still another teacher had the idea to stay with her students for their entire elementary school careers. She began as their kindergarten teacher, and each year she changed grades with them. When she brought them to the conference, participants witnessed a group of articulate, proud, accomplished fifth graders (and their parents) from one of the poorest sections of a major urban school district. The students stood before a room filled with adults and dazzled them with their abilities to recite long passages of oration from African American classics. Some of the children in the class previously had been labeled "retarded" and "speech handicapped." No such "disabilities" were evident in the student performances.

These weeks were exciting and energizing, but we have little data to suggest how much of the learning and sharing from the week finds itself into the classrooms.

The examples of African-centered public schools in Detroit, Indianapolis, and Philadelphia have met with mixed results. Despite the commitment to African-centered philosophy and curriculum, these programs are personnel dependent. Teachers without the knowledge, skills, and dedication to the purpose struggle to implement an African-centered pedagogy. Similarly, teachers who are equipped sometimes find themselves in the midst of public school bureaucracies that renege on promises and constantly change direction and levels of support.

Thus, the work being undertaken in public schools is very fragile. Without being able to demonstrate "empirical" achievement gains, forces outside (and perhaps some within) the community work against this work. Without improved social and cultural commitment and affirmation, community members likely will ask, "What is the point of 'African-centeredness'?" The research community faces similarly daunting challenges. Can we function as advocates while casting a critical gaze on these beginning efforts? Are we willing to acknowledge poor practices along with the good? Are we strong enough to lay bare our own credentials for community scrutiny?

These are but a few of the questions that must be confronted as we attempt to develop and evaluate African-centered curriculum and pedagogy. At this early juncture in our investigations, I am prepared only to suggest that an African-centered pedagogy is a necessary component of schooling that supports and empowers the African American learner. How we teach African children is equally important as what we teach them.

NOTES

1. By *multicultural paradigm* I am referring to the current practice that attempts to "celebrate diversity" by claiming that we are "all ethnic" but does not challenge existing structural and ideological inequities. I am not disparaging scholarly attempts to consider ways that schools might be made more equitable and just for all students.

2. My review used Banks's (1993) notions of the five dimensions of multicultural education—content integration, knowledge construction, equity pedagogy, prejudice reduction, and

empowering school culture—to determine which teacher education programs were attempting to prepare teachers consistent with the theoretical conceptions.

REFERENCES

Apple, M. (1993). *Official knowledge.* New York: Routledge.

Asante, M. K. (1987). *The Afrocentric idea.* Philadelphia: Temple University Press.

Au, K., & Jordan, C. (1981). Teaching reading to Hawaiian children: Finding a culturally appropriate solution. In H. Trueba, J. Guthrie, & K. Au (Eds.), *Culture and the bilingual classroom: Studies in classroom ethnography.* Rowley, MA: Newbury House. 139-152.

Banks, J. A. (1993). The canon debate, knowledge construction, and multicultural education, *Educational Researcher, 22,* 5, 4-14.

Cazden, C., & Leggett, E. (1981). Culturally responsive education: Recommendations for achieving Lau II remedies. In H. Trueba, J. Guthrie, & K. Au (Eds.), *Culture and the bilingual classroom: Studies in classroom ethnography.* Rowley, MA: Newbury House. 69-86.

Delpit, L. (1988). The silenced dialogue: Power and pedagogy in teaching other people's children. *Harvard Educational Review, 58,* 280-289.

Derman-Sparks, L. (1989). *Anti-bias curriculum: Tools for empowering young children.* Washington, DC: National Association for the Education of Young Children.

Erickson, F., & Mohatt, G. (1982). Cultural organization and participation structures in two classrooms of Indian students. In G. Spindler (Ed.), *Doing the ethnography of schooling.* New York: Holt, Rinehart & Winston. 131-174.

Fordham, S., & Ogbu, J. (1986). Black students' success: Coping with the burden of "acting White." *Urban Review, 18,* 1-31.

Foster, M. (1989). "It's cookin' now": A performance analysis of the speech events of a black teacher in an urban community college. *Language in Society, 18,* 1, 1-29.

Freire, P. (1970). *Pedagogy of the oppressed.* New York: Continuum.

Gibson, M. (1993). The school performance of immigrant minorities: A comparative view. In E. Jacobs & C. Jordan (Eds.), *Minority education: Anthropological perspectives.* New York: Ablex Press. 113-128.

Giroux, H., & Simon, R. (1989). Popular culture and critical pedagogy: Everyday life as a basis for curriculum knowledge. In H. Giroux & P. McLaren (Eds.), *Critical pedagogy, the state and cultural struggle.* Albany: State University of New York Press. 236-252.

Grant, C., & Secada, W. (1990). Preparing teachers for diversity. In W. R. Houston, M. Haberman, & J. Sikula (Eds.), *Handbook of research on teacher education.* New York: Macmillan. 403-422.

Grumet, M. R. (1988). *Bitter milk: Women and teaching.* Amherst: University of Massachusetts Press.

Haberman, M. (1991). The rationale for training adults as teachers. In C. E. Sleeter (Ed.), *Empowerment through multicultural education.* Albany: State University of New York Press.

Hollins, E. (1982). The Marva Collins story revisited: Implications for regular classroom instruction. *Journal of Teacher Education, 33,* 37-40.

Hyram, G. (1972). *Challenge to society: The education of the culturally disadvantaged* (Vol. 1). New York: Pagent-Poseidon.

Irvine, J. J. (1990). *Black students and school failure.* Westport, CT: Greenwood Press.

King, J. E. (1991). Unfinished business: Black student alienation and black teachers' emancipatory pedagogy. In M. Foster (Ed.), *Readings on equal education* (Vol. 11). New York: AMS Press. 245–271.

Ladson-Billings, G. (1994). *The dreamkeepers: Successful teachers of African American children.* San Francisco: Jossey-Bass.

Ladson-Billings, G. (1995a). Multicultural teacher education: Research, policy, and practice. In J. A. Banks & C. M. Banks (Eds.), *Handbook of research in multicultural education.* New York: Macmillan. 747–759.

Ladson-Billings, G. (1995b). Toward a theory of culturally relevant pedagogy. *American Educational Research Journal, 35,* 465–491.

Lee, C. (1994). African-centered pedagogy: Complexities and possibilities. In M. Shujaa (Ed.), *Too much schooling, too little education: A paradox of black life in white societies.* Trenton, NJ: Africa World Press. 295–318.

Milwaukee Journal Sentinel. (1998, April 16). Tack to work, lawmakers told. *MJS* online version: *www.jsonline.com/news/0416session.stm*

Ogbu, J. (1993). Frameworks—variability in minority school performance: A problem search of an explanation. In E. Jacobs & C. Jordan (Eds.), *Minority education: Anthropological perspectives.* New York: Ablex Press. 83–111.

Ornstein, A., Doll, R., & Hawkins, M. (1971). *Educating the disadvantaged.* New York: AMS Press.

Ryan, K., & Cooper, J. (1988). *Those who can, teach.* Boston: Houghton Mifflin.

Shujaa, M. (1995). Cultural self meets cultural other in the African American experience: Teachers' responses to curriculum content reform. *Theory into Practice, 34,* 194–201.

Spradley, J. (1979). *The ethnographic interview.* New York: Holt, Rinehart & Winston.

Suarez-Orozco, M. (1987). "Becoming somebody": Central American immigrants in the U.S. inner city schools. *Anthropology & Education Quarterly* (Special Issue), 287–299.

Swartz, E. (1992). Emancipatory narratives: Rewriting the master script in the school curriculum. *Journal of Negro Education, 61,* 341–355.

Tate, W. F. (1995). Returning to the root: A culturally relevant approach to mathematics pedagogy. *Theory into Practice, 34,* 166–173.

Wellman, D. (1977). *Portraits of white racism.* Cambridge: Cambridge University Press.

Wolcott, H. (1987). On ethnographic intent. In G. Spindler & L. Spindler (Eds.), *Interpretive ethnography of education: At home and abroad.* Hillsdale, NJ: Lawrence Erlbaum. 37–57.

Zeichner, K. M. (1992). *Educating teachers for cultural diversity.* National Center for Research on Teacher Learning. Special Report. East Lansing, MI: NCRTL.

$$--- 10 ---$$

Afrocentric Education:
Critical Questions for
Further Considerations

Jacqueline Jordan Irvine

The failure of African American students to achieve in America's schools is well documented. On every indicator of academic achievement—the SAT (Scholastic Aptitude Test), the National Assessment of Educational Progress, college attendance—African American students' performance lags behind their white, Hispanic, and Asian peers (Irvine, 1990).

Although African American and Hispanic students have shown increased performance on standardized test scores, the gains have been relatively small and inconsistent over time. Consider the following data (Bracey, 1992) regarding the SAT: Assuming that white scores remain the same, black students would not catch up with their white counterparts until the year 2100. Or ponder this reality: In 1992, only 1 percent of African American students (as compared to 8 percent of white students) scored 600 or above on the verbal section of the SAT.

The continuing failure of African American students in schools has led to the emergence of many African-centered public schools across the country; among the most notable are the Atlanta and Milwaukee initiatives.

THE ATLANTA PUBLIC SCHOOL AND THE MILWAUKEE
SCHOOLS AFROCENTRIC CURRICULUM PROGRAMS

The Atlanta Public Schools Afrocentric Immersion Project, started in 1989 with a $1 million budget, was located in about 109 schools and affected nearly 60,000 students. A change in school leadership and a focus on improving state-mandated achievement objectives have resulted in only a few schools in the system currently implementing the curriculum. As originally conceived, the Atlanta Afrocentric Immersion Project was based on the philosophy that curriculum should prepare students to live, learn, and work in a pluralistic world. Some of the goals were to:

1. Provide information that will assure that students are presented with a truthful picture of the human experience.
2. Tell the true history of African Americans, not just the contributions of a few isolated heroes and events.
3. Provide an opportunity for educators to integrate the history and culture of African people as they evolved over time.

From these goals emerged nine behavioral learning objectives called Curriculum Learning Objectives (CLOs), Ten Organizing Principles, and *The Baseline Essays* that served as the foundation for the development of instructional activities and the project's evaluation. Teachers in the system spent 30 hours in staff development sessions in preparation for implementing the curriculum. They wrote lesson plans, attended seminars, and participated in field trips.

Unlike the total system implementation plan of Atlanta, in 1990 the Milwaukee Public School Board designated only two of its schools as African American Immersion Schools. The Milwaukee teachers were required to take 18 hours of course credits in African and African American history and culture. In addition to the issue of teacher training and size of the intervention, there were other notable differences in the approaches used by the two systems. The Milwaukee African American Immersion School Project was originally conceived as a school for African American males only and originated as one of many recommendations made by a Task Force to consider the school failure of African American males. However, once the decision was made to establish the school as coeducational, the project's mission took on a more expansive scope. Unlike the Atlanta project, there were changes made in the school structures like extended day and after-school programs as well as school-based staff development programs. New initiatives were combined with the Afrocentric curriculum such as uniforms, rites of passage, mentoring programs, parent coordinators, and home visitations. More important, the Milwaukee program adopted a strong evaluation project that employed a holistic approach involving all the significant stakeholders in the system.

In spite of these differences, the two projects were undertaken as a strategy to reverse the school failure of African American students, and similar immersion projects were replicated in urban districts across the country. This growth has spawned a national debate on their academic credibility and value to African American students. In an attempt to contribute to this discussion and support the Afrocentric education movement as a means to enhance the achievement of African American children, this chapter raises critical questions: *What* is an Afrocentric curriculum? *Why* is it a viable educational curricular alternative? *Who* will teach it? *How* will it be taught?

These are important questions for consideration because the complexity and multiple agendas of the Afrocentric movement are frequently reduced to simple verbs like *immerse, infuse, align, integrate,* and *embed* and nouns like *courses, credits, canons, projects,* and *programs.* Thinking of the Afrocentric curriculum as a course of study or a curriculum revision intervention ignores the what, why, who, and how questions raised in this chapter. The singular focus on Afrocentric education as a curriculum reform may produce virtuous feelings among its advocates but inconsequential and perfunctory results because the curriculum revision approach ignores:

1. The issue of power and control. Issues of power and control engender queries like: How should teachers be prepared to teach? Who decides on what is to be taught? How will money and other resources be allocated? Who defines and controls the reward system? What school structures, practices, and policies need to be put into place to ensure the sustainability of the movement?

2. The psychological and developmental aspects of Afrocentrism that demand that teachers and students reflect upon complicated issues associated with their own personal, cultural, and ethnic identities. Questions related to this issue are, for example: How comfortable and aware is the teacher of his or her own ethnic identity? How does the teacher's racial and personal identity complement each other? How do the goals of the Afrocentric curriculum compare with the teacher's instructional goals and objectives?

3. The mandate of community empowerment that demands that the Afrocentric school curriculum build and develop the communities where African American children and their parents live. Relevant questions to be raised include: Are the students' parents supportive of and knowledgeable about the goals and objectives of the Afrocentric curriculum? What efforts are being made by the school to teach the Afrocentric curriculum to parents? How does the Afrocentric curriculum assist the student's family and community? Are community leaders involved in the development and evaluation of the curriculum?

WHAT IS AN AFROCENTRIC CURRICULUM?

The term *Afrocentric* is used widely, and its definition has taken a variety of meanings. However, most agree that an Afrocentric curriculum is a systematic study of the multidimensional aspects of black thought and practice centered around the contributions and heritage of people of African descent. The principles of an Afrocentric curriculum, as posited by Asante (1991–1992) and outlined in the Portland *African American Baseline Essays* (1990), state that Africa is the cradle of civilization and that the education of African American children should be philosophically based in the African worldview and African thought. Some tenets of this philosophy and worldview as summarized by Boykin (1986) are spirituality, harmony, movement, verve, affect, communalism, expressive individualism, oral tradition, and social time perspective.

There is a strong explicit political agenda in the curriculum (Asante, 1988) as opposed to the implicit political agenda of the Eurocentric curriculum. An Afrocentric education explicitly states that its purpose is to construct a social reality from the framework of African history and culture. In addition, the curriculum places at the center of its work the survival of the continent. Akoto (1994) informs us that the goals of the Afrocentric curriculum are related to issues like self-determination, self-sufficiency, the discovery of truth, and "the mission to humanize the world" (321).

The content of the Afrocentric curriculum in public school systems, frequently based on the Portland model, has evolved in some interesting ways—a curious and often confusing mix of Egypt-centered or Kemetic orientation, west and east African culture, and multiculturalism. For example, in some initiatives kindergarten children count to five in Swahili; sixth graders memorize concepts like pyramids, papyrus, Egypt's climate and distance from their schools; and eighth graders translate fractions into hieroglyphics. Bulletin boards are adorned with pictures of Egyptian kings and queens, kente, and masks. Assembly programs feature dance, musical, and dramatic performances with African and African American themes and schoolchildren dressed as royalty. A statement by an Atlanta teacher quoted in the national educational magazine *Black Issues in Higher Education* (Glenn, 1993) typifies the motivation behind this orientation. She said, "We African Americans are a nation of kings and queens, and our kids need to know that"(22).

Accompanying the Afrocentric curriculum is the attention by some schools to the goals of multiculturalism. A review of some of the Afrocentric curriculum objectives by Manley (1994) discovered that eight school districts that called their curricula Afrocentric actually implemented a curriculum that was multicultural. In fact, the multicultural curricula of these districts were mostly operating at level two of Banks's (1991) typology, that is, infusing information about African Americans and Africans added to a traditional Eurocentric curriculum.

WHY IS THE AFROCENTRIC CURRICULUM CONSIDERED A VIABLE EDUCATIONAL OPTION?

The proponents of the Afrocentric curriculum express its viability and merit based on a number of assumptions about African American children. Among these are several that relate to psychological dimensions of self-esteem and motivation:

1. African American children suffer from low self-esteem.
2. African American children's low self-esteem causes their low school performance.
3. African American children are motivated to achieve by studying their history and the contributions of African American achievers.

African American children suffer from low self-esteem. There are mounting data that, contrary to conventional wisdom, African American children do not suffer from low self-esteem. Previous research that led to these conclusions has been criticized for its methodological weaknesses and failure to understand the cultural worldview of African American children. In a review of the research, Graham (1994) summarized 140 studies concerning motivational characteristics of African Americans. She concluded that "both expectancy for future success and self-concept among African Americans remain relatively high even when achievement outcomes indicate otherwise" (103). Other researchers like Mickelson (1990), Anderson and Senior (1992), and Hare and Castenell (1985) have documented an interesting paradox among African American children—they tend to think highly of themselves and are confident of their abilities even when they perform poorly in school. The evaluation report from the African American Immersion Project in Milwaukee (Pollard & Ajirotutu, 1994) found a similar trend on the PASS (Perceptions of Ability Scale for Students). Why? Researchers speculate that African American students' self-concept is rooted in a nonacademic environment and that school people's evaluations are dismissed by African American children relying instead on the feedback of peers or family members. Adding to the complexity of the issue, researchers have found that African American students who have positive attitudes toward school and have high future aspirations often perform poorly academically.

Mickelson (1990) makes the distinction between African American students' abstract and concrete attitudes toward education. She found a discrepancy between African American students' abstract attitudes (generalized beliefs that schooling is a vehicle for success and upward mobility) and their concrete attitudes (beliefs that their specific hard work and effort will result in success).

African American children's low self-esteem causes their low school performance. Ironically, there are assumptions and theoretical underpinnings of Afrocentrism and racially integrated education that appear to be the same. Both of these perspectives posit a direct relationship between two variables—that is, African American students' higher self-esteem produces higher school achievement scores. *Brown v. Board of Education* (1954) used the doll studies data of psychologist Kenneth Clark to show that black children in segregated black schools were stigmatized by their ethnic group membership. The Court decision stated that black children's poor self-concepts and feelings of inferiority were directly related to their race; hence, they should attend schools with white children where their race would be deemphasized. Some Afrocentric educators make the same direct linkages between self-esteem and achievement except they believe that African American students should attend schools where their racial identity is emphasized and celebrated.

Shujaa (1995) analyzed the responses of 21 white and African American Buffalo teachers in the system's African and African American Curriculum Program. He found that the teachers believed that the curriculum was intended to raise the self-esteem of African American students, never questioning the benefits to non–African American students.

Another example is the Atlanta Public Schools central office administrator who stated in a *Washington Post* interview (Horowitz, 1993), "The person with better self-esteem will accomplish more." The relationship between these two variables is certainly more complicated than this Atlanta administrator's or the Buffalo teachers' statements. Self-esteem and school achievement have a correlative relationship but not a causal one. For example, we know that children who perform well in school appear to have high self-esteem. What is masked in this relationship is the possibility that high achievement fosters and nourishes high self-esteem—and not the reverse, that is, high self-esteem develops high achievement. It appears that children develop a positive sense of self when they perform meaningful tasks and that accomplishment is acknowledged and rewarded by the children's significant others. That is, according to Kohn (1994, 275), students feel good about themselves because they do well rather than do well because they feel good about themselves.

African American children are motivated to achieve by studying their history and the contributions of Africans and African American achievers. What do we know about the relationship between the Afrocentric curriculum and African American students' school achievement? One researcher (Manley, 1994) surveyed and interviewed 340 teachers in 24 of the 29 high schools in the Atlanta public schools. The researcher asked the teachers if the Afrocentric Immersion Curriculum had increased the academic performance of their students. Data analyses revealed that the teachers did not believe that their students' academic performance had improved as a result of the infusion curriculum. The teachers believed that their students were more interested in the subject content when infused with an Afrocentric perspective, but there was no change in standardized test scores or teacher-designed tests. Teachers also said that since the four years the immersion project was instituted, attendance had not improved. This situation in Atlanta begs the questions, Are we using the appropriate tests to measure achievement? How long does it take for the Afrocentric curriculum to produce gains in African American children's test scores?

Murrell (1993, 239) states that the debate on Afrocentrism must move beyond its "trivialized" focus on self-esteem. An Afrocentric education must produce some measurable achievement outcomes, and those outcomes must be identified and negotiated with school people, parents, the students' home community, employers, and the higher education community. I suspect that higher self-esteem and knowledge of one's history are two easily agreed-upon outcomes, but higher test scores on teacher-made, state-mandated, and standardized tests and college admissible SAT scores will dominate these conversations. This focus on standardized test scores is unfortunate and inappropriate; however, educational researchers have been unsuccessful in convincing parents, particularly African American parents, that their children's performance on these measures is of limited value. Afrocentric immersion approaches have to produce achievement and mastery performance if this curriculum intervention is to maintain its credibility and viability.

WHO WILL TEACH THE AFROCENTRIC CURRICULUM?

One area that is often overlooked or minimized is the issue of teachers in immersion schools. Some proponents of the Afrocentric curriculum advocate that teachers of this curriculum must be "cultural representatives" (Akoto, 1994, 325) who advance the cultural and political interest of African people. Lee (cited in Shujaa, 1995, 200) stated that the "conditions necessary for African Americans to achieve ethnic pride, self-sufficiency, equity, wealth, and power" cannot be met in public schools. Given the definition and mission of an African-centered curriculum and the decreasing numbers of African American teachers, Lee's conclusion should be taken seriously.

There must be the recognition that the Afrocentric curriculum can be poorly taught and that African American students need engaged, competent, and efficacious teachers who insist that they learn. Shujaa reminded us that who is teaching is as critical as what is being taught. Research data (Johnson & Prom-Jackson, 1986) revealed that African American children are more teacher dependent than their white counterparts, and studies have concluded that African American students' school success is directly related to their personal feelings about their teachers. Consequently, when African American students believe that they are not liked by their teachers, they do not perform well in school. The converse of this situation is also instructive—African American students often perform well in school for teachers they like. In a synthesis of research on effective practices that enhance achievement for underachieving elementary students, Slavin, Karweit, and Madden (1989) emphasize that the teacher is a central figure. Likewise, Brooks (1987, 59) emphatically states, "The teachers, not the content or methods—important as they are—come first in the learning lives of black children."

There are three points related to teachers. One is the fact that once teachers' classroom doors are closed, they have a great deal of flexibility in the content, the method of instruction, and the time spent on tasks. Unlike other types of organizations, schools do not adhere to a strict bureaucratic model or to the interdependent social systems theory. Performance is seldom monitored, standards are set but rarely enforced, the span of control is large and unwieldy, and goals are diffuse and often ambiguous. If the Afrocentric curriculum is to be successful, dramatic changes in organizational structures, policies, and procedures must also be instituted.

The second point related to teachers is the fact that the diminishing numbers of African American teachers in public schools do not bode well for African American Immersion Projects in any city. Ironically, as the number of minority students increases, the number of minority teachers decreases. By the year 2020, 39 percent of the school-age population will be children from ethnic groups (Hodgkinson, 1989). However, the number of African American students in the nation's urban centers is considerably higher. Orfield, Bachmeier, James, and Eitle (1997) reported that 83 percent of urban schools served a "nonwhite" population and the degree of segregation and racial isolation is deepening. Data conclude that efforts to integrate American schools have failed and left urban schools predominantly African American, Hispanic, and poor. Yet data predict that in the future the teaching force will be less than 5 percent African American, significantly lower than the 12 percent of 1980 (G. Pritchy Smith cited in Rodman, 1985). Smith projected that an ethnically diverse teaching force of 5 percent would mean that the average student, who has about 40 teachers during his or her precollegiate years, could expect, at best, to encounter only 2 teachers of color during his or her entire school career. These research data are not intended to imply that non–African American teachers are ineffective or that they cannot be trained to be effective teachers in African American schools (see Ladson-Billings's [1994] description of Ann Lewis).

In an empirical study Payne (1994) concluded that the most effective teachers of African American students are teachers who have a sense of efficacy; that is, they believe that their students can learn and they can teach. These are confident, at ease, "take care of business," no-nonsense teachers who have positive relationships with their students in and out of school. Payne and other researchers' data indicate that these types of efficacious teachers are more likely to be experienced African American teachers who perceive themselves as parental surrogates for their students.

Evidence of African American teachers' parental roles is documented in the works of researchers like Foster (1997) and Ladson-Billings (1994). Foster quotes an African American teacher: "I'll be their mother at school and they (referring to the children's biological parents) can be the Mama at home" (112). As parent surrogates, these teachers assume familial social relationships with their students. Ladson-Billings described these relationships as equitable, connected to community, and collaborative in nature (55).

One of the most impressive empirical works that illustrates this point is the work of Meier, Stewart, and England (1989). Using all U.S. school districts with at least 1 percent black representation (n = 174), these researchers investigated the relationship between black representation and equal access to education. Specifically, they answered the question, Does having black school board members, black administrators, and black teachers have any impact on black students' school success?

The researchers concluded, "The single most important factor for all forms of second generation discrimination is the proportion of black teachers" (140). In school districts with larger proportions of African American teachers, the study found fewer African American students being placed in special education classes, fewer African Americans receiving corporal punishment, fewer African Americans being suspended or expelled, more African Americans in gifted and talented programs, and more African Americans graduating from high schools. The authors' data supported the finding that "Black teachers are without a doubt the key" (6).

African American teachers are more likely than their white counterparts to decrease minority students' school alienation and contribute to their academic success by serving as cultural translators for monocultural, at-risk African American students who often fail because the culture of the school is vastly different from the culture of their homes and communities. Researchers refer to these differences in cultures as *cultural incompatibility* and *cultural dissonance*. My own work (Irvine, 1990) describes the phenomenon as *lack of cultural synchronization*.

The concept of cultural synchronization is based on anthropological and historical research that advances the finding that African Americans have a distinct culture. Although there are regional and social class variations of the displayed behaviors, there appears to be what Boykin (1986) calls a distinctive cultural deep structure that transcends both regional and class distinctions. Banks (1988) concluded that "while ethnicity is to some extent class sensitive, its effects persist across social-class segments within an ethnic group" (462).

Cultural conflicts are evidence in schools that serve children of African descent. Because the culture of African American children is different and often misunderstood, ignored, or discounted, they are likely to experience cultural discontinuity in schools, resulting in lack of cultural correspondence or "sync." This lack of cultural sync becomes evident in instructional situations when teachers misinterpret, denigrate, and dismiss African American students' language, nonverbal cues, physical movements, learning styles, cognitive approaches, and worldview. When teachers and students are out of sync, they clash and confront each other, both consciously and unconsciously, in matters concerning proxemics (use of interpersonal distance), paralanguage (behaviors accompanying speech, such as voice tone, pitch, speech rate, and length), and coverbal behavior (gesture, facial expression, eye gaze). African American teachers demonstrate unique African American teaching styles that appear to be related to African American students' culture; hence, they facilitate their achievement and school success.

The third point has to do with the issue of how teachers interact with students in the classroom. Scant attention has been given to changing the ways teachers interact with students in classrooms, and, of course, this includes Afrocentric classes. My own research (Irvine, 1990) points to the degree of differential treatment that students can potentially receive in the classroom. Teachers in Afrocentric schools must become aware of their classroom interactions. They must attend to issues like: who is called on and who is ignored; who receives praise, criticism, or no feedback; who is touched and hugged; and who is graded harshly and who receives the benefit of the doubt.

HOW WILL THE AFROCENTRIC CURRICULUM BE TAUGHT?

The *how* question has to do with pedagogy—the teaching strategies, behaviors, skills, and approaches that are most effective in Afrocentric classrooms. This question highlights the point that Afrocentric lessons can be poorly taught. One instructional approach that is gaining prominence is culturally responsive or culturally salient (Hilliard, 1997) pedagogy.

Villegas (1991, 13) states: "A culturally responsive pedagogy builds on the premise that how people are expected to go about learning may differ across cultures. In order to maximize learning opportunities, teachers must gain knowledge of the cultures represented in their classrooms, then translate this knowledge into instructional practice." Smith's (1991) definition extends the Villegas interpretation by noting that student achievement is not the only purpose of a culturally responsive pedagogy. He believes that culturally responsive teaching incorporates the child's culture into classroom practice in order to enhance school achievement.

Other theorists make finer distinctions between culturally responsive pedagogy and critical pedagogy, and culturally responsive pedagogy and emancipatory pedagogy. Ladson-Billings (1992) notes that culturally relevant pedagogy prepares students to effect change in society, not merely fit into it. She advocates a pedagogy that supports students' home and community culture, empowers students intellectually, socially, emotionally, and politically, and urges collective action grounded in cultural understanding, experiences, and ways of knowing. King (1991) pushes this discussion to another level by writing about the concept of emancipatory pedagogy. She believes that emancipatory pedagogists help students by making them "co-creators of culturally affirming emancipatory learning experiences that oppose and transcend it" (263). The elements of a culturally responsive pedagogy prescribe academic excellence, cultural integrity, culturally aware teachers, critical consciousness, community identification, action, and empowerment (Ladson-Billings, 1995).

These various definitions share similar attributes and characteristics. Emancipatory pedagogy is more emphatic in its focus on community empowerment, and culturally responsive pedagogy is more explicit in its descriptions of instructional strategies and methods. Despite these subtle differences, the Afrocentric curriculum as demonstrated in the Atlanta and Milwaukee projects gives little attention to the issue of "how" to teach and provides more focus on "what" to teach. The Afrocentric curriculum rings hollow unless teachers are trained in pedagogical skills and taught to incorporate these elements into their classroom practice.

In conclusion, I want to emphasize that the Afrocentric curriculum is a viable educational option for African American children. However, we cannot reduce the complexities of Afrocentrism's multiple agendas. The Afrocentric curriculum must attend to content curriculum issues but not ignore equally important issues related to schools' values, cultural norms, policies, and practices. An Afrocentric curriculum transforms schools into communities of learners where all students are respected and recognized as individuals and where they feel a sense of connection, intimacy, visibility, and self-worth. The Afrocentric curriculum, as a broader educational and political movement, should not ignore these caring and interpersonal variables.

The Milwaukee effort is an example of how an Afrocentric curriculum can move beyond minimalist efforts. The focus of the Milwaukee effort, appropriately so, is not narrowly directed at the curriculum. This is a total school restructuring project, not just a curriculum addition. Some of the project's noteworthy and replicable features include its attention to:

1. Changing the nature of the interpersonal relationships between and among students, teachers, staff, and administrators.

2. Changing school structures (extended day and after-school programs, teachers remaining with their classes for more than one year, school-based staff development), and adding new initiatives (organization of family classes, full-time social worker, uniforms, rites of passage, and mentoring programs).

3. Attending to the unique and peculiar needs of individual schools' history and context. All of the schools were not required to implement the curriculum immediately and in the same way.

4. Recognizing the need for parent involvement. Teachers were expected to make home visits, and there was a parent coordinator at the middle school.

5. Recognizing the need for a strong and carefully executed evaluation. The Milwaukee project evaluation employed a holistic approach that involved all the significant stakeholders. The evaluation used a wide variety of student outcome measures and several research methodologies and examined several units of analyses (individuals, classrooms, schools) and many data collection strategies, such as classroom observations, interviews, archival data, and standardized assessment instruments.

More Afrocentric schools should be implemented in urban African American schools that understand and address the what, why, who, and how questions raised at the beginning of this chapter. Specifically, we need Afrocentric schools that understand:

1. *What* an Afrocentric curriculum is and *what* its educational and political goals and objectives are designed to address;

2. *Why* an Afrocentric curriculum is more than a self-esteem builder for African American students;

3. *Who* is needed to teach the curriculum—that is, carefully selected, well-trained, culturally conscious teachers; and finally,

4. *How* the curriculum is taught is as important as the content being taught.

REFERENCES

African American baseline essays. (1990). Portland, OR: Multnomah School System.

Akoto, A. (1994). Notes on an Afrikan-centered pedagogy. In M. J. Shujaa (Ed.), *Too much schooling, too little education.* Trenton, NJ: Africa World Press. 319–337.

Anderson, B. T., & Senior, A. M. (1992, February). *African American students' perceptions about academic learning and its impact on academic performance and behavior.* Paper presented at the Eastern Educational Research Association, Sarasota, FL.

Asante, M. K. (1988). *Afrocentricity.* Trenton, NJ: Africa World Press.

Asante, M. K. (1991–1992). Afrocentric curriculum. *Educational Leadership, 49,* 4, 28–31.

Banks, J. A. (1988). Ethnicity, class, cognitive, and motivational styles: Research and teaching implications. *Journal of Negro Education, 57,* 452–466.

Banks, J. A. (1991). *Teaching strategies for ethnic studies* (5th ed.). Boston: Allyn & Bacon.

Boykin, A. W. (1986). The triple quandary and the schooling of AfroAmerican children. In U. Neisser (Ed.), *The school achievement of minority children.* Hillsdale, NJ: Lawrence Erlbaum. 57–92.

Bracey, G. W. (1992). The condition of public education. *Phi Delta Kappan, 14,* 2, 104–117.

Brooks, C. K. (1987). Teachers: Potent forces in the learning lives of black children. In D. S. Strickland & E. J. Cooper (Eds.), *Educating black children: America's challenge.* Washington, DC: Howard University Press. 55–62.

Foster, M. (1997). *Black teachers on teaching.* New York: New Press.

Glenn, G. (1993, November 18). Atlanta pushes inclusive curricula. *Black Issues in Higher Education, 10,* 9 22–23.

Graham, S. (1994). Motivation in African Americans. *Review of Educational Research, 64,* 1, 55–117.

Hare, B. R., & Castenell, L. A. (1985). No place to run, no place to hide: Comparative status and future prospects of black boys. In M. B. Spencer, G. K. Brookins, & W. R. Allen (Eds.), *Beginnings: The social and affective development of black children.* Hillsdale, NJ: Lawrence Erlbaum Associates. 201–214.

Hilliard, A. S. (1997, October). *Perfecting educational practice: An annotated bibliography and index.* Paper presented at the meeting of the Georgia Association of Teacher Educators, Macon, GA.

Hodgkinson, H. L. (1989). *The same client: The demographics of education and service delivery systems.* Washington, DC: Institute for Educational Leadership.

Horowitz, S. (1993, October 17). Afrocentrism has made the grade in Atlanta, From K to 12. *The Washington Post,* B1, B9.

Irvine, J. J. (1990). *Black students and school failure: Policies, practices, and prescriptions.* Westport, CT: Greenwood.

Johnson, S. T., & Prom-Jackson, S. (1986). The memorable teacher: Implications for teacher selection. *Journal of Negro Education, 55,* 272–283.

King, J. E. (1991). Unfinished business: Black student alienation and black teachers' emancipatory pedagogy. In M. Foster (Ed.), *Qualitative investigations into schools and schooling.* New York: AMS Press. 245–271.

Kohn, A. (1993). Choices for children: Why and how to let students decide. *Phi Delta Kappan,* 75, l, 8–20.

Kohn, A. (1994). The truth about self esteem, *Phi Delta Kappan,* 76, 4, 272–283.

Ladson-Billings, G. (1992). Liberatory consequences of literacy: A case of culturally relevant instruction for African American students. *Journal of Negro Education, 61,* 3, 378–391.

Ladson-Billings, G. (1994). *The dreamkeepers.* San Francisco, CA: Jossey-Bass.

Ladson-Billings, G. (1995). But that's just good teaching! The case for culturally relevant pedagogy. *Theory into Practice, 34,* 3, 159–165.

Manley, O. L. (1994). *A study of second grade teachers' perceptions of an Afrocentric curriculum.* Unpublished doctoral dissertation, Emory University, Atlanta, GA.

Meier, K. J., Stewart, J. & England, R. E. (1989). *Race, class, and education: The politics of second-generation discrimination.* Madison: University of Wisconsin Press.

Mickelson, R. A. (1990). The attitude-achievement paradox among black adolescents. *Sociology of Education, 6,* 3, 44–61.

Murrell, P. (1993). Afrocentric immersion: Academic and personal development of African American males in public schools. In T. Perry & J. W. Fraser (Eds.), *Freedom's plow.* New York: Routledge. 231–259.

Orfield, G., Bachmeier, M. D., James, D. R., & Eitle, T. (1997). Deepening segregation in American public schools: A special report from the Harvard Project on School Desegregation. *Equity and Excellence, 30,* 2, 5–24.

Payne, R. S. (1994). The relationship between teachers' beliefs and sense of efficacy and their significance to urban LSES minority students. *Journal of Negro Education, 63,* 181–196.

Pollard, D. S., & Ajirotutu, C. S. (1994, September). *The African American Immersion School Evaluation Report.* Paper presented at the symposium on the African American Immersion Schools Evaluation Project, Milwaukee, WI.

Rodman, B. (1985, November 20). Teaching's "endangered species," *Education Week, 5,* 11–12.

Shujaa, M. J. (1995). Cultural self meets cultural other in the African experience: An analysis of teachers' experiences to a curriculum content reform. *Theory into Practice, 34,* 3, 195–201.

Slavin, R. E., Karweit, N. L., & Madden, N. A. (1989). *Effective programs for students at risk.* Needham Heights, MA: Allyn & Bacon.

Smith, G. P. (1991, February). *Toward defining a culturally responsible pedagogy for teacher education: The knowledge base for educating the teachers of minority and culturally diverse students.* Paper presented at the AACTE annual meeting, Atlanta, GA.

Villegas, A. M. (1991). *Culturally responsive pedagogy for the 1990s and beyond.* Washington, DC: American Association of Colleges for Teacher Education.

Epilogue

The African American Immersion Schools Evaluation Project ended its data collection at the two schools in June 1997. Since that time the two African American Immersion Schools in this city have continued along the paths established during their first five years of existence. The African American Immersion elementary school has continued to refine and solidify its particular African-centered schooling model. Although there have been some staff changes primarily as a result of retirements, there are processes in place at the school to socialize new teachers to the on-going program. New teachers continue to meet the 18-credit education requirement. The school has retained its principal and its focus as an African-centered school. In addition, based on data compiled by the school district, students at the African American Immersion elementary school have continued to attain high levels of achievement as measured by district-level assessments.

The African American Immersion middle school has also continued in the direction established in the first five years. Staff mobility has continued to be high as teachers have not met the education requirements for remaining at the school. Two years beyond the completion of the five-year study period, only six staff members who were present when this initiative began in 1992 remain at the school. In addition, there has been another complete turnover of administrative staff. The new staff and principal have begun a rebuilding process at the school; however, recently, they were given a new mission by the district. Hence, the priority for the development of an African-centered educational model is not clear. Although it is still designated an African American Immersion middle school, a coherent African-centered program is not in place. It remains to be seen what emerges in the rebuilding process.

During the past two years, there have been major changes at the district level that have important implications for the African American Immersion Schools in this city. Two new superintendents have been appointed. As a result, there have been five different superintendents in this district since 1991 when the first African American Immersion School was opened. In addition, there has been a major change in the composition of the School Board. The newest Board and superintendent have expressed support for increasing the number of choice and charter schools in the public schools and reducing the intradistrict busing of African American students. Both of these initiatives raise questions concerning the continued interest in supporting the African American Immersion Schools.

While the future of African-centered education in the public sector is murky in this district, there is some evidence that it continues to be of interest in other areas of the United States. In Detroit, Michigan, for example, three African-centered public schools exist. In Oakland, California, a high school has included a limited African-centered model with other programs. In Washington, D.C., and Chicago, Illinois, African-centered schools that were once independent have become charter schools in the public sector. Furthermore, discussions about the potential of African-centered educational models continue among researchers, practitioners, and policy makers across the country.

The initial five years of implementation of these two African American Immersion Schools supported the conceptual framework undergirding our research. The schools were introduced during a brief period when an elite group of African American decision makers were in a position to have major influence on school reform. However, this engendered considerable debate about the legitimacy of this schooling alternative nationally as well as within the local African American community. Despite the controversy concerning these two particular schools, the idea of an African-centered focus in public schools appears to be increasingly viewed as viable.

Additionally, there is increased interest in African-centered schooling models internationally. This interest has been expressed to us by individuals in Canada and England, both countries that have large populations of children of African descent. Facing many of the same issues existing in urban schools with many students of color in the United States, individuals and groups in these countries have begun to explore the potential of African-centered schooling. In New Zealand, a group has established a culturally centered educational model for Maori children.

There is clear evidence that in years to come schools will have to attend more closely to culture if they are to educate their diverse student populations effectively. African-centered schools provide one cultural option. It is evident from the experience in Milwaukee that much more work will be necessary both to convince people of the value of African-centered educational models and to institutionalize them in the public schools. Yet public schools serve the overwhelming majority of African American children. The Milwaukee experience has important lessons for researchers, policy makers, and practitioners regarding the promise and pitfalls of making African-centered schooling a permanent aspect of the nation's public schools. If we are truly interested in educating African American children effectively, this is one alternative that merits continued consideration.

Index

About the Contributors

CHERYL S. AJIROTUTU is an Associate Professor of Anthropology at the University of Wisconsin–Milwaukee. She is Co-Principal Investigator of the African American Immersion Schools Evaluation Project. Her research focuses on the influences of culture in school and work settings. She has studied institutional and informal learning situations in public schools; the culture of work traditions, particularly in the use of indigenous technology; and language in society. Her research has been conducted and disseminated in publications in both the United States and West Africa. She is co-author of *Traditional Technology in Nigeria*.

A. WADE BOYKIN is a Professor and Director of the Graduate Program in the Department of Psychology at Howard University. He is also Co-Director of CRESPAR, the Center for Research on the Education of Students Placed at Risk. He has done extensive work in the areas of research methodology, the interface of culture, motivation, and cognition; black child development; and academic achievement in the American social context. He has published numerous research and theoretical journal articles and book chapters relevant to his interests. He is currently completing a book entitled *The Psychology of African Americans' Experiences: An Integrity Based Perspective*. Among his honors are a Spencer Fellow of the National Academy of Education and the Distinguished Scholar Award, American Educational Research Association, Committee on the Role and Status of Minorities.

EDGAR EPPS is Senior Professor in the Department of Educational Policy and Community Studies at the University of Wisconsin–Milwaukee and Marshall Field IV Professor of Urban Education Emeritus at the University of Chicago. He has served as a consultant to the U.S. Department of Education and various other federal, state, and private agencies. In 1994, he served as an expert witness in the *Knight v. Alabama* higher education desegregation case, and in 1996, he was a member of the American Sociological Association's expert panel on Social Science Perspectives on Affirmative Action. During the course of his career, he has received a number of awards, most recently the Du Bois, Johnson, Frazier Award of the American Sociological Association (1996) and the Harold E. Delany Exemplary Educational Leadership Award of the American Association of Higher Education's Black Caucus (1997). He is the author of many books, chapters, and journal articles dealing with issues of race in education.

SHIRLEY BRICE HEATH is the Margery Bailey Professor of English and Dramatic Literature at Stanford University, where she also holds appointments in the Linguistics and Anthropology Departments. She is a linguistic anthropologist whose primary interests are language acquisition, sociocultural contexts of learning, and relations between oral/written language across cultures and institutional settings. She is author of *Ways with Words: Language, Life and Work in Communities and Classrooms* (1983), and several other books on language and literacy. Her primary research since the late 1980s has centered on how young people create learning environments during their nonschool hours for themselves and younger peers.

JACQUELINE JORDAN IRVINE is the Charles Howard Candler Professor of Urban Education in the Division of Educational Studies and founder/director of the Center on Urban Learning/Teaching and Urban Research at Emory University. Dr. Irvine's specialization is in multicultural education and urban teacher education, particularly the education of African Americans. Her book, *Black Students and School Failure* (1990) has received the Outstanding Writing Award from the American Association of Colleges of Teacher Educators and the Outstanding Academic Book of 1990 from the Association of College and University Research Librarians. Her most recent books are *Growing up African American in Catholic Schools* and *Critical Knowledge for Diverse Students*. She has presented more than 200 papers to professional education and community organizations and has received numerous honors and awards.

GLORIA LADSON-BILLINGS is a Professor in the Department of Curriculum & Instruction at the University of Wisconsin–Madison and a Senior Fellow in Urban Education at the Annenberg Institute for School Reform. Her research examines the pedagogical practices of teachers who are successful with African American students. She also investigates Critical Race Theory applications to education. She is the author of the critically acclaimed book, *The Dreamkeepers: Successful Teachers of African American Children* (1994), and has numerous journal articles and book chapters. She is editor of the Teaching, Learning and Human Development Section of the *American Educational Research Journal*. Her work has won numerous scholarly awards including the H. I. Romnes faculty fellowship, the Spencer Post-doctoral Fellowship, and the Palmer O. Johnson Outstanding Research Award.

DIANE S. POLLARD is a Professor of Educational Psychology and currently Director of the Urban Education Doctoral Program at the University of Wisconsin–Milwaukee. She is co-Principal Investigator of the African American Immersion Schools Evaluation Project. One of her research interests focuses on understanding cultural, psychological and social factors related to coping and achievement in African American children. She also examines the intersections of race and gender, particularly among African Americans. She is co-editor of the book *Gender and Education* (1993), has published numerous book chapters and articles in professional journals and presented her work at national and international conferences as well as colleges and universities around the United States. She is the 1996 recipient of the American Educational Research Association's Willystine Goodsell Award.

ISBN 0-89789-728-5

HARDCOVER BAR CODE

Advance Praise for

FROM ECSTASY TO SUCCESS

"I recommend this book for anyone wanting to add creativity to their power and power to their creativity."

Joel Roberts,
Media Consultant to
Chicken Soup for the Soul

"From Ecstasy to Success is full of the boundless enthusiasm, dynamic ideas and practical techniques that makes Kala such a powerful teacher."

Serge Kahili King, Ph.D.
Author: *Urban Shaman*

"From Ecstasy to Success presents simple, clear techniques for manifesting love and abundance in your life."

Charles Muir
Author: *Tantra: The Art of Conscious Loving*

From Ecstasy to Success is a beautifully written book of extraordinary insight and originality ...a remarkably clear roadmap to greater prosperity, health and personal fulfillment.

Lee Gladden, Ph. D.
Dean of Graduate Studies, Honolulu University
Author: *How to Win at the Aging Game*

09/00

Aloha nui, Light & Bryan,
Many blessings with your
new book. May Ecstasy
be your dearest companion!
♡ Kala H. Kos

FROM ECSTASY TO SUCCESS

A Simple Guide
to
Remarkable Results

Kala H. Kos

Advance Reading Copy

GGI
Gamma Group International
© 2000

IMPORTANT – PLEASE READ THIS FIRST

Although anyone may find the practices, disciplines, and
understandings in this book to be useful, it is made available
with the understanding that neither the author nor the pub-
lisher is engaged in presenting specific medical, psychological,
emotional, sexual or spiritual advice. Nor is anything in this
book intended to be a diagnosis, prescription, recommendation,
or cure for any specific kind of medical, psychological, emotional, sexual, or spiritual problem. Each person has unique
needs, and this book cannot take these individual differences
into account. Each person should engage in a program of
treatment, prevention, cure or general health only in consulta-
tion with a licensed, qualified physician, therapist, or other
competent professional. Any person suffering from any illness
of his or her sexual organs or prostate gland should consult a
medical doctor and a qualified instructor of sexual yoga before
practicing the sexual methods described in this book.

For information, contact:
Gamma Group International

P.O.B. 441,
Kilauea, HI 96754
USA
Tel: 808-826-1068
Email: kala7s@yahoo.com

#105-1725 Martin Dr.
White Rock,
B.C. V4A 9T5
Canada
Tel: 800-370-7380
(PIN #04)
Internet: www.hawaiiheart.com

ACKNOWLEDGEMENTS

Special thanks and undying love go to my mother, Steffi, and my brother, Bob, for their enthusiasm and encouragement for every one of my projects.

With deep gratitude, I thank my friend and mentor, Serge Kahili King, who taught me the concepts and techniques through which I came to understand the Polynesian practice of Huna that comprise the bulk of this book. *Leis of aloha* go to Gloria King, who has been a steadfast supporter, constantly encouraging me to spread this knowledge.

Mahalo nui loa to my Hawaiian *ohana* that has shared so much heart and wisdom with me — especially to Lloyd Imuaikaika Pratt.

I wish to acknowledge my good friend and fellow teacher Paul Waters, for the insight, wit and advice he provided during my ongoing adventures in writing.

Heartfelt thanks go to my first Tantra instructor, Margo Anand, who opened up a new realm of possibilities within me, and to my other dear tantric teachers and friends who have inspired so much ecstasy.

With great appreciation and love, I thank my editor and dear friend Deanna Brady, whose patience and skill throughout the various projects on which we have worked together have made my life and my words richer.

Thanks also go to Bill Gladstone, whose intuition, skill and generous spirit have guided me forward in my writing career.

Most gratefully, I thank all the people who have read my books, listened to my tapes and attended my workshops, for they have enhanced my life profoundly.

This book is dedicated to the angel on my shoulder,
my dear father, Zvonko Kos,
who always believed in me as a writer…
although he never saw the day my first book was published.

Introduction

THE INNER CAUSE OF OUTER EVENTS

Never before had I known illness intimately. Persistent pain was an unfamiliar sensation to my young body. Each day I prayed that the bus driver wouldn't pull away from the curb while I was laboring to get off the back step and onto the sidewalk. Each evening I persevered, step by step in slow motion, up five flights to my New York apartment. Night after night, I lay in a tub of hot water to relax my spasming muscles.

The disease that had readily been detected in my blood had such a dramatic name: *ankylosing spondilitis*. This crippling arthritic/rheumatic condition seemed much more appropriate to an elderly person than a twenty-six-year-old, and it was already causing painful inflammation of my joints. The doctors explained that it was degenerative, progressive and potentially fatal. They also told me there was no cure. . . .

*   *   *   *

From early childhood I had a secret adventurous streak. I felt that there must be something more to life than the limited view of the world I could see from the small prairie city where I grew up. I was convinced that there were tantalizing mysteries awaiting me elsewhere. I yearned for wonder, awe, a sense of the miraculous. I just knew it existed! This is the path that led me to it:

While studying English literature at a local university, I decided to apply for a position as a flight attendant with a major airline. Although I wasn't sure I was sophisticated enough for what seemed like such a glamorous job, my strong desire to travel and a sincere love of people fueled my enthusiasm in the interview. Suddenly, at nineteen, I found myself living in a major metropolis – Toronto – and flying international routes. The world opened up dramatically as I rode on gondolas in Venice, gazed upon masterworks at the Louvre and danced to the rhythms of steel drums in Barbados. It was a thrilling time of personal growth, and I considered myself highly fortunate.

As I explored the globe, however, my inner horizons also continued to expand. Eventually, I began to yearn for a deeper experience of myself. Although I had continued my education while flying, I longed for a creative outlet that my work as a flight attendant just couldn't seem to provide. After seven years, I had begun to feel the limitations of my job.

When a friend invited me to sit in on her acting class, I had no idea what to expect. As I watched the students practice their craft, I was so inspired that I could hardly contain my excitement. Here was an art form in which I could use all of myself – my body, thoughts, feelings and energy – to express a living character uniquely. How could anything be more creative than that? I knew then that I wanted to study this marvelous form of self-expression.

Little did I know that I was about to encounter the mysterious workings of the universe in a way that would profoundly effect my destiny. I had come to an intersection in my life, and the road I was about to take would alter me in ways I could never have imagined.

It all began during a meal service on a busy international flight with the typical task of pulling a heavy trolley up the aisle. Suddenly, I felt a flash of intense pain in my lower back. Out of necessity, I forced myself to ignore the pain and go on with my work for the rest of the night. By the following morning, the pain was excruciating, and I couldn't even get out of bed. This injury apparently set the stage for my incapacity, as I was faced with the onset of a disease that began to inhabit my body. Unable to continue to fly, I now had a new challenge, as well as an opportunity to change my life for the better.

Since my usual work was out of the question, I decided to try a different direction. It wasn't long before I was attending what was regarded at that time as one of America's most prestigious acting schools, the Strasberg Institute in New York City. There, I learned the importance of becoming highly sensitized, in touch with all aspects of myself and of life.

Feeling vibrantly alive in my new awareness in spite of the debilitation of my health, I immersed myself in fascinating roles. In my study of behavior, I observed people around me and began to perceive that everyone was playing a "role" in the "script" of his or her life. Some "characters" were creating the experience of love, confidence and prosperity; others created disappointment, fear and poverty. It dawned on me that each of us recreates a role every day. I realized that we all have a hand in creating our experience, and the greatest works of art, our ultimate creations, are our individual lives!

One revelatory weekend, during a human-potential seminar, I suddenly realized that the illness I had been enduring for three long years was actually one of my own creations. The power of that discovery lay in my new understanding that I had the ability to "re-create" health. I knew then that I had to take action; the alternative was to end up without a job, poor and disabled, with no hope of acting professionally.

I then set about to create my healing. For the next year, I learned and practiced every discipline I could find that might help my body to rejuvenate itself. I monitored myself and was mindful to acknowledge every sign of improvement. Finally, I returned to the airline administration and was sent to three medical specialists, who each examined me thoroughly. This time, there was no trace of the illness in my body – not even in my blood. I was healthy and vital once again. The specialists pronounced this seeming miracle a "spontaneous remission" – and it continues to this day, nearly two decades later.

Such was the journey that led me to search for the inner causes of outer events.

*   *   *   *

My search brought me to the doorway of the inner world, and once I stepped through, my life was forever changed for the better. That adventure left me with the indelible impression that we each create our experience of reality from the inside out. I was determined to discover how.

As my fascination with the inner workings of human experience grew, my interest in the "business" of acting began to diminish. Imagine my excitement when my search eventually led me to explore an ancient science of manifestation that clearly validated my discovery. Before long, I was drawn to a beautiful Hawaiian island and down the path of the age-old Polynesian art of living known as *Huna*. This began my formal study of the art and science of making things happen. I invested myself in Huna with boundless enthusiasm, and it never lost its appeal or failed to live up to its promise.

Several years after I became a Huna *alaka'i* (a spiritual leader), and a minister, I was led to yet another body of ancient knowledge that also enhanced my life immeasurably. This teaching originated in India thousands of years ago, and it can be practiced alone or with a partner. It is known as *Tantra,* and it is often described as the art of "sacred sexuality," a gateway to spirituality through one's own sexual energy.

Just as I had always felt that there had to be more to life than meets the eye, I felt there had to be something more to sex than just a few fleeting moments of pleasure. Inspired yet again, I became an earnest student of Tantra, exploring the depths of love and sexual energy within my own being. Like Huna, Tantra appealed to me because of its integration of body, heart and spirit. It enabled me to take another step into an even deeper awareness of myself, others and my environment.

I soon discovered the power of combining the knowledge of Huna with the energy practices of Tantra to manifest positive change. I began to design and teach "Ecstasy and Success" workshops based on these elements, and I saw the profound effects these teachings had on the participants. Later, I carried the same effective practices and principles into the arena of prosperity with my "Dare to Create Money" workshops.

That is the journey that brought me to the writing of this little book packed with large ideas. It is a very basic and simple guidebook, distilling just a small portion of the vast knowledge from each of these ancient philosophies. I chose to write it for all the people like myself who sometimes wish for a concise manual that can serve as inspiration on those days when circumstances look a bit grim, and we ask ourselves, "What's it all about?"

Through sharing these ancient teachings, I have been blessed to act as a catalyst for miracles in people's lives, and I am constantly grateful for my own good fortune. Here in "paradise," on the Garden Isle of Kauai, nature shows one and all that there are truly no limits to the beauty, abundance, joy, love and peace that everyone can experience. Come join me on this grand adventure, and become the architect of your destiny. Choose ecstasy and success in all areas of your life. You DO deserve it!

FROM ECSTACY TO SUCCESS

Ecstasy works. Yet for a long time

it has been underemployed.

The time has come to rediscover it.

One moment of ecstasy can transform your life.

– Margo Anand

You are in a rich, green forest. The breeze surrounds you with the scent of leaves, and every cell of your body feels alive. It's as though the grass, the rocks, the trees and the wind are as aware of you as you are of them. They seem to be breathing oxygen into you, infusing you with energy so vibrant that you feel both powerful and peaceful. A friend you haven't thought about in a long time comes to mind, and it's a pleasant thought. Returning home hours later, you find a message on your answering service. You hear the sweet voice of your friend, calling from thousands of miles away, wanting only to say, "Hello – just thinking of you..."

*   *   *   *

Have you ever thought of someone, and suddenly the phone rang, as if that person had read your mind? What if you were able to direct your attention to thoughts of your most cherished dreams and see them simply come true? Imagine feeling empowered, connected with all aspects of yourself and with your environment. Imagine being able to manifest your desires effortlessly!

There is an innate connection between the state of ecstasy and the phenomenon of effortless manifestation. What is referred to here as ecstasy is not synonymous with pleasure or happiness. It is not a reaction to or a result of outside events. It is that state of awe, wonder and bliss that has been referred to as *timeless awareness.*

We assume the basic premise that ecstasy is the nature of *who you are,* that it is available to you at any moment and is not dependent on anything outside you. Once you access your own inner ecstasy – which is part

*Intelligence is the invisible
organizer of all matter and energy,
and since a portion of this intelligence resides
in you, you share in the
organizing power of the cosmos.*

— Deepak Chopra

of universal Intelligence – you also begin to know spontaneously how to bring about positive change in your life.

The key to success, which we will define here as *effective living with effortless ease,* is flexibility. This book will show you how to be flexible in your endeavors. You will learn how to open your thoughts, feelings and body to become more receptive to the way you truly want to be. Using a combination of significant concepts, along with techniques that utilize four essential tools for directing energy (sound, breath, movement, and imagination), you can create your own means to ecstatic ends.

Ecstasy is a state of mind, as well as a tremendous physical experience. The more open you are to new ideas and techniques, the longer and more frequently you can be in this state.

The object of this book is to learn the art of unfolding to ecstasy. Through a doorway of subtle energies, you begin to experience yourself in partnership with the magical forces of the universe. You learn to awaken the ecstatic reflex within yourself and create a life of increased satisfaction, individuality and achievement.

What are the practical benefits of this state? They include new vitality, enduring youthfulness, expanded personal charisma, a deeper acceptance of self and others, a renewed feeling of innocence, enhanced intuition, more experiences of love, pleasure and joy, a richer flow of opportunity and abundance, and improved access to your power in the present moment.

This is an extraordinary kind of living. Not only are daily stresses relieved, but these practices allow you to attract and enjoy blessings greater than you can now

More essentially, this is an

independent inquiry into certain

normal predicaments of human divinity.

– James Agee

conceive. Incorporating these tools and principles into your life, you become more loving, more sexy, more powerful, more peaceful and more successful in every way, with a lot less effort. However, you must practice them persistently. In doing so, you will realize the magnificent and ecstatic nature of the true self!

In *The Seven Spiritual Laws of Success*, Deepak Chopra tells us:

> When you discover your essential nature and know who you really are, in that knowing itself is the ability to fulfill any dream you have, because you are the eternal possibility, the immeasurable potential of all that was, is, and will be...There is no separation between you and this field of energy. The field of pure potentiality is your own Self. . . .
>
> And when you are grounded in the knowledge of your true Self – when you really understand your true nature – you will never feel guilty, fearful, or insecure about money or affluence, or fulfilling your desires, because you will realize that the essence of all material wealth is life energy, it is pure potentiality. And pure potentiality is your intrinsic nature.

As you unfold to more and more ecstasy in your daily life, as you experience your true self, you awaken to the realization that you co-create your reality with the Universal Mind. Experiences of struggle, lack and limitation diminish. When this occurs, it is because your being is in a state of ideal integration.

We cannot live better

than in seeking to become better.

— *Socrates*

THREE ASPECTS OF THE SELF

Think of your consciousness as expressing in three ways: the subconscious self, the conscious self and the super-conscious self (also known as body, mind, and spirit.) These are aspects of you as a whole, yet they have separate functions. At those times when you experience ecstasy, they are interacting harmoniously, as a team.

The manifesting of personal reality requires the cooperation of all three components of your consciousness. The super-conscious manifests your physical experience by using the patterns of your conscious and subconscious thoughts. With the information and tools in the following pages, you will be better equipped to harmonize all aspects of yourself and consciously involve yourself in the process of creating.

When you start using intent – fixed attention in a particular direction with meaning and purpose – you are participating consciously in the process of creating your life. Casually fixing attention on an idea and then seeing it come back to you in form is simply a responsive event (like the phone call). It's what we generally think of as coincidence. When you have a "why," when you have a purpose, then you have intent. Intent has to do with meaningful direction – a formed, purposeful kind of energy and fixed thought.

LIFE IS AN ENERGY EVENT

Quantum physics now confirms what the ancients have long taught, that the universe is made up of energy and consciousness. Therefore, there is no real separation in the universe, and you are connected to everything in

The soul. . . never thinks

without a picture.

– Aristotle

From Ecstasy to Success

a unifying field of conscious energy. When you put your attention on a thought, an object or an experience, a current of energy flows between you and it, drawing the equivalent experience to you (or you to it.)

At the age of twenty-six, I had a dramatic demonstration of the truth of this principle. I was a vibrant and healthy young woman, employed for several years as a flight attendant on international routes, when I experienced what I believed was a "twist of fate." After injuring my back while working on a flight, I contracted an illness known as *ankylosing spondilitis.* I was told that it was a potentially fatal arthritic/rheumatic disease with extremely debilitating effects and with no known cure. Conventional medicine had little idea how to treat it. Unable to work, I learned to cope with ongoing pain and frustration.

After three years, special circumstances provided me with insight into why I had brought that experience into my life, as well as with the motivation to change it. Rallying all my mental, emotional and physical resources, I shifted my attention to the idea and experience of health.

Since the disease was detectable in my blood, and the airline had determined that I was not physically fit to fly while that was the case, I decided to find ways to cleanse my bloodstream. I remember attending a symphony performance during which I used the inspiration and energy of the music to focus my imagination on purifying my blood. I visualized it shooting up from the center of a beautiful white fountain in front of me, cascading down in pure, opaque red. The powerful music seemed to intensify my desire and conviction. As I left the concert that evening, I felt I had taken significant strides toward health and might even have altered my own physical reality.

Always bear in mind that

your own resolution to succeed

is more important than any one thing.

– Abraham Lincoln

From that point on, I continued to direct my attention to the normalcy of my blood, affirming my wellness and participating in every healing modality I could find that might help my body to rejuvenate itself. Finally, after a year of concentrated effort, I fully believed I had replaced illness with health, but I didn't yet have tangible proof. Then the airline for which I had worked, cautious about returning me to active duty, sent me to three specialists who examined me thoroughly. Not one of them could find a single trace of the disease in my blood or anywhere else in my body! Since that day many years ago, I have been free of the incapacitating condition that I was told could potentially take my life.

My own experience taught me that it is possible to change the inner causes of outer events and, thus, actually change the outer events. It also taught me the power of directed attention. Since that time, I have experienced innumerable examples of the same principles at work. By sustaining your focus of attention on thoughts, images and feelings about having what you want, you can manifest the physical equivalents of those thoughts, images and feelings in your life!

At this point, you may be saying to yourself, "I've focused my attention on what I've wanted many times, and I certainly didn't get those things in my life!" Yes, many people have had that experience. Then, what really *is* the key to manifesting your desires?

WHY SOME PEOPLE MANIFEST THEIR DREAMS AND SOME DON'T

Katherine was an attractive, intelligent and independent woman. She had been in several long-term relationships, but she had never felt she could commit to marriage. As she reached her late thirties, she began

The trouble with most people is that

they think with their hopes or fears or wishes

rather than with their minds.

– Will Durant

to yearn for a life-partner and decided she was finally ready to take that step.

Very soon after her decision, Katherine met Todd. Although their connection was obviously strong, she was cautious about becoming involved with him because he was in the midst of a divorce. "I'm at a time in my life when I finally do want to make a commitment," she told him, "and I don't want to find out several years down the road that I'm with someone who doesn't want to get married."

Todd was adamant that his deep feelings for Katherine were genuine and that he had no reservations about marrying again. They quickly discovered a wonderful rapport and became the best of friends and sweethearts. After two happy years together, they made the decision to become engaged. Another year passed, and Katherine felt it was time to make their wedding plans. On the very night they were choosing the date, Todd put up an emotional wall. He still wanted Katherine, but he didn't want to be married.

It was obvious to Katherine that Todd had major fears left over from a painful ten-year marriage and was not able to get past them to make another huge commitment. She felt heartbroken. Realizing that they were not moving in the same direction, nor would they be in the foreseeable future, she chose to leave the relationship.

Later, she had dreams that she and Todd had actually gone through with it. She dreamed that being married was an awful experience, all that she had hoped it would *not* be, and she felt trapped.

She soon began to suspect that Todd's fear was actually a reflection of her own. Delving into her psyche

Experience is the product of the mind,

the spirit, conscious thoughts and feelings,

and unconscious thoughts and feelings.

These together form the reality that you know.

– Seth/Jane Roberts

to make sense of her experience, she uncovered some severely limiting subconscious beliefs.

Not having witnessed many models of what she considered "satisfying marriages" throughout her youth, she had unconsciously come to doubt the possibility of achieving that herself. From a Catholic background in which divorce was considered a sin, she had also grown up believing that even a marriage that wasn't gratifying had to last forever. That belief had instilled a deep fear that if she married and became unhappy, she would be trapped. If either partner did leave the marriage, she would consider herself a failure. Until the time of her dramatic experience with Todd, Katherine had not chosen to be fully aware of her fear of the risks of marriage.

YOU GET WHAT YOU CONCENTRATE ON

There were probably many previous instances when that subconscious fear reflected itself in Katherine's life; however, it had remained a background focus until her experience prompted her to discover it. Her story is a good illustration of a key element in manifestation:

*   *   *   *

The thoughts and feelings you dwell on,
in full awareness or not,
form the blueprint for your experience.

*   *   *   *

The thoughts you think and the feelings that follow them have an electromagnetic reality. The concentration of your attention sets up a vibration of energy in your

Awareness is not the same as attention.

If awareness is like a bulb

that can shed diffuse light over a wide range,

attention is the focus given to it by a flashlight,

for example, which narrows the beam to a

smaller area.

– Deanna Brady

electromagnetic field, which attracts experiences related to what you concentrate on. You may choose to concentrate your attention on particular ideas, yet subconsciously you may have conflicting thought-reactions to those ideas. This conflict is the root cause of what we often label "self-sabotage." It's for this very reason that I so strongly emphasize the importance of identifying underlying beliefs.

Rooting out subconscious beliefs is not a new idea to modern science. Uncovering the effects of past programming is the basis of the field of psychology. However, in this case, your discoveries about your deeply held beliefs will enable you to change your reality.

It is your beliefs — your thoughts, feelings, attitudes and expectations — that actually draw to you everything you experience in form. An electromagnetic field surrounds you. It also flows through you like an electric current, magnetizing your thoughts and feelings so they attract forms that are like them. Every thought you think goes into this field. If you concentrate on an idea, it becomes magnetized more strongly and, thus, has more power to attract that idea in form. How, then, can you reprogram your subconscious with new beliefs for attracting what you truly want?

The conscious aspect of the mind is responsible for programming the subconscious. In *Mastering Your Hidden Self*, Dr.Serge Kahili King, a scholar of the Polynesian philosophy of Huna, writes, "Conscious attention is a matter of choice; subconscious attention is a matter of habit. . . The power to create your own reality is limited only by your conscious or unconscious beliefs about what is possible for you to achieve or

What lies behind us

And what lies before us

Are tiny matters

Compared to what lies

Within us.

– Ralph Waldo Emerson

experience and your ability to focus your attention toward the beliefs you choose...Learning to consciously decide how to direct your thinking and keep the direction of your intent is a marvelous skill because all of your experience comes from that."

The key, then, to manifesting your desires is the directing of both your conscious and subconscious attention toward a particular purpose with as little confusion and distraction as possible.

If you are satisfied with what you are experiencing, the quality of your relationships and the amount of love, creativity and success in your life, that's great. If you aren't, then you need to shift your complete attention, with the help of your vital energy, to a new pattern. The magic happens as you learn how to align your conscious and subconscious *attention* to achieve a specific purpose while directing a clear, continuous flow of energy toward your *intention*.

REPLACING LIMITING THOUGHT PATTERNS

Everything in the universe is composed of energy vibrating in various patterns, and your thoughts are forms of that energy. You are constantly influenced by thought patterns of your own making or those you have adopted from outside stimuli. Continuing to think the same thoughts over time "charges" those particular ideas, which form strong patterns, becoming beliefs. Beliefs that become established in the subconscious mind then act to create your experience of the world.

The mind is its own place,

and in itself,

can make a Heaven of Hell,

a Hell of Heaven.

– John Milton

The principal function of the subconscious is memory, and it learns through sensory experience and repetition. One of the ways in which the subconscious becomes fixed with certain attitudes and ideas is through the repetition of an idea by a figure of authority, especially when an authority is able to engender strong emotion such as fear.

In Katherine's case, the particular thought-patterns about marriage that her subconscious adopted as truth were established predominantly through the authority of her religion and instilled through fears of entrapment and of punishment for sin. Over time, the patterns became so habitual that she no longer thought of them consciously, yet they were embedded firmly enough to form the blueprint for manifesting her experience.

Many subconscious beliefs are formed in childhood from the words and examples of parents. Unfortunately, some parents have subscribed to the "old-school" tradition that it is effective to demean children so that they will endeavor to prove their parents wrong. People who, as children, were repeatedly given such messages as "You'll never amount to anything" or "Can't you do anything right?" often struggle in adulthood with low self-esteem and experience lives of lack and limitation.

The good news is that all of us can create a more satisfying reality through our decisions about ourselves and life, through our beliefs and the actions we choose each day. It *is* possible to replace limiting thought patterns and change external reality. In order to do that, we must make new, positive beliefs firm enough to override the old ones – just as, in the instance of my bout with disease, I was able to replace old beliefs that were generating energy patterns of illness with a new pattern of complete health.

Energy flows where attention goes:
wherever you direct your attention, your
energy flows. Your sustained, focused attention
channels the energy of the universe into
manifesting the equivalent of
what you are focusing on.

– Serge Kahili King

The subconscious craves direction. It relies on the conscious mind for this direction and on the super-conscious for inspiration. If you don't direct your own subconscious, it will take direction from the external world – from parents, friends, authority figures, television, newspapers, books or other outside influences.

Herein lies the importance of Huna – the science of making things happen – because it illustrates how the parts of an individual must work together harmoniously in order to bring the formless into form. As Dr. King writes, "The conscious mind focuses attention on something and the subconscious mind treats the focus of attention as an event and retains a memory of it. The super-conscious uses the memory as a pattern or blueprint to create an equivalent physical experience."

You have control of only one thing in your life, and that thing alone directs the immense power of Universal Energy.

*   *   *   *

The one thing over which you have control
is **how you focus your attention**.

*   *   *   *

The key element associated with this principle is FOCUS. You can create the experience of energy following focus by doing a simple exercise.

*Be aware of the great value of
energy in your body. As your gratitude
increases so will your energy. Energy is the
source of change and transformation,
and is the universal exchange system.*

– Rowena Pattee Kryder

EXPERIMENTING WITH ENERGY FLOW

In order to create a physical reference for this concept, try the following technique to explore how your mind can affect the flow of energy:

Take a deep breath and exhale slowly. Now hold out your hand, palm facing you, with your arm relaxed. Pay close attention to your hand. Observe its size and shape. Look at the color of your skin. Now see all the lines on the palm of your hand. Focus your attention on them so intently that you could even draw them on a piece of paper.

Imagine there is a dial on your palm that can measure the intensity of your concentration. The highest number on that dial is seven, and the needle is now at three. As your concentrated attention becomes more intense, the needle moves to four. Now let's move it up to five as you feel how the intensity of your concentration increases. Now imagine moving it to six. Now go to the highest number on the dial, seven, and feel the sharp focus of your attention. Hold that focus for one more minute.

Now relax your hand, but leave it in front of you, and relax your focus.

Put out your other hand. Do you see or feel any difference between the two hands? You may have noticed heat, tingling, or a change in color, size or plumpness in the hand on which you focused your attention.

These effects are the result of a biological energy-flow following the path between your mind and the object of your concentrated awareness. You have just experienced physically how *attention energizes.*

ATTRACTING WHAT YOU WANT

The above is an example of directing a clear, continuous flow of energy through intention. When

Treat your goals as guides.

They should stretch and challenge you

but not defeat you.

– David McNally

you harbor no doubts or conflicting beliefs about your desires, the current generated by your persistent attention will literally attract what you focus on and manifest it as your reality, using your thought-patterns as templates.

A good friend, Greg, told me a story that wonderfully illustrates this principle in action:

"I had been working with an engineering company for a year, and I realized I wasn't learning anything new. I was overworked and underpaid. I desperately wanted a change; however, positions in my field, photo-voltaic engineering, are usually hard to find and hard to get.

"I decided to try a technique I had learned to help me focus on my goals. On a piece of paper, I wrote a description of the type of work I wanted. I wasn't overly specific, but I *was* definite about what would make me happy. I knew that I wanted an intellectually challenging environment where I could really learn. I also knew that I wanted to be among friendly people, so I described the atmosphere of the place.

"Each night before bed, I read this description several times. Sometimes I'd wake up in the morning to find the paper on the floor, where it had fallen when I had dozed off. I'd been doing this for a week when I noticed a classified ad that really looked interesting. Although the job qualifications were beyond my educational background, I responded anyway and was called in for an interview.

"I discovered that I had a lot in common with the interviewer, whose first love was art. I told him about my solar sculpture, which was touring the country on exhibit at that time. The meeting was a great success. Later, I learned that I was hired because of my creativity and spirit, as well as my engineering qualifications.

It's a funny thing about life;

if you refuse to accept

anything but the best,

you very often get it.

– W. Somerset Maugham

I had been chosen over fifty other applicants, many with Master's degrees and Ph.D.'s!"

Greg's continued focus, positive expectation and lack of doubt led to the effortless manifestation of his desire.

SPHERE OF AVAILABILITY

Both Greg and Katherine had specific goals they wished to achieve, but a major difference affected their success in manifesting their desires. The degree to which each believed that a new experience was possible for them was a determining factor in their outcomes. With her limiting subconscious beliefs about marriage, Katherine couldn't sustain an expectation of success, whereas Greg's open expectation of an ideal situation allowed the universal energy to move in surprising and fulfilling ways.

Whatever it is that you believe is truly *possible* for you to experience right now is precisely what is *available* to you. This is your *sphere of availability* and it is limited only by your beliefs. That is why you must upgrade your expectations.

In the movie *Thelma and Louise*, the two heroines are in the car at the beginning of their weekend adventure, and Thelma is telling Louise about her husband. Thelma's description of his behavior makes it apparent that he's more interested in his own gratification than in her happiness. Louise simply turns to her and says, "You get what you settle for!"

Everything starts

as somebody's dream.

– Larry Niven

As the successful and popular talk-show host Oprah Winfrey says, "You have to move up to another level of thinking, which is true for me and everybody else. Everybody has to learn to think differently, bigger, to be open to possibilities."

You can do this by using the power of your imagination. For many decades, champion athletes have been winning events by continuously envisioning themselves executing certain movements perfectly. This is the reason that world records continue to be superseded beyond what was previously believed possible. If you create a mental picture of your newly conceived self and continue to hold it in your mind, there will come a day when you are that person in reality.

In Jane Roberts' *The Nature of Personal Reality*, Seth says:

> The main image of yourself that you have held has, to a large extent, also closed your mind to other probable interests and identifications. If you think in terms of a multidimensional self, then you will realize that you have many more avenues open to expression and fulfillment than you have been using. . . You, as a personality, regardless of your health, wealth or circumstances, have a rich variety of probable experience from which to choose. Consciously you must realize this and seize the direction for your own life. Your imagination can be of great value, allowing you to open yourself to such courses; you can then use it to help you bring these into being.

The reason imagination can bring these new states into being is that it operates through an interesting

You have to move up to another level of thinking,

which is true for me and everybody else.

Everybody has to learn to think

differently, bigger, to be open to possibilities."

– Oprah Winfrey

attribute of the subconscious mind: *It cannot tell fact from fiction; it cannot tell the difference between a real event and an imagined one.* Whatever it stores as a truth – real or imaginary – the super-conscious will replicate in form.

Since the subconscious learns through sensory experience, use all your senses to imagine yourself in the situations and surroundings that support what you want in your life. Imitate people who have things, qualities or characteristics you desire. "Mock up" the attitudes and essence you admire. Shakespeare wrote, "Assume a virtue if you have it not." The great painter Salvador Dali said, "Those who do not want to imitate, produce nothing."

Put yourself into physical situations that reflect the new condition or experience. Your subconscious is then able to relate more easily to a new way of being, or to the objects of your desires. It expands its parameters of what's possible to achieve, thereby increasing your sphere of availability.

Sometimes a sudden insight shifts the way we see life and opens up our possibilities. During a human development seminar I attended when I was ill and at the height of frustration and pain, I suddenly realized the close relationship between mental and emotional states and physical health. Once I saw the mind-body connection, I knew that I did have the power to change my mind, and, thus, change the state of my body. My sphere of availability expanded to include the possibility of self-healing.

Sometimes information from a source of authority provides the permission people need to open up to new possibilities. Those possibilities, when accepted, then

We don't have to deny our bodies

to discover our spirit.

– Georg Feuerstein

become realities. Through the Kinsey studies of the 'Fifties concerning female sexuality, modern women realized it was possible to be multi-orgasmic. Since then, *the percentage of women who experience multiple orgasms has almost quadrupled from 14 percent to over 50 percent!* The new research into male multiple orgasm (which is *not* synonymous with ejaculation, however) will undoubtedly cause a rising trend in that experience for men.

RIDING WAVES OF POSITIVE ENERGY

In *Centering and the Art of Intimacy,* Dr. Gay Hendricks puts forth a profound concept:

> After a certain point in evolution, it is necessary to use your body to flush out your higher intentions. We can only go so far with our minds, magnificent though they are. As our intentions become higher we have to learn to ride waves of positive energy inside ourselves. As positive energy polishes our inner body, we have to cooperate with it by finding ways to nurture and support its flow. . . .
>
> We believe that at this time in evolution our species is actually creating new channels in ourselves for experiencing positive energy. How to feel good naturally, without chemical assistance, is a new task in evolution.

Now you need to learn how to open additional positive energy channels.

You can think of your physical body as

a device for controlling energy:

it can generate, store, and expend energy.

If you know how to generate, store and

expend energy in an efficient way,

then you can create any amount of wealth.

– Deepak Chopra

THE FLOW OF SEXUAL ENERGY

In childhood, we learned how to limit the amount of energy we expressed. It takes courage to break through the limits of the past and open ourselves to higher levels of positive energy, but it's to our advantage.

Sexual energy is a potential source of incredible power. It is the energy that gives us life – our "life-force." When the flow of sexual energy is strong and clear, we are at the peak of physical health and have abundant energy and strength (and vice versa). We feel happier, and our physical abilities are most efficient. Yet, in many ways – physically, emotionally, mentally – we tend to block off the flow of our sexual energy.

Since the subconscious is drawn toward pleasure and away from pain, let's focus on some of the benefits of sex. What are they? A recent study revealed that women who are sexually satisfied have better health and age more slowly. Sex increases estrogen levels and thereby fights heart diseases. It boosts immunity by lessening stress. It also eases body aches and is a good pain killer and natural sedative. People with active sex lives are less anxious, less hostile and more playful. And…sex burns calories!

The pituitary gland produces a "love hormone" called *oxytocin* that is released in the body during sexual activity. Studies show that it heightens intuition, raises performance levels in aptitude and intelligence tests and increases creativity. This hormone can even augment athletic ability and alleviate depression.

If you don't have a sexual partner handy, don't despair. Studies have shown that oxytocin is also

Just as sexual energy has helped man

out of his spiritual state into the body,

so it can help him to return in full awareness

to his divine primal state of wholeness.

– Elisabeth Haich

released during self-pleasuring and even while simply fantasizing about sex!

Sexual energy rides on the breath. Breath, feeling and energy are entwined. Restricting the breath is a quick way of stopping unpleasant feelings and excess energy. The key to awakening the ecstatic response within yourself is your awareness of your breath while cultivating a deep, consistent level of relaxation in your body so that the energy can flow unrestricted. You can then learn to raise the upper limits of the amount of inner energy you can handle, as demonstrated in the following example.

THE BEAUTY MYTH

As a teenager, Bridgitte was influenced by the popular notion that it is sexy to have a trim body and a flat stomach. In public, she made it a point to be aware of her profile and held in her stomach muscles until this became habitual behavior. Years later, as an adult, she enjoyed a good relationship with her husband, Philip, but was disappointed and frustrated with her sex-life. In spite of Philip's attentiveness, Bridgitte experienced infrequent and fleeting orgasms.

The two of them began to search for ways to bring more fulfillment to their love-making and decided to attend my Ecstasy and Success workshop. During that weekend, Bridgitte discovered that the habit of tightening her stomach muscles had reversed her normal breathing patterns, cutting off her ability to feel sensations fully in the genital area.

It is always important for us
to be aware of our feelings.
Our feelings exist for good reason
and so deserve our attention and respect.

– Harriet Goldhor Lerner

Along with the other workshop participants, Bridgitte was taught the Orgasmic Reflex Exercise (O.R.E.) to bring her focus back to her breath. She needed to re-pattern her breathing habits and re-educate her nervous system. She immediately began to feel stimulation, not only in her genitals, but throughout her body. When she began to feel these new sensations, she wondered, "Do I deserve so much pleasure?"

She became more aware of decisions she had made, through past conditioning, that she did not deserve much pleasure and that too much pleasure would mean that she was bad or "slutty." I encouraged her to put her attention daily on breathing into her belly, practicing the O.R.E. with Philip and using another technique to increase her self-esteem.

In the months that followed, she became more loving and compassionate toward herself as feelings of guilt and shame that had lodged in the muscles of her body began to surface. She was also persistent in focusing her attention on what she wanted as she practiced the techniques. As she has told me many times since, it was well worth it!

CONNECTING TO SEXUAL ENERGY

Breath, sound, movement and imagination are the keys to connecting with the power of your sexual energy. The following exercise will allow you to access this energy and also make a deeper connection with all aspects of yourself. You will find it most effective if you practice it regularly. You may use the energetic force generated by this exercise to power your goals and purpose. (Try it before using the "Triple-A" Technique for manifestation that follows later, and notice the extra power it brings to that process.)

Sex lies at the root of life,

and we can never learn to reverence life

until we know how to understand sex.

– Havelock Ellis

The most important point to remember is to stay as relaxed as possible during your practice. Tension in the face, neck, shoulders, abdomen or hips will inhibit your breathing and the flow of energy.

ORGASMIC REFLEX EXERCISE

This exercise was drawn from bio-energetics by Tantra teachers Lori Grace and Robert Frey: "The orgasmic reflex is a reflexive movement that occurs when you are releasing sexual energy, most often experienced at the time of genital orgasm. It is a quick, involuntary contraction of the *abdominus rectus* muscle combined with an exhalation of breath. By practicing this reflex voluntarily, you reeducate your nervous system to access orgasmic energy at will."

Among the benefits of doing the O.R.E. for just a few minutes every day are these: it strengthens your body's energy field; it allows your body to become more comfortable with higher charges of energy; it promotes stronger orgasms and extends their duration.

NOTE: It is recommended that you practice it for 5-15 minutes, but no more. It can stir up deep feelings and generate a high degree of energy. Please read the "IMPORTANT" message at the beginning of this book before proceeding.

THE TECHNIQUE:

Lie down on the floor with your legs bent, your knees pointing toward the ceiling and the soles of your feet flat on the floor. Now inhale as you rock your pelvis downward, creating a little archway under the small of

The truly sensuous takes time
and a feeling for the deliberate,
undulating rhythms of the body
and of nature.

– George Leonard

the back. Exhale as you lower the small of your back toward the floor again (and even press into the floor with the small of your back), tilting your pelvis upward so that your genital area rises toward the ceiling. Do NOT lift your pelvis off the floor. Practice this movement with the breathing until you don't have to think about doing it correctly.

It is important to keep your abdominal muscles relaxed. If you are tensing your abdominal muscles as you practice the motion, press into your feet and knees as you bring your genitals upward, to assist you in moving your pelvis.

Now, while bringing your pelvis upward, make a sound as you exhale. This can be a sigh or a guttural sound, for example, but let it come easily so it doesn't interfere with the full exhalation of breath. Again, the movement of the breath and the pelvis is this: inhale/downward, exhale/upward (vocalized). Practice this combination until it is automatic. Think of the movement as wave-like and allow the free motion of your neck.

To intensify the energy flow, consciously tighten your genital muscles as you bring them upward and relax them as you bring your pelvis downward. Make sure you're not holding your breath when you squeeze these muscles. As you squeeze and bring your genitals up, exhale with sounds, fully expressing any emotions such as sadness, anger or joy that may be surfacing. Your body will recognize this movement of your pelvis as an expressive, assertive act.

You have to be definite with the Infinite.

The Infinite can only become definite

when you become definite.

You have to define and declare

the good you want

before you can get it.

– Reverend Ike

After several rounds, relax, take a deep breath and imagine breathing the energy up your spine. Remain quiet and relaxed for several moments with your eyes closed, feeling the effects of the process.

NOTE: If you experience uncomfortable feelings accompanying this technique, realize that they may be an indication of some subconscious limitations that could be undermining your capacity for creativity and ecstasy. In the event that you experience strong and disturbing emotions, do not hesitate to seek counseling.

One of the great benefits of the O.R.E. is the energetic charge you build, which can be used to power your goals and purpose. Now that you have generated this energy, think about where you most want to direct it.

CLARITY

If you understand that your physical, emotional and spiritual energy flows in the direction of your focus, then doesn't it make sense to focus on *what you want*, not on what you *don't* want? Yet, so many people have so little clarity about what they want. Clarity and focus go hand in hand.

The quest of every person is to be happy. If you don't know what you want, ask yourself what would fill your heart with joy and enliven you, while allowing you to be a growing, contributing human being. Imagine this in vivid detail, using all your senses. Once you are clear about what you want, the trick is to keep your mind on it, in a positive frame, as much of the time as possible. Divert potential distractions. To the degree that you are

To be what we are, and to become

what we are capable of becoming,

is the only end in life.

— Robert Louis Stevenson

distracted, your energy isn't flowing in the direction of what you want, so it takes that much longer to manifest it.

You may already be familiar with popular techniques like "treasure-mapping" and affirmation. In themselves, these techniques have no special power. They are simply tools you can use to help yourself stay clearly focused on your intention. They do this by helping you create as much visual, auditory and emotional stimulation as possible in order to impress your subconscious. These kinds of techniques must be utilized frequently until you *know and feel* the new facts to be true.

This is also the purpose of making a plan to arrive at your goal. You create on all four levels of reality: spiritual, mental, emotional, and physical. On the physical level, you must clarify your goals, make plans, then take appropriate actions to carry them out. The following Manifestation Process is an effective way to convince your subconscious mind that what you want is already a fact in your life and is in the process of manifesting itself in form.

THE MANIFESTATION PROCESS

To begin, let me introduce you to the Power Breath, which will charge you energetically, bring you into the present moment and signal your subconscious that something important is about to happen. The subconscious responds more quickly to your direction when you consciously use your breath to energize or to relieve tension. Your conscious breathing clears the path for an effective flow of life-force energy to help bring about the changes you want.

Think like a man of action,

act like a man of thought.

—Henri Bergson

You can practice this technique at any time, with your eyes open or closed. Simply begin by noticing your breathing. Now, as you inhale, put your attention on the crown of your head, and as you exhale, put your attention on your navel. Keep shifting your focus of attention from crown to navel with each inhale and exhale. Since *energy flows where attention goes,* the mere focus of attention on these two areas will start the flow of energy between them. Continue the Power Breath for at least four rounds.

Now that your subconscious self has been alerted, and you are in a more relaxed and energized state through your conscious breathing, you are ready to begin the process.

The following manifestation process is known as the "Triple-A" Technique: Affirm, Assume, Act.

1. Affirm the outcome of your desire. Declare it succinctly in positive, pleasurable, emotional language. (For example, *I am a millionaire, and I love it!*)

2. Assume the final result, as if it has already occurred. Imagine yourself vividly in this desired condition. Feel and picture your surroundings while generating strong enthusiasm. Verbalize it for reinforcement.

3. Act to anchor this state in your subconscious by using symbolism. For example, raise your arms with hands pointing upward to the heavens, the invisible realm. On the count of three, pull your hands down into fists, and imagine bringing your invisible desire into visible, physical reality, while shouting "Yes!" Take appropriate actions in the world to further your desired outcome. Make it important to you!

We cannot become what we need to be

by remaining what we are.

– Max De Pree

Do this process consistently, at least once every day. As often as possible, speak to your subconscious, recalling the new state, and tell yourself *Yes! You can do it...you can do it!* It can also be very effective to give your subconscious (your body-mind) a name you can use when speaking to it, like a nickname you might call yourself with fondness. (Remember that there is no actual separation between your conscious and subconscious mind. For that reason, choose an endearing or empowering name that does not create a sense of separation.)

Fill up your energy field with this positive programming until you identify with it completely. Then you will find your life reflecting your new identity. Through this type of repetitive reprogramming, you are creating an energy-charged idea that will form a stronger pattern than that which was previously in place. The strongest of the patterns is the one that determines your image of yourself and the reality you create.

The new words, images and feelings will support your new ideas and instill a sense of their reality in your subconscious mind. The more you focus your attention on these new ideas, the more they will seem to be true. When you convince your subconscious mind that they are true, they will be true in every way!

MOTIVATION

You may be familiar with much information about what it takes to create your life the way you want it to be, yet you may not be striving to change your old thoughts and habits, to plan and to follow through with action. In fact, you may be asking yourself, "Why aren't I doing those things?"

Great works are performed not by strength

but by perseverance.

– Samuel Johnson

"I really *want* to do them." Perhaps – but not as much as you *don't want to do them!* You'd rather do something else or think about something else because your motivation isn't yet strong enough. Maybe you're dealing with the fear of failure, or you haven't made the goal important enough. You must become more excited about succeeding than you are afraid of failing. The motivation to change has got to be stronger than the motivation to stay the same!

Motivation is the moving force; it moves you to act. Your motivation is based upon the strength of your desire, which is based upon the importance of what you want and your determination to achieve it. The more important the goal is to you, the more you're motivated to go for it.

DESIRE AND CONCENTRATION

When you really want something, you tend to concentrate your attention on it intensely until you get it. To concentrate is to think persistently and clearly about your objective. You then experience the results of your most dominant and consistent thinking — in other words, you get what you most concentrate on.

A prime example of this comes from one of the most talked-about films of the 'Seventies, *Kramer vs. Kramer*, which starred Dustin Hoffman and Meryl Streep. It dramatically illustrates the power of heightened concentration. The film is about a major transition in the life of a man whose wife leaves their marriage unexpectedly. Because the emotional strain and the additional demands of caring for his son disrupt his

Vote with your life. Vote Yes!

– Das Energi

work, Ted Kramer is fired from his position as art director at a major advertising agency.

He then learns that his estranged wife, Joanna, is suing him for custody of their son, Billy. Wanting very much to keep his child, Ted hires an attorney who tells him that if he's unemployed, he has no chance of winning the case. In desperation, he manages to make a last-minute appointment with a small ad agency on the last working day before Christmas. Though the head of the agency is obviously impatient to begin his vacation and reluctant to hire someone so over-qualified, Ted's intense desire and sheer determination land him the job.

The more important the goal, the stronger the desire. One of the most powerful factors in bringing ideas into form is the intensity of the desire. *Kramer vs. Kramer* is a perfect example of the power of increased concentration, motivation and desire. Devotion to his son made Ted Kramer's goal urgently important. Focusing intensely on his goal – to care for and be with Billy – moved him to take every available action and overcome every apparent obstacle.

Since the intensity of your desire is so important, how can you increase it? Make the end result, the goal, more important by *deciding* that you must and will have it. Give it importance through your own personal authority. This desire – the passion about it, the fierce determination to achieve it – is not the same feeling as a yearning, which implies the idea of wanting something you feel you don't deserve or cannot get. Rather it is the kind of feeling that says: *"This is what I want, and this is what I'm going to have!"*

I learned this, at least, by my experiment:

that as one advances confidently

in the direction of his dreams and endeavors

to live the life which he has imagined,

he will meet with a success

unexpected in common hours.

– Henry David Thoreau

Building your desire to achieve your goal will build your motivation. You can amass so much energy this way that when you focus your attention, it has much more power. Greater motivation will help you increase your concentration. You can also use reinforcement tools, such as affirmations and pictures, to keep your sights on the goal and inspire positive feelings.

Concentration increases focus, which gives you the power to change your reality. Another effective way to increase your focus is by increasing your confidence. It's important to remember that where there is less doubt and fear, there is naturally more confidence. Therefore, the best way to increase your confidence is by finding practical ways to deal with doubts and fears. These feelings increase stress, which greatly limits both energy and effectiveness.

THE PATH TO CONFIDENCE

You have already learned that a current of energy is generated between you and wherever you put your attention. An effective way to increase the energy current between you and your goal is to remove any resistance.

The primary cause of resistance is SDUF: Stress, Doubt, Unhappiness and Fear. When these are not present, your confidence level is high, and your desires can manifest effortlessly.

Notice the events in your life that seem to unfold easily and the skills and talents you demonstrate without much effort or strain. These things generally have very little SDUF related to them (like the phone call from the friend you thought about).

We can learn to soar only

in direct proportion to our

determination to rise above the doubt

and transcend the limitations.

– David McNally

The less SDUF you have in your life, the more confident you are. The higher your state of confidence, the greater the flow of energy available.

REPLACING THE SDUF WITH CONFIDENCE

What can you do to optimize the state of confidence? Here is a technique for replacing SDUF with strong and positive new beliefs. This technique prepares you for a new reality. It also allows you to project your intentions to others physically, and they automatically respond to your new self-image. Through your new body language and other subtle means of communication, others read your increased confidence and automatically feel more willing to cooperate with your clear intent.

1. Become aware of the condition or experience you would like to change (for example, fear, anger, depression, illness, poverty.)
2. Acknowledge whatever you are feeling in regard to the condition or experience. Tap your breastbone slowly with your fingertips, at the point about a hand's-width down from your clavicle bones, while saying *I deeply accept myself even though I... (...have fears about...* or *...am experiencing...).* This technique engages the thymus gland while stimulating the immune system, relieving stress as you reprogram the subconscious with your words.
3. Now, declare the positive opposite of the state or circumstance you have been experiencing (change *fear* to *courage, anger* to *happiness, depression* to *enthusiasm, illness* to *health, poverty* to *abundance.)* Use all of your senses to imagine yourself in the desired state. How does it feel, sound, smell, taste? Choose an attitude and a posture appropriate to this state, and practice them as often as possible.

We must see our own goodness,

appreciate our assets and abilities,

and celebrate our humanness.

– Dennis Wholey

4. Since the subconscious works best with symbols, pick a symbol that represents the new state or condition, and carry a picture or drawing of it in your wallet or purse, or put it someplace where you will see it frequently.

Through this form of repetitive reprogramming, you will notice an improved energy flow. Negative attitudes can produce inner stress, which translates as muscular tension. It is this stress that directly inhibits the flow of your energy and can even make you physically ill. To change your energy, change your attitude.

While working with the SDUF, it is important to direct energy through *positive attitude* and *positive expectation*, both of which supply you with a super-charge of *positive emotion*.

CULTIVATING A POSITIVE ATTITUDE

Let's observe how you relate to yourself, others and the universe through your thoughts, feelings and imagination. What are some of the energy-charged ideas that affect your attitude?

Think of your body. Do you like it? What do you say most often about it to yourself and others? Such negative phrases as these have become part of contemporary culture: *My body is so flabby. I'm so overweight. I look terrible. The older I get, the less attractive I am.* What images of yourself do you create? What things do you tell yourself that hurt your self-esteem? Do you imagine yourself saying or doing something foolish and feeling humiliated? Do you find yourself thinking thoughts like *I'm so stupid; I never get anything*

If you keep on saying things are going to be bad,

you have a good chance of being a prophet.

– Isaac Bashevis Singer

right or *I'm just not highly educated enough* or *I'm just lousy at managing money?*

What do you tell yourself about other people, life, and the world around you? *You just can't trust most people. Life is a struggle. The world is not a safe place. Rich people are greedy. Sex is dirty. Money is the root of all evil. The government is out to get us.* These kinds of ideas are so common that they can begin to sound like truths, but they're not.

Did you notice that just reading some of these statements made you feel uneasy? Negative suggestions or statements tend to increase your fears, anxieties and self-doubts, whether they come from you or from external sources – from other people or from media such as television. If you accept them, they can adversely affect your health, your emotions and your self-confidence. Accepting negative thoughts makes people SAD: Sick, Angry and Depressed. You can choose to reject them and their influences.

COUNTERACTING NEGATIVE SUGGESTIONS

You don't have to accept negative suggestions or allow them to program your subconscious mind. Here is a way to counteract them:

First, get in the habit of paying attention to what you're thinking, hearing and saying. Second, whenever you become aware of a negative thought or statement that might act as a suggestion, say to yourself, aloud or silently, "Cancel that!" It helps to visualize a cancellation sign – a circle with a diagonal line running through it. You can reinforce the cancellation by taking a deep breath.

The poet writes his truest lines

upon his own countenance.

– Grayson

The third step is to replace the idea with a positive statement that affirms the opposite of the original one – a statement that you want to believe is true (even if you don't believe it yet). Say it aloud or silently to yourself. If the original suggestion was accompanied by a strong negative emotion, see yourself surrounded with white light, and imagine that this field of light has the power to dissolve and neutralize any negativity.

This method works beautifully for counteracting unwanted suggestions from others, as well. Silently "cancel" any criticism directed at you and praise yourself with a statement of the positive opposite. Neutralize any negative emotions by imagining yourself within a sphere of white light that harmonizes the energies around you. In this way, you are not energetically reinforcing the idea that you need to protect yourself.

In order to have a consistently positive attitude, you must be diligent about neutralizing negative suggestions and focusing on positive thoughts and desires. This is not because "negative" thoughts, suggestions or beliefs carry more power than beneficial ones do; no one thought has more power than another. Those thoughts which have been accepted as true by your subconscious mind are the thoughts that form your reality, and it's your choice to replace the ones that limit you with those that benefit you. This is simply a matter of surrounding yourself with thought vibrations that are more effective for materializing the type of life you desire so that they may solidly replace the old programming. If you find that you are putting out negative energy through worry, criticism, judgment, anger, resentment or guilt, don't put out more by being angry at yourself for it. Simply choose to acknowledge some of your own positive traits and praise them instead

Unless there be correct thought,

there cannot be any action,

and when there is correct thought,

the right action will follow.

– Henry George

of demeaning yourself. I am not suggesting it is easy, but it *is* do-able!

Project your best self every day in the way you look, walk, talk, and act. Look for the good in yourself and others...and if you can't find it, invent some! People tend to respond to others in kind. You'll see people reacting to you in a new, more positive fashion. Since everything is connected energetically, others will also pick up your thoughts subconsciously and begin to react to you in a new way. Do everything with an attitude of ecstasy and success, as if you are already ecstatic and successful, and you will reinforce that reality.

DE-STRESSING THE WORKPLACE

Often, the workplace presents its own unique challenges to our intention of experiencing ecstasy. When there are difficulties in this area, I suggest a technique that has been very effective for turning unhappy situations into happy outcomes. It requires the use of your imagination and the directing of your focus in a particular way. First, be willing to assume that all things are connected and interdependent as part of a living system, and second, assume that what you imagine within this responsive system has its own ability to influence.

Having said that, I would like you to imagine yourself surrounded with a sphere of light. If you want, you can choose to give this light a particular color, depending on the result you desire. For instance, you could use pink for friendliness or love, green for cooperation or healing, blue for calming or confidence. Choose what feels good to you, understanding that

If we lose affection and kindliness from our life,

we've lost all that gives it charm.

— Marcus Tullius Cicero

there is no right or wrong way to interpret the colors. What matters is what feels best and is most suitable for you.

Now you can imagine this light responding to your direction and focus. Begin to expand it outward to permeate the environment and the people around you. If you like, imagine the light filled with particular patterns, soothing sounds, loving feelings or sensations. Now, mentally or verbally state, with deep desire, that the light is indeed having the effect that you want. For instance, *"The people in my workplace are now cooperative and harmonious."*

Here are some examples of the positive effects of this exercise, with slight variations, illustrating the limitless possibilities with which you can apply your own creativity.

Jesse, an engineering designer in his early sixties, tells how effectively this technique worked for him at his office in Los Angeles:

"During the beginning stages of my spiritual search, I experimented with ways of establishing harmony. Physical confrontation wasn't very effective because I was still answering criticism with anger. At a Huna lecture, the speaker suggested that I send loving light to influence a troublesome coworker. Since I associated pink with love, I envisioned him surrounded with a pink aura. I also incorporated genuine feelings of love. After doing this a few minutes a day for three days, my coworker displayed a surprisingly happy disposition, yet he couldn't account for his new harmonious attitude. We eventually became good friends!"

There is a fountain of youth:

It is your mind, your talents,

the creativity you bring in your life

and the lives of people you love.

— Sophia Loren

Another example comes from Paul, who was working in marketing and sales for a Chicago company:

"Every morning as I arrived in the parking lot, I would envision a green light around the building in which I worked. Along with the light, I used the phrase *"Harmonize the energies between us."* As I entered the building, I sent the light to all four corners and said, *"Harmonize the energies around me."* A feeling of calmness would come over me, and the day always started out on a positive note. It worked equally well when I met and talked with business associates and during times when I felt tension in the air."

As you can see by the results, this method has exciting possibilities for inviting more ecstasy into everyday situations. Since we are all connected, it is possible to influence others in beneficial ways and to improve conditions at home, at work and within the larger environment.

It is not possible to control others against their will by doing this; however, the more positive and consistent your thoughts, the greater your influence. The reason for this is simply that the subconscious minds of all individuals move toward pleasure and away from pain. Therefore, other people will be drawn to cooperate with your loving thoughts.

This concept may bring up the question of using a technique like this to impose negative suggestions or influence others negatively. People who attempt this consistently soon find themselves energetically weakened and eventually experience very debilitating effects. This is because the subconscious experiences itself as part of everything in the universe.

Keep your face to the sunshine

and you cannot see the shadow.

— Helen Keller

When you criticize or curse another, your subconscious takes it personally, feels attacked and draws in its life-force energy, thereby weakening you. You then have less energy to manifest your own dreams. This effect has been demonstrated repeatedly through applied kinesiology, or muscle-testing.

To enjoy the benefits of heightened life-force energy and more harmonious relationships focus your loving attention in the moment. By choosing to keep your focus on the present you are not diverting energy through thoughts of the past or the future. In disagreements with others, look for what does work and deal only with the current situation. Do not bring up the past.

THE POWER OF POSITIVE EXPECTATION

Another element that is key to increasing confidence is to cultivate the positive expectation that your desire is already being fulfilled. I've learned to focus my attention with positive expectation in many situations in my life, such as having harmonious, trusting relationships with others – and I am delighted to find many helpful and friendly people in my everyday experience. If you expect the worst, you are energizing that particular idea. Why not expect the best?

Positive expectation is supremely important in directing energy. To help you remind yourself to expect the best, here is an acronym I learned that you can use throughout the day: EWOP – Everything's Working Out Perfectly.

A successful relationship with reality

must be learned as a dance is learned –

not by contemplation but by participation,

by exercise of will, by movement,

action and response.

— Deane Juhan

You can "EWOP" everything. Whenever you find yourself focusing on SDUF (stress, doubts, unhappiness or fears), just think of the word *cancel* or imagine a cancellation sign, and then EWOP it! Tell yourself that you can stop worrying because *Everything's working out perfectly, and I don't even need to know how.* This is an opportunity to trust your super-conscious self (also called the High Self), to bring about the desired events in the best possible way. You can give yourself an emotional break from agonizing over outcomes. When you are more relaxed, you will also be less reactive and more effective.

EWOP EXERCISE

Think about something in your life with which you have a concern. Now decide to turn this situation over to your High Self to handle the details. Say silently or aloud, *"High Self, I'm turning this over to you. Take care of this in the best way possible."*

Now, inhale with your attention at the center of the earth, and exhale with your attention at the heavens. With each ensuing exhalation, imagine that any problem, challenge or difficult emotion is being released to your High Self to be resolved. Allow yourself to let go.

To the full extent of your current ability, begin to expect that the best outcome is already happening. Have confidence that everything is working out perfectly. You will do whatever may be appropriate to do in the future, but right now you can just settle back and trust that everything is turning out beautifully. This helps you to remain in a calm and clear state of positive expectation more of the time.

When a man's willing and eager,

the god's join in.

– Aeschylus

POSITIVE EMOTION

Both positive attitudes and positive expectation generate positive emotion. The energy of positive emotion can break through all kinds of blocks, overriding existing beliefs that interfere with the manifestations you desire. By consciously generating positive emotion, you can increase your life-force energy exponentially.

Earlier I spoke of directing energy to a given result. Now we're emphasizing the building up of such a strong force that when you direct your attention, it has greater power. The more energy you have available when you focus, the stronger the effects of that focused energy. One of the best ways to build your energy is through enthusiasm and excitement.

Henry Ford credited the powerful emotion of enthusiasm as one of most important factors in achieving success. One way to generate strong, positive emotion is to get very enthusiastic about the benefits of your dream or desire. This enthusiasm actively motivates your subconscious to cooperate with you in achieving your goal precisely because of a behavior pattern I referred to earlier that often *appears* to sabotage your wishes.

Another acronym that has recently become popular best describes the basic idea that engages and motivates the subconscious: WIFM –*What's In It For Me?* Whatever you do, there is always some subconscious benefit in the doing of it. For some people, there are even benefits (however well hidden from the conscious mind) to being poor or being a failure. There may be an idea hidden in the subconscious mind that it is dangerous to be rich or that only bad people succeed. Whatever

A happy person is not a person in

a certain set of circumstances,

but rather a person with

a certain set of attitudes.

– Hugh Downs

your subconscious is doing, it is doing for a benefit. It may seem as though it is sabotaging your efforts, yet it is really trying to help by always moving toward perceived pleasure and away from perceived pain!

If you want to change your subconscious attitudes and behaviors quickly, dwell upon the benefits of the change. What are the benefits of having more ecstasy in your life? What are the real benefits of being rich, of being successful? If you would like greater prosperity, think about the pleasure of having all the money you want and being able to do everything you want to do. Psyche yourself up!

Consciously make yourself emotionally excited and enthusiastic. Feel how much fun it's going to be to have and do those things. Dwell on the satisfaction and the rewards of having achieved your goal. Use mental rehearsals to see and feel yourself enjoying those benefits now! Using your imagination in this way can literally pull you toward ecstasy, prosperity and success.

BRINGING ECSTASY INTO DAILY LIFE

Focusing on ecstasy will bring ecstasy into your life. My friend Jwala, a teacher of Tantra, suggests in her book *Sacred Sex* the following exercise to release more creative, ecstatic energy. Once you complete this exercise, you may be very surprised to find just how miserly you have been in allowing yourself the things that give you pleasure. The time to begin focusing on ecstasy in your life is now!

Each day, and the living of it,

has to be a conscious creation in which

discipline and order are relieved with

some play and pure foolishness.

– May Sarton

I highly recommend that you make the opportunity to do this exercise and the follow-up that she advocates. Also, deliberately choose some activities that are childlike. *Be* a carefree child again, and experience your innocence and aliveness.

1. To begin, take a look at your top ten turn-ons in life. Make a list of the things that totally absorb you when you do them – that make you lose track of time and space. These are the things that give you the most satisfaction, that keep you in the moment so you are not thinking about the past, the future or what's for lunch. Write down the things that bring you joy, contentment, fulfillment.

2. Now prioritize the things on your list in the order of their importance to you. Which one is the most essential in your life? Which one is next? And so on.

3. After you have put the list in order, write down how many hours a week you spend doing each of the things on your list. If you are like most people, you will find you are not spending much time, if any, on most of the activities on the list. If you're feeling some frustration and discontent, could that be part of the reason?

   Once you find what turns you on, do it, no matter what obstacles lie in your path. If you love to paint, paint. If you like to swim, do it. If you love to play sports or ride horses or take long baths, make sure you create the space to do those things. Do at least one thing on your list every day. Treat yourself. Celebrate. As you do these things more often, a sense of inner satisfaction grows, and you become more content and begin to glow. In this state you become a fuller cup and eventually overflow. You become less needy and more able to give love.

Sexual energy, or ching-chi *in Chinese,*

is one of the most obvious and powerful

types of bioelectric energy.

– Mantak Chia

You will find that the more ecstasy you experience the more energy you will have available to you. Ecstasy is inherent to your nature, which has at its disposal an infinite supply of energy. This is one of the greatest benefits of experiencing the ecstatic state. The more energy you have available to you when you focus, the stronger the effects of your focus and the better the results you can produce. You will also find that you are more magnetic to others when your energy is heightened.

CREATING CHARISMA

Not only does *energy flow where attention goes* but *attention goes where energy flows*. When our senses are stimulated by intense energy in any form, the source of that stimulation attracts our attention. This attraction occurs with loud noises, bright lights, strong aromas, pungent flavors and other such stimuli. Similarly, we tend to be attracted to some individuals because they project such powerful energy. This is often referred to as *charisma* or *animal magnetism*.

Marilyn Monroe is most definitely associated with the phenomenon of sexual charisma. In fact, she was able to turn this characteristic on or off at will. In an article in *Ms.* magazine, Gloria Steinem relates the following: Actor Eli Wallach is one of many colleagues who remember her sitting completely unnoticed in a room, or walking down the street, and then making heads turn in sudden recognition, at will. "I just felt like being Marilyn for a moment," she would explain.

In the perennial bestseller *Think and Grow Rich*, Napoleon Hill writes, "A teacher, who has trained and directed the efforts of more than 30,000 salespeople, made the astounding discovery that highly sexed men are the most efficient salesmen. The explanation is that

Sex energy is the creative energy of all geniuses.

There never has been, and never will be

a great leader, builder, or artist

lacking in this driving force of sex.

– Napoleon Hill

the factor of personality known as 'personal magnetism' is nothing more nor less than sex energy. Highly sexed people always have a plentiful supply of magnetism. Through cultivation and understanding, this vital force may be drawn upon and used to great advantage in the relationships between people."

The following is a technique for enhancing your personal magnetism by increasing your energy field through focused breathing. It is similar to the Power Breath, but in this case you shift your attention between the crown of the head and the genital area rather than the crown and the navel. As the electrical current of energy flowing through you increases, the magnetic field around you increases.

The Charismatic Breath can be done anytime and anywhere. You need not close your eyes; simply focus on the shifting of your attention. Remember, you are breathing in the pure energy of the universe, which is always available to you – even while standing in those dreary lines at the bank!

1. First, simply notice your breathing. Now, slowly and consciously inhale through your nose and focus your attention on the top of your head. As you exhale through the nose, move your focus of attention down to your genitals. Continue this, shifting your focus back and forth from the crown of the head to the genitals with each inhalation and exhalation.

2. Once you feel the relaxing effects of this process, imagine that the electromagnetic field that surrounds you is increasing with each exhalation. You may even want to see this field as a cloud of light or color that expands with every outflow of breath.

Clear sexual energy is spiritual energy.

Both come from the same source – God.

— Joan Gattuso

This exercise can be continued for any length of time you like. Pay attention to any physical sensations that occur. For example, you may feel a tingling in various parts of your body or a current of energy moving through your spine. This is perfectly normal and only means that your physical sensitivity to the accumulation of life-energy is increasing. This feedback is immensely valuable to your self-development.

HINT: To magnify the effects of this technique, you can go through the process silently, with eyes open or closed, while at the gym using repetitive exercise equipment. The added physical stimulus is highly impressive to the subconscious mind!

Anyone can expand sexual charisma and use that energy effectively. If you have concerns about attracting people whose attentions you would rather not have, direct your subconscious to attract only those who are in harmony with your highest good. Choose to direct this part of yourself with images and feelings of safety and security, regularly reinforcing the idea that the world is a safe place. Request that your High Self guide you wisely in all situations, and always pay attention to your intuition.

HARMONIZING RELATIONSHIPS

It is possible to improve your relationships with others through the use of the Charismatic Breath. This and all of the exercises work best when you are most relaxed, so always take a few moments first to instruct your body to release tension wherever you are aware of it.

The view that sex has a spiritual dimension

is so alien to everything we have been taught

that it takes most people completely aback.

– Rianne Eisler

It is most effective to experience the following guided imagery with your eyes closed. I would suggest reading the material into a tape recorder and then playing it back for yourself.

1. Close your eyes and focus on your breathing. Inhale with your attention at the crown of the head, then exhale with your attention at the genitals. Repeat at least eight times, until your breathing is slow and even. Visualize the merging of the universal energy coming through your crown with the sexual energy through your genitals. Know that as you exhale, they flow together throughout your aura, expanding it and extending it outward into the room around you. Be aware of your body. Notice any sensations of warmth, tingling or relaxing muscles. Now focus on your inner power. Notice that you are feeling more confident and grounded in the present moment.

2. Take this feeling into a relationship you currently have. Imagine bringing into your energetic field the form and essence of a spouse, friend, work associate, lover, child, parent...or even yourself. Envision your relationship with this person, and change it for the better. See and feel harmony between you. Hear yourself praising and acknowledging this person, and feel him or her responding with appreciation, love and acceptance. Imagine a cocoon of green, healing light enveloping both of you. Now, take a deep breath and say to yourself, *"I am in total harmony with..."* Complete with a closing word or phrase such as, *"So It Is."* Take another deep breath, and open your eyes.

Love is the secret key;

it opens the door of the divine.

— Rajneesh

Enjoy this experience of harmony, and know that you can draw upon this feeling anytime you wish. For the greatest effect in improving a relationship, it is recommended you practice this exercise privately in its entirety once a day. Remember that everything in the universe is interconnected. Therefore, your focused intention to harmonize yourself with others can bring about positive change.

ATTRACTING YOUR IDEAL MATE

If you so choose, it is also possible to use focused breathing with intent to magnetize your ideal mate to you. You cannot know exactly what your true love looks like, so it's counter-productive to visualize a particular face or body. Instead, go fully into your feelings of love and passion, desire and longing, eagerness and joy. Bring your whole being into the state of pure love for yourself and for the person you seek. Let your ideal mate feel your love intensely!

Remember to enlist the help of that aspect of yourself most directly connected to the Universal Intelligence – your High Self – by turning over the selection process to that part of you. Request that the upcoming relationship be for your highest good, trusting that this wise component of who you are truly knows all the necessary characteristics of the person who is best suited to you.

The following is a variation of a magnetizing exercise that appears in my book *The Power of Aloha, The Hawaiian Guide to Love, Health and Wealth.*

Lovers don't finally meet somewhere.

They are in each other all along.

– Rumi

In it, you begin by building up your inner charge of vital energy while repeating specific statements so that you're more highly empowered to accomplish your intent. Then you focus on your heart as you accept your new love into your life.

1. As you INHALE with your focus at the crown of your head, say to yourself, *"I am receiving love,"* and feel the universal energy flowing into you.

2. As you EXHALE with your focus at your navel, say to yourself, *I am sending love,"* and imagine your love flowing out to your sweetheart.

Continue with this receiving/charging procedure for at least eight breaths. Now, with this raised charge and ongoing flow of energy, you will be repeating messages of self-love and love for your approaching mate while focusing your attention at your heart.

Inhale with your mind quiet and your focus on the crown of your head.

1. As you EXHALE with attention at your heart, think to yourself, *"Here I am – I love myself!"*

Inhale with your mind quiet as these words resonate through your being.

2. Now EXHALE with attention at the heart, saying, *"I accept you in my life – I love you!"*

Love is the miracle cure.

Loving ourselves works miracles in our lives.

—Louise Hay

Inhale with your mind quiet as these words resonate through your being.

Repeat this process at least eight times, or as long as it feels appropriate. Then stop and quietly enjoy the afterglow.

Through regular repetitions, you are establishing an energy link with the person who is in resonance with you on the deepest levels. Your success will rest on how powerfully you desire the results and how often you return your attention to this process with utmost confidence.

THE ROAD WELL TRAVELED

You have come a long way on the path of ecstasy and success. You have learned how to direct your focus and energy to a given result through increased concentration, confidence and positive expectation. You have also learned to build up the force of your vital energy through breath, movement and positive emotion so that when you direct your focused energy, it has greater power. You are now able to direct the three aspects of yourself, the conscious, the subconscious and super-conscious, as partners in the art of creation. You have also taken steps to experience more often the core of who you are: an ecstatic, abundant, creative being.

On your path, however, you may encounter something that is a major inhibitor of the ecstatic state. This impediment has become more prevalent in recent years with the full-blown onslaught of the "information age." This culprit cannot only deplete your energy and fray your nerves, it can also reduce your life span. The culprit's name is *ongoing stress*. It is the result of accumulated tension in the body.

How can one consent to creep

when one has the inclination to soar?

– Helen Keller

We know that continuous stress causes disease. It over-stimulates the heart and weakens the immune system. In women, it can interfere with the reproductive system by disrupting the hormonal balance. Over the past fifty years, research has shown that stress even quickens the aging process. Equally as significant, stress undermines confidence, and it is the state of ultimate confidence that correlates with effortless manifestation.

When you are in the stress mode, your coping skills are diminished. The buildup of tension in the body interferes with your memory, feelings and awareness. The more this repression occurs, the more fear is engendered within the subconscious, for it begins to experience a sense of separation that leads to insecurity. Fear and doubt arise, rather than confidence. The fear mode leaves no room for inner guidance and wise decision-making. The conscious and subconscious are thrown into disharmony. As you can see, stress is antithetical to the ecstatic state.

However, there is one mind-body technique that can alleviate the stress response directly. It is known as meditation. Many people profess to have difficulty in maintaining a meditative discipline. For those who do rise to the occasion and practice meditation regularly, there are exquisite benefits: an improvement in health and vitality, strengthened coping mechanisms, as well as access to inner guidance and profound inspiration. However, one of the greatest benefits of meditation is a reversal of the aging process! The research two decades ago by physiologist R. Keith Wallace indicated that meditation has profound rejuvenating effects on the body.

According to Deepak Chopra in *Ageless Body, Timeless Mind*, "Beginning in 1978, Wallace researched the effects of meditation on human aging. He used three markers for biological aging as shorthand for the aging

The biggest surprise in my search for
the inner self was finding that it could be
experienced by any human being whenever
his desire for it was sufficiently sincere.

— Tim Galway

process as a whole: blood pressure, near-point vision, and hearing threshold, all of which typically decline as people grow older. He was able to show that all these markers improved with long-term practice of TM [a form of meditation], indicating that biological age was actually being reversed. Meditators who had been practicing the TM technique regularly for fewer than five years had an average biological age five years younger than their chronological age; those who had been meditating longer than five years had an average biological age twelve years younger than their chronological age. These results held good for both younger and older subjects."

Certainly the lowering of biological age is a fabulous benefit! Yet there is another even more significant benefit.

THE STILLPOINT ZONE

The process of meditation serves as a vehicle to create a strong, harmonious, rapport between the three selves that opens the pathway to fantastic abilities. Perhaps you have heard the term *"the Zone"* used by athletes or others who have achieved feats of exceptional accomplishment. *"The Zone"* refers to that state of *stillpoint* or *pure potentiality* which emanates from the integrated core of our being and from which arises all effortless manifestation.

It is no wonder that one of the greatest basketball coaches of all time, Phil Jackson — the former coach of the Chicago Bulls and current coach of the Los Angeles Lakers — instructs his team in the art of meditation and insists that they practice regularly. He is undeniably aware that this routine is instrumental in their success.

Create a balance.

The outer and the inner are not opposed.

They are movements of the same energy,

two banks of the same river,

and the river cannot flow with only one bank.

— Osho

When you relax into the state of *stillpoint,* and your skills correspond with your new beliefs and expectations, you witness *instant* success. Occasions of "mysterious coincidence" increase, and you find yourself in awe of the seeming "miracles" that unfold before you.

WHAT IS MEDITATION
AND HOW DO YOU PRACTICE IT?

One dictionary definition states that to meditate is to engage in contemplation. However, it could also be said that the contemplation, or conscious directing of your attention, is done to alter your state of consciousness. Meditation is simply about where you direct your attention and how it alters your consciousness. There's no limit to the things you can direct your attention toward: objects, breath, symbols, colors, sounds, odors, uplifting thoughts, or spiritual masters.

In beginning a meditation practice, you may discover that it opens up an intimate relationship with yourself that is very deep. You may also find yourself fearful of exploring that intimacy. However, if you choose to stay with the practice, your rewards will be great. You will begin to experience more frequent states of ecstasy in the midst of your everyday routine, and you will be amazed at the countless instances of unfolding miracles — especially if you take time to dwell briefly on a goal or intention before you begin your practice.

In order to establish a new subconscious habit pattern, it is often recommended that you set up a meditation schedule. The best time of day to meditate is when you can be free of interruption and distraction. You may want to experiment with different times to see which is optimal for you.

The alchemical process

of transmutation of lead into gold

is simply a metaphor for

the transformation of ourselves

into awakened self-mastery.

— Elizabeth Kelley

Once you set a specific meditation time, do it no matter what. You will then become accustomed to being quiet at those times and you will find the practice easier. If you are a beginner and you wish to meditate consistently, begin with 10 to 15 minutes each day. Within a short while, you may want to increase that to 20 minutes once a day, or 10 minutes twice a day. However, do not let this suggested time frame deter your practice. Even five minutes, three times a week, is better than nothing.

You may find that your experiences during meditation range from ordinary to extraordinary; from boredom to bliss. Don't worry about doing it right, and let go of your expectations about what *should* happen — just accept whatever occurs.

I have found that it is advantageous to begin with a *stillpoint exercise* before the actual meditation. By bringing you to your calm center, this prepares you to remain in a meditative state more easily. From the *stillpoint exercise*, you will transition into a simple meditation technique. Within this method, the repetition of shifting your focus will lead your mind out of its normal thinking process and into the silent gap between thoughts. Don't try to force anything to happen or to chase your thoughts away in an effort to make your mind blank. Simply breathe deeply while bringing your focus to the inhalation and the exhalation.

To begin, allow a certain period of undisturbed time for this process. Recording the directions onto a tape will allow you to keep your eyes closed throughout this experience and more easily follow the instructions:

In receptivity we are capable of opening to radiant gardens of energy.

— James N. Powell

Be seated with eyes closed, spine upright and hands turned palm up, resting comfortably on your lap. Simply turn your awareness to your breathing. Take a deep breath and hold for five seconds. Exhale and tell yourself to *relax*. Be aware of the air moving in and out of your nostrils.

THE STILLPOINT EXERCISE

Focus on your dominant hand.

Simply pay attention to that hand.

Begin to focus on both hands simultaneously.

Begin now to focus on the top of the head.

Shift your focus now to about an inch above your head.

Focus now about an inch in front of your forehead.

Focus now about an inch in front of your throat.

Focus now about an inch in front of your chest.

Focus now about an inch in front of your navel.

Focus now about an inch in front of your pubic bone.

Focus now about an inch behind your tailbone.

Center your focus on your dominant hand once again and allow the energy to build.

Begin to focus on both hands as you fill them with the energy created by your conscious attention.

Begin to focus again at the top of the head and feel this triangle of energy.

Now relax your focus and keep your eyes closed.

As is the human body, so is the cosmic body.

As is the human mind, so is the cosmic mind.

As is the microcosm, so is the macrocosm.

As is the atom, so is the universe.

– The Upanishads

THE STILLPOINT MEDITATION

With your eyelids still closed, allow your eyes to rest comfortably downward. Notice your breath becoming more rhythmic. Now begin to shift your focus as follows:

1. As you INHALE, breathe in with attention at your crown.

2. As you EXHALE, breathe out at with attention at both palms.

Feel the energy that builds with each breath. When thoughts come into your awareness, acknowledge them and release them. You may choose to visualize a word such as "love" as a focal point before each exhalation.

If you wish to shift to a simpler form, begin the following:

1. As you INHALE, breathe in with your attention at your navel.

2. As you EXHALE, breathe out with your attention at your navel.

Continue to shift your focus from the outward to the inward movement of your navel as you inhale and exhale.

Enjoy the experience of silence; enjoy the energy and relaxation generated within you. When you are prepared to come out of this state, return with an attitude of gratitude for all the good in your life and all

To love is to return to a home we never left,

to remember who we are.

— Sam Keen

the good that is about to come into your life. Now, take a deep breath, and open your eyes.

Ground yourself by looking around the room and noticing particular colors, shapes (for instance, circles or squares) and the spaces between the shapes. Let yourself integrate this experience for several moments before returning to your regular routine.

If this simple practice feels effective for you continue with it. If you feel that this particular form doesn't suit you, be flexible and try a different method. There are many forms of meditating and there will be one that suits itself perfectly to your own needs. Just persevere until you find it!

CONNECTING TO COSMIC ENERGY

Meditation is one of the oldest known paths human beings have taken to explore realms of experience beyond the conscious self. Practicing a form of meditation on a regular basis is one of the most loving things you can do for yourself. By taking time to be at peace, in quiet connection with your breathing and with your inner being, you are able to attune with the Cosmic Mind. This is your opportunity to be guided to great acts of creativity and high states of love.

As you quiet your mind, you are better able to sense subtle energies and sensations in your body and, thus, expand your ability to experience pleasure. Practicing meditation and then bringing that calm and focus to your interactions with a partner is also one of the greatest gifts you can give.

In reality, we are divinity in disguise,

and the gods and goddesses in embryo that are

contained within us seek to be fully materialized.

True success is therefore the experience of the

miraculous. . . When we begin to experience our

life as the miraculous expression of divinity –

not occasionally, but all the time –

then we will know the true meaning of success.

– Deepak Chopra

THE BIGGER PICTURE

There is nothing greater than your connection with the Source of all of life. As you grow in the realization of your true dimensions as a being, you will experience a bliss greater than you can now imagine. So much more than material wealth and success – even more than what you normally perceive as love – can be yours as you awaken to your true self. As your consciousness unfolds, the unlimited universe is able to express ever more of itself through you. Your ideals and your whole identity can expand to include a larger context for yourself and the rest of the world. The tools you have been given to help you focus on and fully manifest the experiences you desire are also stepping stones to experiencing the greater reality of life.

As you learn to master your physical reality, you can begin to trust that there is a power within you that is universal and infinite. This is the cosmic energy out of which everything is created. As you use it to create ecstasy and success in all areas of your experience, you will come to discover that there is a divine purpose to your life, far grander than you might ever before have considered.

My simple blessing to you is expressed through the words of Jonathon Swift: "May you live all the days of your life."

EPILOGUE

Love is the wind beneath the wings of ecstasy. Ideally, this little book has given you a new appreciation for the vast, energetic power of love by bringing more of an experience of it into your everyday life.

What can guide you back into the state of ecstasy each day? You can return consistently to the primary concepts you have learned here, allowing them to express themselves practically in your relationships with yourself and others. These concepts can be defined as follows:

1. *BE AWARE* of ecstasy. Define it with words, images, feelings and movement. Actively advance your positive beliefs about ecstasy so that they can support the truly limitless, ecstatic spirit that is you. . .

2. *BE FREE* of limitations related to ecstasy, love and the creative life-force energy. Use positive feelings, positive affirmations and positive movement to travel beyond your limitations to your goal. . .

3. *BE FOCUSED* on the benefits of ecstasy. Imagine the actual positive benefits that come from having ecstatic relationships. Bring sensory imagination fully into play so that energy grows and flows in that desired direction. . .

4. *BE HERE* in the present moment where ecstasy abides, and practice being ecstatic, loved and loving. Rehearse this through the manifestation process by talking, feeling and behaving as if it were true right now. This activity will move your desire into physical reality. . .

5. *BE HAPPY* with yourself and with others. Silently praise yourself and the person or persons with whom you want to have good relationships. Look for the good in all things, and praise it. . .

6. *BE CONFIDENT* in your ability to make changes. Nurture your sense of inner power as you learn to connect with your spiritual self more fully. . .

7. *BE FLEXIBLE* in your attitudes toward new circumstances, people and experiences. Actively replace negative with positive in your choice of words, images and postures.

You may wish to copy these concepts and place them where you will see them often. Reading them at the beginning of your day will help to keep them in mind as you go about your regular routine. Or you may choose to focus on one of these concepts throughout the week and see what begins to show itself in your world as you supply energy to that particular idea.

ABOUT THE AUTHOR

Kala H. Kos is the author of *The Power of Aloha, The Hawaiian Guide to Love, Health and Wealth*. She has been a freelance writer for the past twenty years, having completed her undergraduate studies in English literature at the University of Saskatchewan and University of Toronto. Kala received her M.A. in Psychology from Honolulu University and is currently a Ph.D. candidate in their doctoral degree program. She also enjoys the position of adjunct faculty member at Honolulu University.

For several years, Kala produced the popular *Mastery of Self-Expression* workshops in Canada and Australia. Trained at the well known Strasberg School of Acting in New York, Ms. Kos also hosted and produced numerous television shows, including her Los Angeles-based program "From Hawaii With Love." She has presented numerous lectures, taught many classes and has been interviewed extensively regarding the principles presented in *From Ecstasy to Success*.

While a leader in the human-potential movement, Kala turned her attention to ancient traditions of self-fulfillment, apprenticing with Serge Kahili King, renowned author and teacher of Hawaiian shamanism. She has studied and taught the Polynesian Huna tradition for fifteen years and is expert in the application of these practical processes of life-transformation in such a way that they can be integrated easily into daily life. Her Huna and prosperity workshop, *Dare to Create Money*, is enjoying international acclaim.

Ms. Kos has also studied and taught Tantra, the age-old Indian philosophy and practice of sacred sexuality. Among her teachers were Margo Anand, author of *The Art of Sexual Ecstasy*, Charles and Caroline Muir, who wrote *Tantra: The Art of Conscious Loving*, and Bodhi Avinasha, co-author of *The Jewel in the Lotus*. After trainings in this discipline, she created an ongoing series of "Huna/Tantra" workshops entitled *Ecstasy and Success*.

The founder of Hawaii Heart Institute, Kala offers a unique program of professional trainings, residential intensives, public workshops and teleconferencing classes.

FOR MORE INFORMATION:

To order Books or Audiotapes by Kala H. Kos
Or register for Live Events and TeleClasses
Or to book Speaking Engagements
Call toll-free

1-800-370-7380 PIN #04

BOOKS

The Power of Aloha by Kala H. Kos
The Hawaiian Guide to Love, Health and Wealth
Die Huna-Lehre by Kala Kos and John Selby
Published by Wilhelm Goldman Verlag, Munchen
From Ecstasy to Success by Kala H. Kos
A Simple Guide to Remarkable Results

AUDIOTAPES

Dare to Create Money
A 4-Week Formula for Magnetizing Riches to You
From Ecstasy to Success
Meditations and Exercises from the Book

LIVE EVENTS INCLUDE

Dare to Create Money
On-Site Workshop
Ecstasy and Success
On-Site Workshop
Dare to Create Money
Teleconferencing Course
The Inner Road to Riches
Teleconferencing Course

FOR MORE INFORMATION CONTACT:

Gamma Group International Seminars
#105-1725 Martin Dr.
White Rock,
B.C. V4A 9T5
Canada
Tel: 800- 370- 7380
(Pass code: 04)

P.O. Box 441,
Kilauea, HI 96754
USA
Tel: 808-826-1068

Visit the Kala H. Kos website at:
www.hawaiiheart.com
Email: kala7s@yahoo.com

Please write to us and share your personal results regarding use of the principles and techniques within these pages. Your stories may be selected for the next book that is already in progress.